AT THE CHEF'S TABLE

AT THE CHEF'S TABLE

Culinary Creativity in Elite Restaurants

VANINA LESCHZINER

Stanford University Press
Stanford, California

Stanford University Press
Stanford, California

Printed in the United States of America on acid-free, archival-quality paper

Library of Congress Cataloging-in-Publication Data

Leschziner, Vanina, author.
  At the chef's table : culinary creativity in elite restaurants / Vanina Leschziner.
    pages cm
Includes bibliographical references and index.
  ISBN 978-0-8047-8797-0 (cloth : alk. paper)
  1. Celebrity chefs—United States. 2. Creative ability in cooking—United States. I. Title.
  TX649.A1L47 2015
  641.5092'2—dc23

                    2015004654

ISBN 978-0-8047-9549-4 (electronic)

Typeset by Bruce Lundquist in 10.5/15 Adobe Garamond

Contents

Acknowledgments

Writing a book is unlike professional cooking in most respects. Above all, I could hardly expect this book to offer even a fraction of the pleasure I have had eating at many of the best restaurants in New York City and San Francisco during the fieldwork that led to the book. But writing a book is like professional cooking in that the final product is associated with an author, even though it is the outcome of a collective endeavor. Nobody was more indispensable for making this book possible than the chefs who gave of their time generously, allowed me to prod them with questions, and gave me access to their kitchens to watch how they worked, even during the busiest times. Elite chefs are constantly approached for interviews by high-profile media so I am grateful that they agreed to my requests for interviews, even though they got nothing in return. Unfortunately, the mores of sociological research prevent me from acknowledging chefs by name, which is particularly regrettable in the case of those chefs who, beyond agreeing to be interviewed, let me observe the kitchen during dinner service and invited me to observe other parts of their work (staff meetings, visits to farmers' markets, work on new dishes). The biggest thanks are due to those who called up their friends to tell them that giving me an interview was worthwhile. Without their help, I would not have had access to some of the chefs who were critical to a study of high cuisine in New York and San Francisco.

Much intellectual, professional, and emotional support made this book possible. Nobody deserves more gratitude than John Levi Martin, who has long been a mentor. John's contributions to my work and well-being far exceed what could be acknowledged in these pages. I could have not dreamt of more or better intellectual and professional advice and support, nor of a more unwavering friendship.

I am also fortunate to have met Karen Cerulo, Paul McLean, and Ann Mische, whose input is all over this book. I am grateful to Viviana Zelizer for her early feedback, and to Eviatar Zerubavel for his support during my time at Rutgers. A special thank you to Karen, who is always there when I need her advice.

Over the years since this project started many people have contributed to it in all sorts of ways. Some read and commented on one, various, or all chapters; others helped through discussions and conversations; still others offered advice or support; and quite a few provided welcome and necessary distractions along the way. Thanks go to all my friends who have served as regular reminders that there is an exciting life besides book writing. Here, I wish to thank those who have given feedback or support for this book: Shyon Baumann, Claudio Benzecry (a big thank you for reading the whole manuscript!), Joseph Bryant, Clayton Childress, Eduardo de la Fuente, Mustafa Emirbayer, Rick Fantasia, James Farrer, Priscilla Ferguson, Adam Green, James Jasper, Sherri Klassen, Anna Korteweg, Monika Krause, Jennifer Lena, Paul Lichterman, Omar Lizardo (a special thank you for various readings in addition to the whole manuscript!), Jeff Manza, Alexandra Marin, Neil McLaughlin, Ashley Mears, Daniel Menchik, Philippe Monin, Craig Rawlings, Arturo Rodríguez Morató, Krishnendu Ray, Erik Schneiderhan, Daniel Silver, Jeremy Tanner, and Andreas Wimmer.

I have also benefitted from the feedback of audiences at conferences where I presented parts of this book, including several American Sociological Association annual meetings, Eastern Sociological Society annual meetings, International Sociological Association Forums of Sociology, and also at invited presentations, colloquia, and workshops at McMaster University, Rutgers University, Sophia University, the University of California, Los Angeles, the University of Chicago, the University of St. Andrews, the University of Toronto, and Yeshiva University.

The research for this book was supported, at various stages of the process, by an award from the Graduate School at Rutgers University, a fellowship from the Center for Cultural Analysis at Rutgers University and a Connaught Fund start-up award and other research support from the University of Toronto.

Four graduate students helped with research for this book—thank you to Terran Giacomini, Sarah Knudson, Lance Stewart, and Lawrence Williams.

Two anonymous reviewers for Stanford University Press took the time and effort to read the manuscript carefully (and promptly), and provided thorough and insightful feedback that greatly helped to improve the book. If I ever had an ideal of an editor, Kate Wahl, my editor at Stanford University Press, is that ideal personified. Her advice and support has been constant and wonderful in every single instance, and her endless patience and positive disposition are beyond my comprehension. Thanks are due also to Elspeth MacHattie and Gigi Mark at Stanford University Press.

I wish to dedicate this book to the memory of my mother, Gisèle Ebel, who loved food and books almost as much as she loved people. She put up with me as I worked through many drafts of this book, but regrettably, did not live to see that work finally come to fruition.

Preface

This book is about the creative work of chefs at elite restaurants in New York and San Francisco, an empirical subject I chose in order to examine the (much more abstract) analytical question of how and why individuals act the way they do. Areas of life rife with ambiguity, uncertainty, high pressure, and contradictory forces are especially good for exploring how individuals make choices about their actions. Creative work in cultural spheres is one such case. In such work it is not always easy to make products that satisfy the taste of audiences *and* create something original. In addition, the evaluation of quality is not clear-cut but has the power to make or break one's career nonetheless. Creators must navigate competing forces—including their own habits and inclinations, economic pressures, and status constraints—in coming up with new ideas and managing their careers.

Why explore these issues in high cuisine? When I began the research that led to this book, chefs' work was still largely unexplored in sociological and organizational research (particularly in the Anglo-Saxon world), so there was much to learn. In the world of elite restaurants, there are especially strong and competing pressures to have a creative and distinctive style and at the same time to navigate market forces to run a profitable business (of a type characterized by high costs and low profit margins). That creativity and commercial forces are both at the center of chefs' jobs means that chefs have to make difficult choices to manage their work and careers. For analytical purposes, it means that high cuisine combines areas that are often separated in scholarly research, namely the business world and the spheres of culture and the arts. Chefs cannot choose either the value of artistry or the incentives of the economic market. That is, there may be "starving artists," willing to forgo material comforts for the sake of their art, but there cannot be such a thing as a starving chef (a metaphor that surely applies to more than economics when it comes to chefs). Chefs risk not only losing their restaurants if they cannot run a profitable business but also damaging their reputations. These conditions turn the world of elite restaurants into a particularly good case for studying the dynamics of cultural creation and examining the major theories and perspectives that we use to explain the workings of cultural spheres and organizational configurations.

That the main question that drove this study is about creative work means that the focus of this book is on how chefs create dishes and manage their culinary styles. To understand how they do so, I made use of several lines of research, addressing cognition, categories and classifications, literature on work and occupations, theories of action and practice theories, field theory, and organizational analysis. No book can address all the factors that make an area of life what it is, and this one is no exception. Though I focus on the creative part of chefs' jobs, chefs do not create dishes on their own but collaborate with staff (and rely on them for cooking). Neither do they spend much of their time on the creation of dishes, for management activities and overlooking the kitchen staff take up a good part of their day. These factors inform my understanding of high cuisine and the analysis I developed, but little information about them is provided in the book.

Though broad analytical questions guided the research project that led to this book, the book itself is about chefs in elite restaurants in New York and San Francisco, and its goal is therefore to convey how these individuals understand their own world. This approach entails several implications, critical among which is the delimitation of that world. To make choices about their work and manage their careers, chefs orient their actions to those chefs they see as potential competitors (those who are not potential competitors serve for inspiration, but getting inspiration from others and orienting actions towards others are two very different processes). Chefs in other cities are not competitors (i.e., if I am in New York today, I cannot go out for dinner in Tokyo, however great the dining scene is in that city). Those preparing food at fast food restaurants or the corner joint are not competitors either, and neither are chefs at *ethnic* restaurants (a term I understand phenomenologically, following chefs' own understanding). This means that chefs' mental maps of their world, which they use to orient their actions, have relatively narrow boundaries, and therefore that this book has the same narrow boundaries.

That I describe the contemporary world of elite chefs, and that a large part of the information I discuss is drawn from New York City, has the unfortunate consequence that I use mostly male pronouns throughout. There are not many elite female chefs in New York now, and there were even fewer several years ago when I conducted the research. Following the standards of scholarly writing and switching between male and female pronouns when making generalizing statements about individuals would have drawn an inaccurate picture of the world inhabited by the chefs I interviewed.

Having conducted the research several years prior to the publication of this book has other adverse consequences. Major changes have drastically changed the landscape of the restaurant industry. The phenomenon of the celebrity chef has exploded since the mid-2000s, when I did the fieldwork, bringing about a dramatic growth in media and popular attention to chefs that is quantitatively and qualitatively different from the way they were regarded previously. There are now many more television shows, magazines, websites, blogs, and apps about chefs, and many more social media on which diners can share reviews and photos of their meals, and all this has changed the culinary profession. Among other things, it has made culinary careers more socially desirable (which they were not when the chefs I interviewed entered the occupation) and has increased enrollment in culinary schools. Food trucks, very much part of this phenomenon, are also a development of the past few years. And some of the major trends sweeping the culinary world as I write these pages had either a minimal or nonexistent presence in New York and San Francisco when I did my fieldwork, including the New Nordic cuisine, nose-to-tail eating, and foraging.

The restaurant industry is fast changing; restaurants open and close at a rapid pace, and fads and fashions last only a few seasons. The trends that mattered most in the mid-2000s, particularly in New York, have receded by now—even the names of some of those trends have changed. Molecular gastronomy was what all chefs talked about then, and foams were in menus all over town. Few foams grace dishes these days, and if chefs talk about this cuisine now, they call it modernist cuisine. The change of nomenclature aside, chefs in New York spend less time talking about this cuisine these days or about the most famous modernist chef in the city. However, if the social sciences help us predict anything, we should expect that chefs still all talk about the key trend of the day and the major chef who represents that trend, whether the trend is foams or foraged foods or the chef is modernist or New Nordic. That is, though the cases in this book represent a particular moment in time, in particular locations, the fundamental patterns derived from those cases should be expected to characterize the dynamics of high cuisine in times and locations beyond those discussed in these pages.

AT THE CHEF'S TABLE

CHAPTER ONE

Exploring the World of Elite Chefs

Creativity should be a protected commodity; only some should be entitled to have it. But those entitled should be self-centered, because it is about their creativity, so they have to do what feels right to them.

THIS ADVICE, shared with me by one of the most prominent chefs in the United States, looks odd and even contradictory at first glance. Creativity should not be for everybody because, the chef explained, some chefs are so enthralled with innovation that they forget about flavor. Yet chefs should concern themselves only with their own creative inclinations when they design dishes.

The chef was not being illogical or even contradictory. A chef of long standing in New York, renowned for his refined food and for running a successful business, he has a thorough knowledge of the intricate world of elite restaurants. The advice he offered, somewhat humorously and offhandedly, conveys some of the basic principles that guide the work of elite chefs. If they want to succeed in a city with exceptionally high costs and fierce competition, they must offer original dishes that stand out in the market but not so original that they will not appeal to customers. That chefs should be self-centered and do what feels right does not mean that they should indulge their foibles, but that, after years of working in restaurants, they can intuitively rely on the knowledge they have accumulated over that time. They have an intuitive sense of the flavors that work well together, the techniques required for a dish, and customers' preferences, and all these skills effectively work as a good corrective for any excessive flight of creativity.

How and why chefs make choices about the dishes they put on their menus is the question I explore in this book. I examine a range of areas to answer this question, including the career paths of chefs, the classification of their culinary styles, their social connections, the ways they exchange information, the work processes behind the creation of dishes, and the ways in which status influences chefs' work and careers. I look closely at how elite chefs in New York and

San Francisco go about their work to explain how they shape their culinary styles and develop their careers. All the factors that go into running a restaurant inform the analysis in this book, but discussion in the chapters focuses on the creation of dishes and culinary styles because the goal is to explain the nature of culinary creation, and nothing is more central than the food.

The Elite Restaurant Worlds
of New York and San Francisco

For those who enjoy fine dining, few cities equal New York and San Francisco in terms of the quality and number of restaurants showcasing high-end food and the newest trends in cuisine. New York is typically considered the best culinary city in the United States and among the best in the world, and a hothouse for innovation. San Francisco, viewed as the second best in the country, is the birthplace of the so-called California cuisine, a unique style that has spearheaded the seasonal, farm-to-table cuisine now popular across the country. Both cities possess a great range of restaurants, from the most exclusive to casual bistros, from classical French cuisine to gastropubs, from strictly regional cuisines (e.g., Tuscan, Provençal, or Basque) to culinary styles unbound by any region. Beyond fine dining, the two cities are also a rich source of so-called ethnic foods.

The restaurant worlds in New York and San Francisco differ in significant ways. First, the restaurant industry is much larger in New York City than in San Francisco, with about 8,500 restaurants in 2012 (the latest data available at the time of this writing),[1] compared to about 1,800 in San Francisco (Berkeley and Oakland, two cities in Alameda County included in the study, have a combined 600 restaurants).[2] Along with its greater size and number of restaurants, New York also has higher real estate costs than San Francisco, and all these factors heighten the pressures on chefs trying to survive in the New York market. San Francisco has a sunny and temperate climate, with great access to local fresh ingredients year-round. New York has more limited access to local ingredients, so chefs in this city must sometimes ship in ingredients and find ways to deal with the loss of flavor in these less fresh or ripe ingredients.

Cooks rely on technique to compensate for ingredients that are less flavorful than desired. This principle is typically used to explain the difference between French and Italian cuisines.[3] As the explanation goes, French cuisine has developed a large set of techniques and complex combinations of flavors that minimize the impact of a comparatively limited availability of fresh ingredients. By contrast, with regular access to a wide variety of fresh ingredients, Italian cuisine highlights the flavor of foodstuffs through a relatively simpler technical grammar. Something similar applies in New York compared to San Francisco. There is a predominance of complex culinary styles in New York, with chefs always looking for the latest techniques and intricate combinations to make innovative food, and a focus on simpler styles that showcase fresh ingredients in San Francisco. What is more, the restaurant world of New York is profoundly influenced by French cuisine, whereas that of San Francisco has a stronger Italian influence.

Chefs and Culinary Styles

Chefs at elite restaurants in New York and San Francisco are a varied bunch. Some have the renown of Hollywood stars, and others are unknown outside the local community. Some serve intricate tasting menus at a cost of $400 per person, and others offer simple meals in casual environments for no more than $40. Some are employed by restaurant owners to cook in the styles of those already established restaurants, and others open their own business, selecting the culinary style and whole design of the establishment. Even chefs who own their restaurants are a varied bunch. Some own only one restaurant, and others own an army of them. Some open restaurants in only one city, whereas others open restaurants across the country, and still others extend their business across the globe. Some chefs have television shows, a plethora of best-selling cookbooks, a line of cookware or brand of grocery products, and spend their time shuffling between restaurants or among their various lines of business, while others are fully devoted to one restaurant.

Most elite chefs fall between the two extremes. For one thing, even chefs who are in the kitchen every night rarely cook. Save for those who serve simple food at small establishments with minimal kitchen staff, chefs *expedite* during service; as orders come from the dining room they call them out to the kitchen staff, and they check dishes to make sure they look right, sometimes adding finishing touches such as herbs or sauces before sending them to the dining room.[4] Chefs sometimes cook during the day, in the preparatory stages before service, especially if they are developing new dishes, but they generally spend a good part of the day managing the business and overlooking the kitchen. Some may go to farmers' markets, deal with purveyors, or run around purchasing supplies, and those who own multiple restaurants mainly oversee operations and management. Chef-owners spend a larger proportion of their time on business than those who are employed by others.

Elite chefs also vary widely in the kind of food they serve.[5] Some work within the confines of a regional cuisine, others combine cuisines of varied origins, and still others have no attachment to any region.[6] Some keep to tradition, others modify classic recipes slightly to re-create them, and still others assemble dishes inventively, sometimes so innovatively that the dishes hardly look like recognizable food. For the sake of analysis, I classify restaurants, and therefore their chefs, into three status categories—middle, upper-middle, and high status—and consider two categories that comprise culinary styles: regional origin (e.g., Italian, Spanish, or Californian) and innovativeness; the latter I reduce to a binary category—innovative or traditional.[7] While restaurants are classified according to regional style in reviews and restaurant guides and not by innovativeness, the latter must also be considered because it is critical for a restaurant's success and a chef's career. In effect, restaurant reviews and ratings hinge largely on a chef's innovativeness. The processes for creating dishes, from how chefs understand food to how they make a dish, also differ along with the innovativeness of their culinary styles.[8]

Like many artists, elite chefs must design products with creative appeal and develop a style that is distinctive enough to be recognized as their own. But unlike many artists, they must navigate market forces and ensure profitability, not only to keep their jobs but also to earn a reputation as a chef. Even renowned chefs who serve noteworthy food to a full house every night will lose their reputation if their restaurants are not financially viable operations. These conditions introduce a host of pressures into culinary work, and turn chefs into an especially good case to examine the duality of creativity and constraint that characterizes many fields of cultural production. Though being a starving artist may be the choice of few in any area of activity, some artists *can* work without remuneration or concern for profit, but this is not the case for those who create cultural goods in the context of day jobs, a world about which still relatively little is known.[9]

Joining the Kitchen

This book is based largely on ethnographic research with forty-four chefs in the most highly rated restaurants in New York and San Francisco, where I interviewed chefs and observed each of them at work in their restaurant's kitchen. While these restaurants range from the most elite to casual bistros, they are all renowned and highly acclaimed. Interviews were with chefs, and not cooks, because chefs have the biggest role in the creation of dishes. Chefs often consult with their staff when creating dishes; some create dishes on their own and then ask the staff for feedback, and others collaborate more actively to develop new ideas. Cuisine is a collective endeavor in terms of the social organization of the work, but chefs are solely responsible for the food they serve, even if they do little of the creation or cooking. They sit at the top of the hierarchy in a restaurant, managing the business with a general vision for the restaurant and its culinary style; those in lower ranks mainly follow orders to accomplish specialized tasks.[10] Most significantly, the food served at elite restaurants is tightly associated with chefs' names.

Although chefs are the main source of the information in this book, culinary professionals in lower ranks provided important complementary information about the nature of culinary work. I interviewed staff in the ranks below the chef, in particular chefs de cuisine, sous-chefs, and cooks.[11] I also interviewed restaurateurs, restaurant managers, food writers, service staff, and professionals working in the restaurant industry such as food purveyors, lawyers, and architects, who provided a supplementary perspective on a variety of areas central to the success of restaurants. Beyond the formal interviews, I had plenty of informal conversations with chefs and culinary professionals about their jobs, careers, and restaurants. Lastly, I used information from restaurant menus and reviews, as well as articles on food and chefs in New York and San Francisco, in order to paint a thorough picture of the two cities.

This is not a comparative study of New York and San Francisco. The goal that drives this book is to identify characteristics of culinary creation that should be common across locations and to explain how and why the social and organizational dynamics of culinary creation may differ across locations, rather than to systematically compare and contrast two cities. A large proportion of the information I discuss in this book relates to New York. San Francisco plays the role of control case, helping to elucidate whether the patterns of culinary creation in New York have to do with characteristics particular to that city or are to be expected given the mode of cultural production in cuisine.

The Mode of Cultural Production

The kinds of dishes chefs create are shaped by many factors, not least of which are the styles and status of their restaurants. But chefs have room for choice in creating dishes, and their creative inclinations to introduce changes to their cooking or to keep to tradition inform their choices. At the same time, decisions to innovate are significantly influenced by the risks they perceive, as well as by the nature of their work and the social conditions attendant on it.[12] Indeed, how chefs understand the risks of innovating for their restaurants (i.e., will innovative dishes attract attention from the media and customers, or scare clientele away?) significantly inform their choices.

Patterns of culinary creation are shaped by five key attributes. First, the creation of dishes is individualized. Whether chefs consult with the kitchen staff when creating dishes or not, they are perceived to be the sole creators of the food and *responsible for* it. Culinary creation thus becomes an individualized activity, turning a chef's name into highly valuable capital and increasing the significance of status.[13] Second, chefs are also seen to be *responsible for* the execution of dishes. They may not do most, or any, of the cooking, but customers and critics typically associate cooking with the chef, and collapse the cooking into the creation of dishes in assessing the food.[14] This means that, unlike individuals working in areas wherein the creation and the execution of cultural products are separated into two different jobs (e.g., playwrights and performers), chefs risk their reputation if they make dishes that are conceptually interesting but poorly executed. Third, chefs' jobs involve the management of their restaurants, which impinges on the culinary side of their jobs in two ways. For one thing, chefs spend a good deal of time on administration, and this limits the time available to create new dishes. And managing the business makes them acutely mindful of issues of cost and profit, which constrains the types of dishes they create.

Fourth, the creation of dishes is an invariably commercial endeavor; no chef can design a menu without concern for the financial viability of the restaurant. The ingredients and labor required for complex dishes must be kept in check to guarantee a profit margin. As a commercial endeavor, the creation of dishes is targeted at a varied audience, comprising customers and food critics, who are not all necessarily discerning.[15] Fifth, chefs find inspiration in dishes created by other chefs, but there is no way for them to give public credit for the ideas they borrow (neither plates nor menus come with footnotes or references). This influences the dishes they create because it limits the kinds of ideas they can safely derive from peers while avoiding the impression that they are copying them. In short, the exchange of information in cuisine is not legally regulated but is controlled through normative behavior.[16]

Just like musicians, painters, filmmakers, or scholars, chefs must convey a sense of authenticity in their styles to legitimate their work. If they continuously change their styles, they give the impression of not being genuine; contrariwise, if they keep to tradition without renewing that style at all, it appears as if they have no ideas of their own. But chefs have more constraints on their creativity than many artists do due to the varied range of their duties and the commercial aspect of their work that is invariably present. Creators in areas with a mode of cultural production akin to that of cuisine (e.g., fashion, product design, or architecture), facing homologous work conditions, should be expected to make similar kinds of choices about their work. Existing research shows that patterns of creation differ across areas of activity, but there are conflicting theories about what explains such patterns.[17] Scholars have looked at a variety of areas but have not paid attention to the mode of cultural production, and this has limited the understanding of the nature of cultural creation.

Cultural Fields

Chefs face competing pressures to emulate the ideas that are popular in their environment to ensure a customer base on the one hand and to differentiate from peers to stand out in the market on the other.[18] They look closely at what other chefs with a similar customer base are doing to make choices about their dishes, and they respond to both pressures. This means that professional cooking must be situated in a social context as well as in a temporal dimension. Chefs look at what others around them do to create dishes, and they modify their food when the social environment changes and when they change jobs, acquire more experience, or are exposed to new ideas. Indeed, chefs create dishes *as* they make career moves, and make career moves *through* the dishes they create. They come to occupy positions in their social environment through their culinary styles, the status of the restaurants where they work, and their social connections. And they make choices about their food and career moves from their social positions. Insofar as their choices shape their culinary styles and status, they constrain future actions.

Many elite chefs have more than one restaurant, and many have restaurants in more than one city or country. However globalized and prestigious they may be, though, they must adapt their culinary styles to the local environment, to local tastes and preferences. Chefs are tied to a customer base that is largely local (i.e. most diners are confined to their geographic location when going out to eat), and are also bound by their immediate competitors, namely chefs at elite restaurants in the same location.[19] They therefore look at what local chefs are doing and orient their actions to them. They may look to chefs in other geographic locations for inspiration, because it helps them *get ahead* in the game. But they do not need to know what these chefs are doing to *stay* in the game. This means that culinary fields are geographically bound social spaces.[20]

This attribute makes culinary fields especially good cases to advance the current knowledge of cultural production and the dynamics of fields. In localized fields, social relationships have a more concrete nature; individuals have face-to-face interactions, socialize, have awareness of one another's whereabouts, and are connected through third parties such as staff, purveyors, and customers.[21] Physical co-presence means that these relationships, even when mediated by third parties, are much less abstract than social relationships in nonlocalized fields, and therefore that individuals report on actual relations rather than theorizing about their relationships in the field. In nonlocalized fields—which are the ones most commonly studied (such as academia, literature, music, and the arts)—individuals orient their actions to those of others who do similar work regardless of where they are located.[22] A fiction writer, for instance, does not write books for local audiences, and neither is she bound only by the actions of writers in her geographic area. Because the extant knowledge of fields was built on these kinds of areas, it led to a narrow understanding of fields as social spaces that are despatialized or, worse, abstract.

Because in fields of high cuisine individuals must create products with creative value but cannot disattend to economic costs and profit, the impulses towards artistic consecration and commercial success are fused. This characteristic stands in contrast to the typical understanding of fields of cultural production as social spaces structured around an opposition between the two impulses, and a trade-off between them that is well understood by those working in a field.[23]

Navigating a Field

The nature of the field, status, social connections, and the actions of field members all introduce constraints to which individuals must respond in creating products.[24] But social constraints are not the whole story. For one thing, *constraints*, an abstraction used to account for varying degrees of patterning in social action, are constraining only to the extent that individuals perceive them as such and respond accordingly. Whether individuals perceive cues as more or less constraining is associated with their social positions but also with how they understand their environment and their own place in it, and their disposition to respond to it habitually or creatively. Information about these factors is therefore necessary for explaining dynamics in a field.[25]

Chefs have mental maps that represent the field where they work, which help them understand the positions they occupy vis-à-vis others and orient themselves. The maps are structured around the coordinates of traditional cuisines and originality as well as around status. And they have a microscopic culinary analogue that guides chefs in creating dishes. That is, traditional cuisines and originality constitute the basic principles chefs follow to create dishes, always in view of the status of their restaurants.[26] From their understandings of the environment and their own jobs, chefs develop theories about where they are in the field, where they want to go, and what they need to do to get there. These theories come to form their self-concepts, and guide them in making choices between competing incentives and constraints.[27] Chefs cannot equally satisfy the pressures to serve food that is familiar to customers and to create original dishes to differentiate themselves from competitors. They either lean towards traditional styles and prioritize the value of *flavor* in their approaches to cooking (i.e., to the extent that traditional dishes have passed the test of time, there is no question that they have good flavor), or lean towards originality and prioritize the imperative of *differentiation.* In making these choices, they gradually shape their culinary styles and, in turn, build their careers.

Even when chefs sometimes put dishes on their menus due to factors that are beyond their control (e.g., when they are hired at an existing restaurant, with already established dishes and styles), they generally have a degree of choice and follow their self-concepts to make that choice. Self-concepts combine descriptive and prescriptive understandings inseparably (e.g., what kind of chef am I? what kinds of dishes fit with my style?), equip chefs with a sense of direction in and through the field, and give them a compass for navigating the field and making choices. Self-concepts are informed by the choices chefs make, and are therefore dynamically adjusted to the changing positions chefs occupy in the field.

Culinary Careers

It takes many years of very hard work in kitchens, with little pay, to reach the position of executive chef (what I call *chef*). Kitchens are organized around a rigid hierarchical occupational structure that clearly distinguishes the job of the highest occupational ranks from the routine and menial work of the lower ranks. Cooking on the line (i.e., working as a *line cook*), and holding any job below this rank, entails following orders and learning to do a few specific things consistently, technical tasks that have little to do with creating dishes, developing menus, or management. During their first years in kitchens, culinary professionals have only limited knowledge of what a chef's job involves. Knowledge of what it is like to be an elite chef is also limited by the types of restaurants where individuals work during their first years in the occupation. For many chefs, these early jobs have been in small town establishments with low-quality Italian American food, pizza joints and the like. The types of dishes, ingredients, and techniques; the presentation; and the overall quality of the food in these establishments are nothing like what is standard at elite restaurants in New York and San Francisco.

Culinary professionals move gradually from the lowliest positions to the highest ranks in a kitchen (see Figure 1 for the occupational structure in kitchens). The lowliest position is held by the dishwasher, followed by the *prep cook*, who is in charge of the menial tasks of peeling and chopping and other preparation of ingredients for cooking. In elite restaurants there are usually

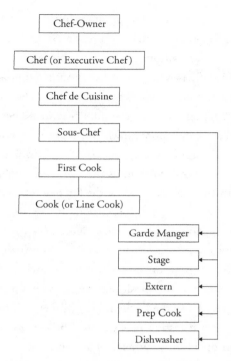

FIGURE I. Occupational Positions in a Restaurant Kitchen

also externs, who are culinary school students, and interns, often referred to by the French term *stages* (which can mean either "interns" or "internships"). *Stages* are culinary professionals training in a kitchen but are not employees and therefore do not command pay. Both externs and interns do menial tasks, similar to those done by prep cooks, but they are hierarchically above the prep cooks because they are on a professionalizing career path, whereas prep cooks, often illegal immigrants in New York and San Francisco, frequently take their jobs as temporary employment (even if they sometimes end up turning them into permanent careers). The next rank up is *garde manger*, dedicated to the preparation of cold appetizers and salads. After this comes the first job that involves actual cooking, the *line cook*, or *cook*, who is assigned to a specific technical task (e.g., making pasta or sautéing). In general, culinary workers commit to the occupation only after being in the line cook position for a while. Some then move to other, perhaps better, restaurants, and some others go to culinary school, typically a two-year program (but some schools offer a four-year bachelor's degree program) that requires an externship in a restaurant.

After line cook, occupational ranks vary by restaurant status and the number of kitchen staff, as well as by other specific restaurant characteristics. Whereas larger restaurants have larger numbers of kitchen staff (but not necessarily more occupational ranks), restaurants with higher status have both larger numbers of staff and more ranks. Most commonly in high-status restaurants there is a *first cook*, or *chef de partie*, responsible for a cooking line (e.g., pasta or sauté). Above this rank is the *sous-chef*, a direct assistant to the chef who can substitute any position in the kitchen when needed. The sous-chef works closely with the cooks because he is the highest-ranked person involved with actual cooking (this is why Figure 1 displays lines—indicating authority—going from the sous-chef to all the ranks below). The responsibilities associated with this position vary depending on whether or not there is a chef de cuisine (the next higher position); the sous-chef may manage kitchen operations, lead a section in the kitchen, help with expediting, and work with the chef developing and testing new dishes. The *chef de cuisine* is responsible for all kitchen operations. Whereas high-end restaurants always have a sous-chef (or several) and a chef de cuisine, lower-status establishments may have only a sous-chef. The top position is the *executive chef*, or *chef*. Some of the larger or higher-end restaurants also have an *executive sous-chef*, or *chef tournant* (French for "turning chef"), who is skilled enough to replace anyone in the kitchen.[28] When the chef is also an owner, and especially if he owns more than one restaurant, he may appoint someone else to the role of executive chef or name this person chef de cuisine.[29]

Occupational positions are arranged by rank in Figure 1, and as mentioned earlier, the lines connecting positions indicate authority—that is, which position is responsible for those below. In addition to being divided into ranks, kitchens are organized into stations, akin to departments, with a hierarchical division of labor.[30] Some kitchens are organized by cooking method, with the most common stations being grill and sauté; there may also be more specialized stations, such as wood-burning oven. Other kitchens are organized by ingredients, typically with stations for fish and meat, and perhaps stations for items like vegetables or pasta. Cooking stations are ranked according to the technical difficulty of the cooking method and the centrality of the cooking method or ingredient for the restaurant; a fish station will be highly ranked in a seafood restaurant but not necessarily in an Italian restaurant known for pasta. A kitchen will also have a pastry department, and the most elite restaurants generally have a baking department as well. The pastry department is semi-autonomous in relation to the rest of the kitchen, with a similar but smaller internal structure, consisting of a pastry chef, pastry sous-chef, and cook(s). In effect, pastry constitutes a different career line, with its own culinary program, and should be considered a different field.[31]

Most restaurant kitchens have the basic stations, but the larger kitchens have more specialized cooking lines. All restaurants have a cold station where cold appetizers and salads are prepared; it is the station requiring the least skill, and therefore it is the lowest-ranked and the entryway for new cooks. At the other end of the kitchen hierarchy is the expediting station, where dishes are finalized and checked for consistency before service staff pick them up to take them into the dining room. Either the executive chef or the chef de cuisine is in charge of this station. The structure I outline here applies to restaurants with a larger number of kitchen staff; in a kitchen with three staff members, a chef and a cook do the cooking, and the third person is the dishwasher.[32]

Kitchens have a long apprenticeship structure, training those in the lower ranks to be competent at basic cooking skills under the high-pressure conditions of restaurant kitchens. These culinary professionals do delegated work for a long time, stripped of power, personal gratifications, and affirmations, a context that gives them an experiential understanding of the hierarchical structure in the occupation.[33] The organizational structure and power dynamics in kitchens subject new members to discrediting and humbling experiences with denigrating work, as well as making them vulnerable to pranks and psychological and physical abuse, all of which operate as an initiation process into the occupation.[34]

The initial job positions in kitchens are considered training, whether that training is the long-term formal apprenticeship that is the traditional form of culinary education in Europe, the short-term formal apprenticeship (or externship) required by most culinary schools in the United States, a *stage* (internship), or the regular employment and mobility through the ranks that constitutes a culinary career. *Stages* are fairly common in the early careers of elite chefs in New York and San Francisco; they are internships at prestigious restaurants obtained through the social connections of the chefs for whom up-and-coming culinary professionals work, taking place most typically in European kitchens (or in top New York kitchens in a few cases), ranging in time from a week to a couple of months, and always unpaid. Whatever professional training cooks obtain in a matter of days (*stages* of a week or two are common), there is no doubt that they acquire prestige from these experiences, which is instrumental for career advancement.[35] The restaurants where chefs have done *stages* are generally referenced along with the restaurants where they have been employed, whether by chefs themselves or in their public bios in the media. And these references rarely specify whether the position at each restaurant was a *stage* or employment, or the length of tenure, which indicates in and of itself that *stages* afford prestige. Furthermore, the strenuous work and financial costs involved in an internship that not only has no economic remuneration but can also be costly, especially when it entails going to Europe, underscore the value of such experiences for a career in high cuisine.

Stints in good restaurants also provide social ties, and these are essential for accessing jobs in high-status establishments, especially when changing jobs as frequently as culinary professionals do. Restaurant jobs are almost never perceived to be an end in themselves; they are stepping stones to higher goals, whether higher ranks in the kitchen, positions in better restaurants, or restaurant ownership. There is a common understanding that tenure in a restaurant should be long enough to learn all there is to learn from the kitchen but no longer. High mobility rates are common across service occupations, and the intensity of mobility in cuisine cannot be overstated. Restaurants are among the occupations with the highest staff turnover.[36] It is rare for culinary professionals in any position below executive chef to stay in a restaurant for over two years. As employers, chefs understand that one year is a reasonable time for cooks to stay with them, and two years is a sign of loyalty, a quality they value highly. Mobility is a serious concern for chefs, since it takes a fair amount of time and resources to properly train new personnel.

Even the position of executive chef is seen as transitional (so long as it does not involve ownership of the restaurant), and chefs tend to stay at a restaurant for only a few years. A chef's job consists of tasks at odds with one another, including the creative work of conceiving dishes, the intense work pace during service in the kitchen, and the tedious routine of making the same food over and over again. Chefs like their jobs because of the creativity, and they like the intensity of the kitchen, but their daily work is steeped in routine. A good part of their time is spent ensuring that dishes taste and look exactly the same every time they are ordered, and the same dishes may be on the menu for days, months, or years. Reasonably, chefs experience a need for change after some time. The harsh realities of the restaurant business notwithstanding, all chefs plan to open (or at the very least dream of opening) their own restaurants.[37] Restaurant ownership need not be the end either, for it opens the door to plans for further ownership—a second, third, or fourth restaurant.

Cooking was often deemed a blue-collar job until recently when, with the development of the *nouvelle cuisine* in France in the 1960s and 1970s, chefs "came out of the kitchen" and their names and faces became recognizable.[38] This entailed a transformation of cuisine from an occupation organized around dishes and the restaurants where they were served (i.e., information centered on renowned dishes offered by specific, renowned restaurants) to one structured around chefs and their careers (i.e., what matters now is who the chef is and where he has worked). Areas of activity structured around individuals and their careers are more highly organized than those structured around objects and locales, because it is not single actions that constitute careers and the field as a whole but the sum of actions undertaken throughout individuals' careers.[39] The dramatic expansion of media devoted to food and of reviews, ratings, rankings, and awards; the growth of culinary schools; the rapid changes in fads and fashions; and last but not least, the phenomenon of the celebrity chef (itself a sign of an area structured around individuals' careers) show a more organized, and also more dynamic, world of high cuisine than existed previously.[40] With these changes, professional cooking gained social status, and chefs' names became valuable capital for restaurants. Such a context encourages culinary professionals to accumulate experience and prestige from the early stages of their careers, requiring them to move fast and early to get the "right" jobs.[41] Prestige becomes more dynamic in a field structured around individuals and their careers because individuals are better able to control their prestige when they move from one job to another.[42]

In effect, a successful career in cuisine requires skillful management, because it is through that career path that a culinary professional accumulates and conveys status, and therefore also through that path that he can arrive at the top positions in the occupation. This is thus where one must start in order to understand the world of high cuisine. In the next chapter, I describe how culinary professionals enter the occupation and move from one job to another—from their first stints in restaurants to their current jobs—and how they manage their careers to arrive at the highest positions in the culinary fields of New York and San Francisco.

CHAPTER TWO

Career Paths in High Cuisine

"A CHEF DECIDED TO BECOME ME," a celebrity chef in New York said to explain his career choice. As a kid growing up in a tough part of New Jersey, he liked playing sports and had talent, and he also liked people. He obtained a job as a dishwasher through a cousin. "Dishwashing was just mind-blowing," he remarked, "because then we'd go out to dinner, we'd go for pizza or something." Even at the lowliest rank in the kitchen, he was part of a team, a meaningful feeling for him. He was hard-working and capable in the kitchen and gradually moved up in rank, and then moved on to better restaurants and more prestigious locations. He eventually attended the Culinary Institute of America, in Hyde Park, New York, which opened access to jobs in elite restaurants in New York City.

This story is emblematic of how a good proportion of elite chefs begin their careers. For many, the culinary profession has an unintended and early beginning, a convenient job taken as a teenager that eventually and unwittingly becomes a lifelong career. The culinary profession in the United States is thus somewhat atypical.[1] In Europe, in contrast, culinary professionals typically begin their careers with a formal apprenticeship during adolescence, which entails a career choice and therefore an intended beginning.[2] One could think of many factors that might lead individuals to turn to the culinary profession, including a sense of vocation, an aptitude for cooking, or a lack of better options in their social context. However, when I asked chefs about what turned them to a career in cuisine, they told one of two archetypical stories.[3] "Falling into" cooking unwittingly, as happened to the chef in the above example, is one of them, and the other one involves the experience of growing up in a food-loving family and learning to appreciate food at an early age.[4]

These stories are told over and over again, with the result that they become common sense; they are thus easily available to new entrants to the occupation to explain (both to themselves and others) a nonnormative career choice.[5]

Beyond the initial choice, careers in kitchens do not follow a standardized path. There are multiple ways to enter the occupation and a variety of means of moving up the ladder, a process that may occur within a single kitchen, across restaurants, and across culinary fields. Even for those moving up within a kitchen, virtually no position is requisite for becoming an executive chef. Careers in cuisine are episodic and feature particular highlights, typically jobs obtained somewhat randomly (by virtue of the strength of weak ties) that help to advance careers.[6] Career paths also take particular forms across culinary fields, since individuals respond to the conditions of their environment when they change jobs and make career choices in view of how these choices are understood in their environment. In this chapter, I look closely into the career paths that lead to the executive chef position in elite restaurants in New York and San Francisco to show how culinary careers unfold and explain why they take particular patterns in each city.

Becoming a Chef

Becoming a chef is unlike entering law, medicine, or business in that the latter are, by and large, normative occupations. It is also unlike going into the diamond retail business or politics, where the social and symbolic capital required for entry, such as connections with suppliers or brokers and trust from customers or audiences, makes these occupations less accessible to those who do not inherit or cannot otherwise access the requisite capital.[7] Becoming a chef is also unlike turning to carpentry or clock making because the technical skills required in these occupations are often transmitted from one generation to the next. It is also unlike going into farming or mining in that these career choices are often bound by geographic location.

All sorts of capital, from economic resources to social connections and from cultural knowledge to reputation, are potentially useful in a culinary field, and some of them are inheritable, including money, restaurant ownership, management know-how, social connections in the culinary world, and family cooking traditions. Nonetheless, these assets are not necessarily convertible into a chef's career. Indeed, very few elite chefs have parents who were chefs, and *none* with whom I have talked, whether in formal interviews or informally, had a parent who had been a chef. A few interviewees had relatives in the restaurant business but in service or restaurant ownership, not cooking, and few of the chefs I interviewed grew up in a family from whom they might have learned culinary know-how useful for their restaurants.

There is strong evidence that cooking in elite restaurants is not an inherited occupation, nor was it normative for the chefs I talked with (professional cooking had little status when they entered the occupation)[8] or geographically bound (a large number of the chefs in New York and San Francisco did not grow up in those cities). A cook in the corner family restaurant in his hometown might, once he had found the job, stay on for lack of better options in the area, but this is not the case for elite chefs in big cities. Getting to the higher positions in top culinary fields requires, at a minimum, a good measure of determination and ambition because it takes years of hard work, long hours, stressful conditions, and low pay to move up the ladder.

STUMBLING INTO IT

Given how onerous careers in high cuisine are, one might expect chefs who have attained great success to convey an active, purposeful decision in choosing the occupation. Yet most chefs I talked with experience their occupational choice as accidental. *How* they started working in cuisine might be fortuitous—for example, a matter of convenience for those who took up a job at the local restaurant in their hometown—but this does not account for *why* they turned that job into a lifelong career. Accomplished and successful chefs' perception of their careers is that "it happened," "I stumbled into it," "I fell into it," "a chef decided to become me," or "I didn't really decide." Several chefs stated that a convenient job *became* a career. A chef at a high-status restaurant in San Francisco offered this explanation:

> Well, I didn't really decide. I don't know. I went to art school. And then, at a point during my art school, I had to get a job, and the easiest place to be employed is a restaurant. They accept all varieties of people.

What is characteristic of this typical story is that it does not describe or explain a choice but only narrates events, circumstances, and conditions surrounding the choice. Other chefs do not even acknowledge that a convenient job turned into a career but simply make reference to a seamless succession of jobs that, in the aggregate, constitute their careers; they took up a job and never left the trade. Indeed, only three chefs I interviewed chose the occupation without prior work experience, and two of them grew up in France, where they had to make a career choice at age fourteen to pursue formal training in cooking in lieu of high school. A few others chose to pursue cooking after their very first job in a restaurant, but they did so either through a process of elimination, because they were not interested in anything else and restaurant jobs were attractive enough options, or through a process of correspondence, because they saw cooking as similar to other things they liked, such as the fine arts.[9]

The chefs I interviewed rarely had any interest in, or even knew anything about, a professional career in cuisine before being on the job, so they began their careers in cuisine with no intention or awareness of doing so. Little information about professional cooking was available when they were young. Cooking was not (and is still not) taught at elementary or secondary school as part of the standard curriculum, media attention to food was scant, and the chefs I talked with had no personal connections or any contact with chefs (personal contact with chefs, as one comes into contact with teachers or doctors, was unlikely).[10] What is more, most chefs with whom I talked had never dined at elite restaurants before working in these establishments and did not even know restaurants of this kind existed. A renowned chef at a prestigious middle-status restaurant in New York, for example, talked about how little he knew about this world.

> But when I began, I had no idea that there were restaurants like this [*pointing to Fig & Olive, a casual but upmarket restaurant next to where we were sitting*]. I lived in the suburbs. This level only existed for the very wealthy French, French chefs, for the most part. So there wasn't a dream to be a chef in a restaurant. My dream was to be a *good cook.*

He was a very ambitious kid, working hard in kitchens to learn as much as possible and be the best, but the best of *cooks.* Like many, he portrayed following the path to become a chef as an automatic process. Several others offered similar accounts of their career choice, quick, matter-of-fact narratives uttered in a tone that connoted that there was not much to say about the topic. A few chefs made reference to the ways in which skills, preferences, and inclinations had informed their career choice, even if they also portrayed the process as contingent and automatic. A chef at an upper-middle-status restaurant in New York explained:

> I needed a job, for the most part. And I started working in a restaurant when I was fourteen . . . dishwashing and stuff. But really the thing, after high school, I liked it. I liked cooking. I got a good job at The Harvest [in Cambridge, Massachusetts] and I learned a lot. And I really excelled there, fast, in the kitchen from prep to like doing, like grill within a year. So, I liked it. So I fell into it, you know. The rest is history; that's all I've ever done.

Getting satisfaction from their jobs and feeling competent are sentiments shared by many chefs, although not many point to these as factors that inclined them towards the culinary profession. This ought not to be surprising, because in the phenomenological experience of everyday life, their careers are experienced as a succession of everyday actions and events that, like much else in life, follow one another without deliberative thinking, purposeful decisions towards predefined ends, or awareness of what those ends may be.[11]

THE SOCIAL DIMENSION OF COOKING

Chefs who grew up in a family household with good homemade meals tend to identify this as a factor that contributed to their career choice. Whereas more than half of the chefs I interviewed said they fell into the job, most of the others suggested that learning to appreciate food early on was significant in their becoming a chef. The two narratives differ substantially, but they are alike in that they highlight a social dimension associated with food. Most chefs underscore the reward of cooking for others, bringing together friends and family around the table, the camaraderie in restaurant kitchens, or the recognition awarded to the cook. Those who grew up with homemade meals evoke affectionate memories associated with the family table, experiences that had a deep impact on them. A chef at a high-status restaurant in New York painted a vivid image of such experiences:

> I think, I think, that I became a chef because I was very early exposed to good food. And what food is bringing along with good food is dinner, lunches on Sundays. . . . The house used to smell of the cooking. And that

was to me an awakening of the sense. Awakening of both the taste buds but also the nose. . . . But you know what? It was very important also, it was a matter of feelings also. The family was there . . . we used to celebrate some holidays and things like this. So good food is always connected to other things as well, sense of smell, joy, tenderness. So that's why in a way, little by little, I became interested to become a chef, to become a cook. So, that's it.

This chef is from France, and his words convey the stereotypical image of life in that country, with food and family around the table over leisurely meals. Most French chefs I interviewed made reference to family traditions and the emotions associated with them, but those from elsewhere who grew up with homemade family meals also made similar comments. Socializing with co-workers, and in particular experiencing the camaraderie that accompanies the long and intense hours of kitchen work, is another social dimension of cooking meaningful to chefs. They often point out that early restaurant work (as a temporary job during high school or college) opened access to a new world, a world of adulthood, with a salary that allowed them to afford goods that were previously out of reach, the chance to socialize with older coworkers, and the symbolic capital that comes with all this. "Hanging out" with colleagues after work, working in a team, and the pace of kitchen work are experiences that commonly lured chefs to the occupation. A chef at an upper-middle-status restaurant in San Francisco talked about this:

> I just fell in love with, not only the food and the creative process, but working with my hands. . . . But I also loved the camaraderie in the kitchen and the adrenaline and the feeling part of a team. And I remember when I was in high school, I loved working and being independent and feeling, you know, like I was an adult. . . . It was so great, it was so much better than school.

The long and odd hours of restaurant work leave relatively little time or opportunity for a social life with individuals outside the restaurant industry, which helps create a tight social network and strong occupational identification among chefs.[12] This occupational identity begins to be fostered early on and continues to be cultivated over years of training. It is also fostered by culinary schools, given that, unlike colleges, they offer only specialized technical knowledge and thereby constrain the potential development of other intellectual interests. Arguably, the strong professional identity contributes to the low out-mobility rates typical of cuisine. Some individuals move to cuisine from successful careers in other areas, especially finance or the corporate world, but it is rare for culinary professionals to leave the occupation once they have arrived at the higher occupational ranks.[13] Countless conversations with culinary professionals and stories about chefs published in the media have not produced even one story about a chef who left the occupation before retirement. Chefs sometimes suggest that, if they were to end their careers as chefs, they would remain in cuisine as restaurateurs or entrepreneurs in catering, the food import business, or the production of tableware or kitchenware.[14]

Occupations with options for upward mobility give employees incentives for staying in them.[15] In addition, the technical skills, knowledge, and social networks accumulated over years of work in kitchens are not easily transferable to other occupations, making it difficult to start anew.[16] The tight social networks and occupational identity also constrain the options available to chefs; they are likely to have limited access to information about other occupations (an organizational constraint), or deeply embedded in their social world, they may not even think of a career in another area (a cognitive constraint).[17]

The Labor Market in Cuisine

Chefs may rarely move out of their occupation, but they frequently move within it and signal their social standing through their moves.[18] Highly consequential, career moves are part of a trajectory that can unfold in multiple ways. There is vertical mobility, including moving in terms of occupational rank, restaurant status, or culinary field status, and mobility across culinary styles, which is largely horizontal but also entails hierarchy, given that some culinary styles have higher status than others. There are also multiple entry portals for culinary careers in New York and San Francisco; individuals may enter their careers by taking the lowest positions in kitchens in these cities, by acquiring formal education that includes an externship, or by moving from restaurant jobs in other geographic locations. Further, although restaurant kitchens have a multilayered occupational structure, some positions can be skipped. Cuisine constitutes what is called an internal labor market, wherein individuals enter an organization at the lowest occupational positions, undergo a long process of training, and move up in rank. This is an investment for employers, so they have incentives to promote their employees to fill higher positions rather than hire new staff, both to make the investment worthwhile and to more reliably fill the positions with already trained staff. This in turn gives current employees an advantage in competing for higher positions, hence their likelihood of being promoted and moving up the ladder within the organization.[19]

Culinary professionals also move up the occupational ladder through jobs in other restaurants. These, particularly in the higher ranks, are generally obtained through social ties, such as coworkers, friends, or acquaintances who have information about job openings and extend recommendations. Culinary professionals often obtain jobs through chefs for whom they work, who can place them in top restaurants thanks to the chefs' own social connections. They also sometimes obtain jobs through culinary school because externships can lead restaurants to extend a job offer once the training is completed. In short, social ties are essential for mobility opportunities.[20] To the extent that there is no standardized occupational ladder, and openings in restaurant kitchens are unpredictable, mobility is not gradual but rather stochastic, occurring in spurts as opportunities present themselves. There is, however, a core set of positions that few culinary professionals skip: cook, sous-chef, and executive chef. It is especially rare for culinary professionals to skip the sous-chef position—or the structural equivalents of first cook or chef de cuisine—on the path to executive chef. Becoming a chef-owner without the experience of being an executive chef is even more rare.[21]

Whether individuals move up through internal promotion or by going to another restaurant depends on occupational rank and restaurant status. Individuals in the lower ranks are likely to move up to higher positions through internal promotion, regardless of the status of the restaurant where they work. When it comes to moving to the executive chef position, the process varies by restaurant status; those who work at upper-middle-status restaurants tend to become executive chefs through internal promotion, whereas those who work at middle- or high-status restaurants generally obtain their first executive chef positions by moving to another restaurant. Although internal promotion in the higher ranks is regular at upper-middle-status restaurants, it is almost nonexistent in middle- and high-status restaurants in New York and San Francisco.

A variety of skills allow culinary professionals to move up the ladder. Technical skills are of course key, especially for jobs in the occupational ranks below executive chef because these jobs are dedicated to specific technical tasks. But skill is not easy to assess when hiring new staff; consistency, especially under pressure, is critical but can only be tested over time, not in an interview. Other qualities, chief among which are social attributes, therefore become more helpful for assessing potential employees. Social attributes are not only easier to assess than skills are, but they are also important for cooking jobs. If social networks and internal promotion are common means for mobility in cuisine, it is at least in part because they effectively convey information about social attributes.[22] Among all the social attributes, status and trust are the most central in the labor market in cuisine.

To the extent that individuals learn good technical skills at good restaurants (a reasonable assumption shared by chefs), past employment—which signals status—provides the most reliable way of assessing potential employees.[23] The restaurants where culinary professionals have worked therefore function as one of the best proxies for skill.[24] Social and psychological skills are also highly valued because cooks spend so much time together in close quarters, under pressure and high stress, and last but not least, with potential weapons to hand.[25] As a result, chefs highlight personality traits as the most important attributes in hiring staff, in part because healthy social and psychological behavior is not as easily taught as technical skills.[26] Because a brief meeting provides only a limited impression, chefs rely on status and long-lasting personal contact to discern social and psychological attributes. Recruiting employees who are reliable—with good technical and social skills and also loyal so that they stay on the job—is significant because training cooks entails big investments of time, money, and effort.[27]

Social ties matter for mobility at least in part because they convey status, but they only work because they also convey—and are built on—trust. Chefs rely on personal trust when they promote cooks to higher positions or recruit new staff. For those who have the requisite social networks, obtaining jobs seems easy—jobs come to them without apparent effort. When chefs narrate how they moved through the ladder, they often tell of their chance encounters with someone who offered them a job, and of being fortunate to have been "in the right place at the right time." A chef at an upper-middle-status restaurant in New York casually commented on how he had obtained many of his jobs:

> There was an opening at Bouley [a high-status restaurant in New York], a friend of mine had a friend who was working there and who said, "if you want the position, come in.". . . [Eventually] I left and went to The Brass Rail [in New Jersey]. . . . That was another accidental thing, it was a waiter . . . and he had just bought the business. . . . So I went and I interviewed. . . . And then from there I went to Yonkers in New York. I ran into someone, again, it seems like my whole career is by chance. . . . So now they were opening a restaurant without a chef. I was at the right place at the right time, if you will.

These chance encounters that lead to jobs are of course less the product of pure contingency and good fortune than the workings of social ties and the trust that sustains them.[28] This is the typical way whereby culinary professionals obtain jobs; so the more social connections—and the more trust—they have, the easier it is for them to have access to jobs. That status and trust matter for obtaining jobs is not surprising, but what *is* somewhat surprising is that chefs rarely mention skill as one of the attributes they consider when hiring staff. Having specialized skills (e.g., in Italian cuisine, fish, or modernist techniques) demonstrates specific training, an attribute that is necessary but that also leads to what in occupational classifications is considered a simple identity. A simple identity allows for differentiating members of the occupation from outsiders as well as making distinctions among culinary professionals—that is, typecasting.[29]

Simple identities are instrumental in an occupation with multiple entry portals because there are no credentials to easily distinguish those who have invested time and effort to develop their expertise from newcomers,[30] but the downside is that they constrain individuals to a particular category and thereby limit career options. In cuisine, however, the long apprenticeship effectively serves the purpose of protecting existing members of the occupation from newcomers.[31] Moreover, typecasting is not so salient here because culinary professionals move frequently within a kitchen (e.g., from grill to sauté) as well as across restaurants (e.g., from an Italian to a Mediterranean restaurant) during their training, and do so precisely to learn different techniques, regional cuisines, and styles of cooking. At the higher ranks, chefs also switch from one cuisine to another when they change jobs, and also sometimes when they open new restaurants. Whereas competence in a variety of areas—what can be called *generalism*—can be seen as lack of skill in labor markets where specialization in one category is a salient positive attribute, in cuisine not being specialized in one technique or culinary style is viewed as choice rather than failure.

The case of cuisine suggests that risks and rewards for individuals with multiple identities vary by status, an underdeveloped aspect in the literature about labor markets.[32] Having multiple identities may entail higher risks for newer professionals because it can be confused with lack of skill, but will not be so risky for those who have already proven their skill, and even less risky when they have high status; in effect, for elite chefs, a simple identity can be negatively perceived as narrowness.[33] By the same token, skills and social ties also have a role that varies by status. In the absence of formal credentials to provide social closure, skills and social ties are especially useful for low-status individuals, who have yet to acquire the reputation or a distinctive occupational identity (e.g., expertise in high-end New American cuisine) that can help them obtain jobs. In contrast, chefs with more prestige and high status have well-defined occupational identities, so being typecast can be instrumental for being offered jobs.

Entry Portals

Formal education is not a requisite or the first door to a culinary career, and neither is it highly valued by chefs.[34] Whether they attended culinary school or not, the chefs I interviewed uniformly dismissed it on the grounds that it does not provide real training because this can only be acquired on the job. They maintained that formal education only gives a foundation: knowledge of the techniques, stocks, sauces, and dishes of the classical canon. A chef at an upper-middle-status restaurant in San Francisco commented on his own experience in culinary school:

> I learned a lot of codified basics, you know. . . . The cooking was good, it was good. I learned, I definitely learned. If I had to do it all over again, I don't know that I would have gone to culinary school. . . . I would go work in Europe for a long time.

Chefs' critique of culinary school is also largely based on the high cost of tuition, which can go up to well over $100,000 for a four-year program at the top schools in the United States. If tuition were lower, as it used to be, culinary school might be a more worthy investment in chefs' eyes. Just about everyone I interviewed suggested that traveling abroad to eat (mostly in Europe) would be a better use of time and money. While costly, it exposes young cooks to a variety of cuisines, including traditions and novel ideas, that are afforded high prestige. However limited culinary schools may be, they nonetheless have an essential, if latent, function, namely providing social ties that lead to future jobs.[35] Culinary schools, and particularly the better ones, facilitate a high-status entryway to the field because they set up externships for students, typically at high-status restaurants. Externships may or may not lead to job offers from these same restaurants, but even when they do not, they open access to other high-status restaurants through the social connections acquired in and through them.

Culinary programs range widely in terms of social networking opportunities, just as they range in cost of tuition and reputation—three attributes that co-vary. The most prestigious school is the Culinary Institute of America (CIA), located in Hyde Park, New York, followed by Johnson & Wales University, located in Rhode Island.[36] Somewhat further behind are the International Culinary Center, until recently called the French Culinary Institute, and the Institute of Culinary Education, both in New York City. As in any hierarchically structured field, the better culinary schools provide better social networks because they have connections with the best chefs, who make their restaurants available for externships. The top school, as is typically the case, is criticized by chefs for its poor training and the arrogance it breeds among students. No chef I have interviewed claimed to have preference for hiring CIA graduates, and some even said they favored anyone but CIA graduates. Chefs say they care most about a positive learning disposition and good attitude. A chef at a high-status restaurant in San Francisco, trained at the CIA, expressed these views:

> In my kitchen I have two currently enrolled at culinary school, and I have one who is doing my sauces right now, and he's never gone to culinary school. . . . For me, what I hire on is personality, desire to learn, how they are going to work well with others, how they are going to make my kitchen a better place to be, you know. I want them to come to work and want to be here. I want to be here with them. . . . No attitude and no ego.

Despite chefs' apparent disregard for culinary schools, elite restaurant kitchens are filled with culinary school graduates and externs, and especially from the CIA. Having externs is understandable under any circumstance because they are free labor and fairly risk-free given that they do the most menial work. This is an asset because labor costs constitute a large proportion of restaurant budgets, and more so at the highest-status restaurants because their food is highly labor intensive. In effect, these establishments have a much higher number of externs; they are also better able to attract externs due to their reputation. However, restaurant kitchens are also staffed by cooks and chefs with culinary school diplomas, and this is not because many externs are hired by the restaurants where they trained. Of the thirty-five American chefs I interviewed, twenty-three had received formal training, and fifteen did so at the CIA.[37] Even more significantly, there is a correlation between restaurant status and the proportion of chefs with formal training, *and* with CIA degrees. The high-status restaurants included in this study have the highest proportion of chefs with formal training (85% of all chefs and 77% of American chefs), as well as the highest proportion of chefs with CIA degrees (67% of American chefs).[38]

Furthermore, whereas the proportion of formally educated chefs varies only slightly across restaurant status (72%, 70%, and 85% at middle-, upper-middle-, and high-status restaurants, respectively), the proportion of chefs educated at the CIA varies more widely (28%, 23%, and 46% for each status category, respectively). The association between educational credentials and restaurant status is especially clear when only American chefs are included, since all foreign chefs I interviewed had formal education. There is a significantly higher concentration of formally educated, and CIA educated, chefs at high-status restaurants (the proportion of formally educated chefs among Americans is 65%, 55%, and 78% for each status category, respectively, and that of CIA educated chefs is 29%, 33%, and 67%, respectively). At the same time, in New York, the likelihood that the chef was born and trained in Europe and that the chef de cuisine and sous-chef were born in Europe as well increased along with restaurant status. In short, educational credentials clearly matter for careers in the culinary fields of New York and San Francisco.

Of the more than 550 culinary programs in the country, few are represented in elite restaurants in these two cities. In total, the chefs I interviewed attended only seven U.S. culinary schools, as mentioned above, and a large number of them attended the CIA. Besides the fifteen chefs who studied at the CIA (at the Hyde Park campus), two studied at Johnson & Wales University (at the Providence, Rhode Island, campus), two at the French Culinary Institute (New York City), two at the New York City Technical College (Brooklyn), one at the Institute for Culinary Education (New York City), one at the California Culinary Academy (San Francisco), and one at City College of San Francisco.[39] Overall, middling credentials, and the level of prestige and social networks associated with them, are not effective for advancing careers in elite restaurants in New York and San Francisco, so it takes the most highly recognized credentials, or none at all, to succeed.[40]

In the face of this clear context, it is puzzling that chefs manifest such dismissive attitudes about educational credentials. There is no question that culinary schools can provide only limited training for the fast-paced work of restaurant kitchens and that they are a costly investment, but they do ensure a minimum level of technical competence, and better schools provide better training. If chefs hire staff with culinary degrees in practice, but state in their discourses that they favor other criteria, it is in part because they deliberatively attend to information about social and psychological attributes when they assess candidates, with the result that the more taken-for-granted information (and information they knew beforehand, from candidates' resumes) becomes backgrounded in their consciousness.

Moving Upwards and Sideways

The restaurants where chefs have worked are even more consequential than culinary schools for careers in cuisine because they make up chefs' occupational identities. Shaping one's occupational identity is key earlier on, and the first move to the executive chef position is the most important transition in this regard.[41] Becoming an executive chef means not only that the culinary professional is suddenly responsible for a restaurant's operations, but also that he has to demonstrate he is a chef in his own right, distinct from those who trained him. This is particularly important when chefs have previously worked for renowned personalities, so they often switch to new culinary styles when they get their first executive chef position.[42]

However, just as scholars begin to shape their professional identities in graduate school and do not switch from one subdiscipline to another upon obtaining their first faculty positions (e.g., from demography to ethnographic research in sociology, or string theory to condensed matter in physics), culinary professionals' careers are also significantly shaped by their training. Chefs who commented on the jobs where they obtained their training conveyed a clear sense that they knew the skills they wanted to learn (whether culinary, managerial, or financial) and where to learn them. Some even suggested that they made career moves during their training to enact social ties, so that they would be able to say they had worked with this or that renowned chef. At the same time, many of the acclaimed young chefs I interviewed expressed the fear of being typecast as a renowned chef's disciple, which would amount to being perceived to be lacking in ideas or skills of their own. Some noted that they sought to work with several prominent chefs during their training, and to stay for a relatively short time with each, to avoid the risk of becoming too closely associated with anyone. For individuals to approach jobs with the kind of instrumental mindset that enables them to move from one establishment to another as they see fit requires what Robert Faulkner calls a *detached concern* with their jobs.[43] That is, frequent mobility—whether in the early phases of culinary careers or among executive chefs—is facilitated by individuals' having a stronger loyalty to their careers than to employers.

As they become more established, chefs face less pressure to distance themselves from any particular culinary style. However, if being competent in more than one style is a positive value, they should be expected to expand their repertoires to other types of cooking when they open new restaurants, whether laterally to other cuisines or vertically to other status categories. Research on status constraints would indicate that opening restaurants in lower-status categories is an undesirable move. Joel Podolny, for instance, argues that the economic advantages that help high-status individuals in their positions are not transferable to lower categories, making lower-status businesses less economically profitable.[44] These advantages include lower financial costs in the form of better credit (creditors see high-status individuals as lower risks), lower labor costs (employees are willing to work for lower salaries in exchange for status), and lower advertising costs (high-status individuals attract customers based on their reputation alone, thus requiring less publicity). All this would seem to indicate that chefs should open more restaurants across cuisines than in lower-status categories, but this is not the case. First, high-end restaurants are less profitable than lower-status establishments because they have higher food and labor costs (owing to more costly ingredients and a higher staff-customer ratio) and a lower volume of business. More importantly, high-status chefs *can* transfer some of the economic advantages that accrue to their status to restaurants in lower-status categories. Owing to their reputation, they obtain financial backing more easily, attract employees willing to work for lower pay, have preferential access to good foodstuffs through their connections with the best purveyors, and attract customers easily to whatever type of restaurant they open on the basis of their renown alone.

Structural, institutional, and cultural conditions explain mobility in an occupation. First, occupations with few options for upward mobility often have a higher rate of turnover.[45] Turnover is also higher where upward mobility rarely occurs through internal promotion.[46] Horizontal mobility varies in accordance with the symbolic meanings and values fostered in an occupation. It is easier for individuals to move when they are in occupations that facilitate the formation of professional ties with colleagues across subareas or firms, because then they are likely to build stronger and more loyal ties with colleagues and their own careers than with employers.[47] Tenure is generally longer for individuals who are physically constrained to the space wherein they work because they tend to develop social ties within that space.[48]

However, these conditions do not explain the high rate of mobility in cuisine. Although there are ample options for upward mobility and internal promotion is common, turnover is very high, especially in the lower occupational positions, where options for upward mobility and internal promotion are most plentiful. The long and intense hours spent in kitchens should encourage strong social ties with employers and colleagues in the workplace, as well as loyalty to that workplace, and all this should decrease turnover. Strong ties do develop in kitchens, and are sometimes maintained throughout chefs' careers, whether informally by socializing with (past or current) bosses and colleagues, or formally by continuing to work for former bosses or building business partnerships with them. But social ties or loyalty to the workplace do not typically prevent culinary professionals from moving on. Culinary professionals rarely stay at a job due to their relationships with employers or coworkers; this occurs only when chefs work for restaurateurs or chef-owners not involved in the day-to-day operations of the restaurant for a long time, and when they are in dependence relations that allow them to apply their own ideas to the restaurant, so that they have high job satisfaction. A chef at an upper-middle-status restaurant in New York who had worked for the same restaurateurs for ten years explained:

> Well, the people that own this restaurant are like family to me now. . . . They respect my loyalty. They respect my integrity, the decision making I'm making and the love that I put into what I do and the passion that I have here with what I do. . . . But at the same time . . . I'm working on a project right now which is going to, maybe opening in February if everything goes well. . . . But also, when I do other things, I don't just do it, I involve the owners here and I let them know what I'm doing.

Even in the extremely rare case where a chef has had a long and satisfactory relationship with restaurateurs, it does not stop him from pursuing other plans. Chefs rarely convey a strong attachment to employers, but rather an investment in furthering their own careers. The unfavorable conditions of restaurant jobs make this not so surprising, including, as they do, long hours, low pay (especially for the ranks below executive chef), and stressful and hazardous work environments.[49] A chef who had recently moved to San Francisco to work at a high-status restaurant commented:

> It got to a point when, you know, after three and a half years it was like, I feel like I really need to move again, not only for myself but I've taken so much, you know, I've gotten so much from there that it was really time to move on professionally and creatively. . . . I need to push my cuisine, and to continue to learn I need more . . . and I felt I put in a fair amount of time, three and a half years is a good amount of time for a chef when he is in his twenties. So that, I sort of wanted to close that chapter and start a new life.

When jobs are stepping-stones to other and better positions, there is always an incentive to move onto another job to learn new things, accumulate prestige, and get closer to the goal of becoming a chef-owner, as the chef just quoted went on to remark later in the interview. The routine nature of the job—something chefs mention often—is another factor that should be expected to increase mobility. Trying to fight such routine sometimes leads chefs to create new challenges for themselves, and moving to a new restaurant is an effective way to do so. Individuals in occupations perceived as creative, with expectations of intellectually or artistically rewarding work but highly routine daily tasks, will be especially inclined to try to break free from those routines.[50] Looking closely at career patterns in the culinary fields of New York and San Francisco will help us to better understand the factors that contribute to mobility in cuisine.

Career Paths in New York and San Francisco

Chefs' career paths are singular, but they also clearly show the effects of social forces on individual trajectories.[51] They are not purely contingent, even though contingent events can lead to new jobs, and neither are they the outcome of causal chains of events, even though particular types of jobs can open doors to others.[52] Career paths develop in interdependence with the careers of others, affected structurally by *vacancy chains*,[53] institutionally by the means of mobility common within the labor market in question, and organizationally by the ways that individuals orient their career strategies to those of others and therefore around the symbolic meanings associated with career moves within the labor market. Career paths of culinary professionals in New York and San Francisco show clear patterns, and are remarkably different between the two cities, so I first examine careers in New York and then contrast them to those in San Francisco.[54]

CAREER PATHS IN NEW YORK

Career patterns in New York vary significantly by chefs' current status. Overall, chefs with lower and higher status have worked at restaurants of similar status throughout their careers. Renowned chefs currently at prestigious middle-status restaurants (high-profile restaurants that are modestly rated for their type of establishment and thus borderline with the upper-middle-status category) have the most fluctuating paths, followed by chefs currently at upper-middle-status restaurants.[55] That they are at the border between two status categories explains why their careers have constantly fluctuated between status levels. Career paths of chefs currently at middle-status restaurants tend to be more consistently middle status; these chefs had limited experience in high-status restaurants during their training, which constrains them to the middle-status level for their executive chef positions. On the other end, chefs at high-status restaurants tend to begin their professional careers at relatively high-status restaurants and remain on that level. What is more, chefs at the most elite restaurants (those with four stars in the *New York Times*) have the most stable career paths, working constantly at high-end restaurants.

Figures 2 through 6 outline typical career paths at the different status levels and provide detailed information about the progression of careers, from the first kitchen jobs until chefs' current positions. First, Figure 2 displays the career path of a chef who is now at a middle-status restaurant (see the figure key for the coding for the figure). In his youth, this chef obtained a job as a prep cook in a middle-status restaurant in a small town in New York state. After a few years, he was hired as a private chef in another town on the East Coast, where he only stayed for about a year. He then found a job as a sous-chef in a high-status restaurant in a nearby town, where he was later promoted to chef de cuisine. Through social ties, the restaurant's chef-owner arranged a job for him as a chef de cuisine at a restaurant in France. This international experience facilitated his finding a job in New York, where he became a sous-chef at a restaurant that was high status but somewhat lower within that category than the previous two establishments where he had worked. This job enabled an

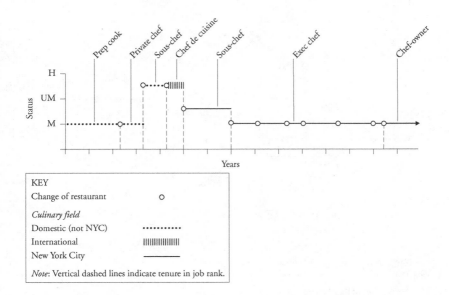

FIGURE 2. Career Path of a Chef at a Middle-Status Restaurant in New York

upward move in rank to the position of executive chef at a different restaurant, though at the expense of restaurant status. He has remained at middle-status restaurants since then and, after several years as executive chef at various establishments, opened his own middle-status restaurant.

As Figure 3 shows, the career path of a chef at a prestigious middle-status restaurant could not be more different. There is a significant contrast in the career path's general flow, since this one has numerous status fluctuations, and short tenures in each job. The chef has also held more ranks in kitchens than the chef in the previous case. Like him, however, he started out in a small town in New Jersey, attended culinary school, and held externships at a few restaurants across the country. This record led to a brief job as a private chef abroad, after which he returned to a town in New York state to work at a restaurant of higher status than the previous ones, where he was hired as first cook and shortly thereafter promoted to sous-chef. He secured a *stage* in France thanks to the social connections of the restaurant's chef, after which he was able to obtain a job in New York City at a restaurant of the same status level as the previous establishments where he had worked (including the *stage*), but at a lower occupational rank. After a few moves from one position

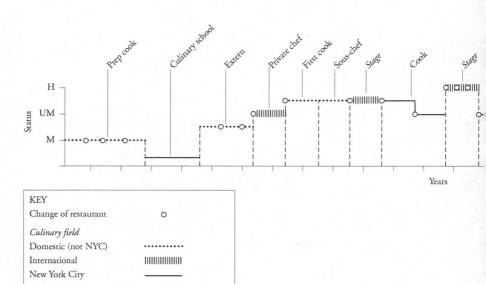

FIGURE 3. Career Path of Chef at a Prestigious Middle-Status Restaurant in New York

and status level to another, as well as further *stages* in France, he became an executive chef at a prestigious middle-status restaurant in New York. Following years as executive chef in a couple of restaurants at the same status level in that city, he opened his own prestigious middle-status restaurant.

In contrast to this career path, the career path of a chef at an upper-middle-status restaurant (see Figure 4) is steadier, yet not as steady as that of a middle-status chef. This career path has fewer status fluctuations; the chef attended culinary school, after which he worked mostly at prestigious middle-status and upper-middle-status restaurants. The steadiness in status levels is accompanied by longer tenures in each job. This individual also moved through fewer occupational ranks, and fewer jobs, before becoming an executive chef. After graduating from culinary school, he gradually moved up in rank at the same restaurant; the restaurant's chef sent him to several countries abroad for *stages*, which enabled him to find a job as a cook in Washington, DC, at a restaurant similar in status to the establishments where he had been appointed previously. After this job, he moved up to chef de cuisine at a restaurant of somewhat lower status and, through social connections, found a job as an executive chef in Italy; after a brief tenure there, he was able to

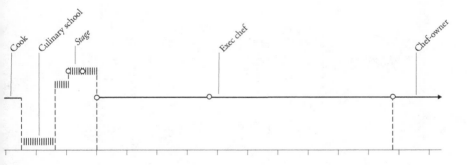

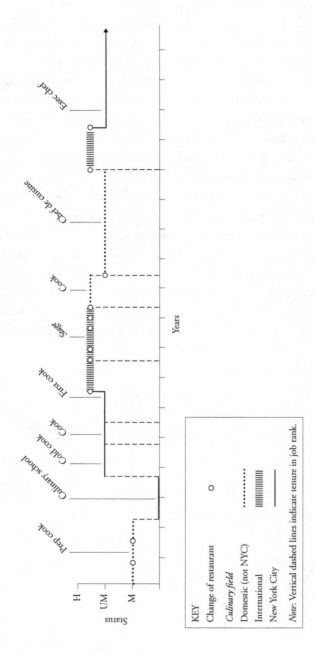

FIGURE 4. Career Path of a Chef at an Upper-Middle-Status Restaurant in New York

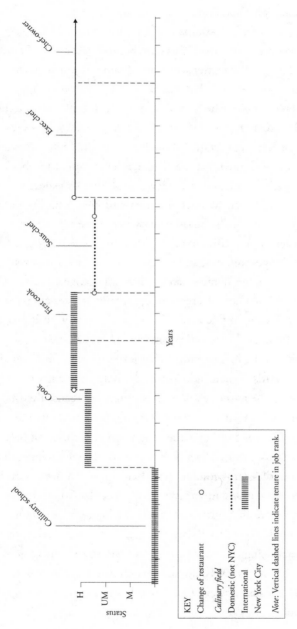

FIGURE 5. Career Path of a Chef at a High-Status Restaurant in New York

obtain an executive chef position in New York at a restaurant of slightly lower status than the Italian restaurant.

The career path of a high-status chef (represented in Figure 5) differs noticeably from the previous three. This chef began his career in France, where he attended culinary school, after which he obtained a job as a cook at a high-status restaurant, and he never left this status level. He worked at a couple of restaurants in France, where he held long tenures, and moved up to first cook. He then came to Washington, DC, where he obtained a job as sous-chef at a slight expense of restaurant status, though still on the high-status level. This job provided him with the social ties and symbolic capital to obtain a job in New York at the same rank and status level, a job that was shortly interrupted by an offer to be the executive chef at a high-end New York restaurant. After several years of work there, he became an owner of the restaurant. In contrast to the previous examples, this chef held few jobs, moved through few ranks, maintained the longest tenures, and always at the same status level.

In general, the careers depicted so far show a negative association between status and occupational rank. Careers go up in rank and restaurant status only to the positions of cook or first cook. Then, for the higher positions, advancement in rank comes at the expense of restaurant status. This is especially the case in the move to the first executive chef job; careers tend to remain steady status-wise afterwards. When individuals move up in occupational rank *and* restaurant status in the lower positions, it is generally because they have moved down to a culinary field with lower status, typically a small town or a U.S. city other than New York or San Francisco. The negative association between rank and restaurant status is especially salient in the oscillating career paths of chefs at prestigious middle-status restaurants. Their upward moves in rank usually come with a decrease in restaurant status; in particular, when they move from sous-chef to executive chef, they trade a job at a high-status restaurant for one at a prestigious middle-status restaurant. On this status level, moving up in rank requires sacrificing restaurant status.[56] Obviously, steady careers, whether at middle- or high-status levels, do not have this negative association between rank and status, because upward mobility is less likely to come at a salient status cost (or, expectedly, gain).

Status is also inversely associated with tenure. Frequent fluctuations in status generally come with frequent mobility, what amounts to a succession of brief tenures in each job—a particularly clear pattern in the career of the chef at a prestigious middle-status restaurant (Figure 3). This is not, theoretically, a necessary association: a career with status fluctuations could in principle be constituted by long tenures in each job. By the same token, a career steady in status could in theory be constituted by short tenures in each job. Nevertheless, chefs at the two extremes of the status hierarchy have the steadiest careers status-wise and long tenures, and chefs at the high-status level, with the steadiest careers in terms of status, have the longest tenures (Figure 5). Because chefs at prestigious middle-status and upper-middle-status restaurants have short tenures, they have worked at more places in total.

Individuals advance their careers through moves that are meaningfully oriented to the actions of others in their environment and are largely in line with the sociocultural models of careers salient in that environment. New York chefs who begin their careers in Europe (as in Figure 5), where careers have traditionally been approached as lifetime projects, have longer tenures in each job and fewer jobs in the end.[57] A few of the foreign-trained chefs are currently at high-end restaurants, where all chefs tend to have longer tenures, but foreign chefs now at middle and upper-middle-status restaurants tend to have longer tenures as well. Conversely, European chefs trained in the United States have trajectories that mirror career strategies typical of this country; they approached their careers more entrepreneurially, and this resulted in less steady career paths. In contrast to Europe (and Japan), for instance, individual achievement in the United States is signaled through mobility, not tenure.[58] Individuals have more sense of control over their careers in this more flexible occupational model, and they move more often given that mobility is a means to control their careers.[59] Having multiple restaurant jobs, provided they are status-affording jobs, constitutes what is perceived as a successful culinary career in the United States. It signals a strong foundation of skills, given the (reasonable) assumption that varied skills are acquired at different restaurants.

As one would expect, it takes fewer positions to become an executive chef at a middle-status restaurant than at an establishment of higher status. Data from all the chefs I interviewed show that it took those currently at middle-status restaurants an average of five positions to become executive chefs, and those at high-status restaurants an average of eight positions. Although it took slightly more positions to become an executive chef at a high-status restaurant than at an upper-middle-status restaurant, the difference was, in total, not as significant because several chefs at high-status restaurants were born and trained abroad, so they had longer tenures and lower mobility. The variance in career paths prior to the executive chef position is also partially explained by the kinds of ranks chefs held, and in particular whether they held *stages*.[60] On one end of the spectrum, chefs with middle-status careers are unlikely to have held *stages*, and on the other end of the spectrum, high-status chefs are likely to do *stages* only if they were not trained abroad—being trained in Europe makes *stages* somewhat unnecessary. The large number of foreign chefs in high-status restaurants in New York results in a low total number of *stages* for individuals in this status category, with the result that those with careers at the prestigious middle-status and upper-middle-status restaurants are the most likely to go through *stages*. Overall, the lower a chef's current status, the less likely he is to have had work experience abroad, whether a *stage* or a paid job. A causal explanation might posit that international experience leads to high-status careers, but by the same token, high-status careers lead to international experience because access to jobs abroad is attained through social connections that are more likely to be acquired through high-status restaurants.[61]

The co-constitutive nature of international experience and high-status careers partly explains why higher-status culinary professionals generally undertake a *stage* or brief work experience at high-end restaurants relatively late in their careers, before moving up in rank or restaurant status—by that time they have the requisite social connections. Only those with careers that have led them to upper-middle- or high-status restaurants do *stages* later in their careers; through these *stages* they can move beyond their basic training and acquire expertise in specific techniques. If individuals with lower-status careers have any international experience, it is earlier in their careers; they likely lack the social connections to attain the kinds of placements at the top restaurants in the world that allow chefs to move beyond their basic skills, a characteristic that is reflected in their careers.

Just as international experience is positively associated with status, national experience outside of New York or San Francisco is negatively associated with it. A job in most domestic locations other than these two cities negatively affects careers.[62] It is rare for chefs in New York to work in lower-status locations once they have obtained a job in this city; when that does occur, it is among chefs who end up at middle-status restaurants. Since working in other domestic locations signals low status, it is unlikely to enable chefs to reach the higher social positions in the top culinary fields in the country. For a better understanding of the implications of career patterns in New York, I describe the typical career paths in San Francisco below, and draw a comparison between the two cities.

CAREER PATHS IN SAN FRANCISCO

Career paths in San Francisco differ significantly from those in New York. First, they are overall steadier in terms of status and generally have much longer tenures, even for positions such as line cook, which are typically brief in New York. This results in careers with fewer positions held prior to the executive chef position. Status fluctuations and length of tenure are associated in San Francisco, but in contrast to New York, they are *positively* associated: more status fluctuations come with longer tenures in each job. In addition, individuals tend to move up steadily in both occupational rank and restaurant status, if not throughout their entire careers, at least for a good portion of them. Thus, compared to the occupational ladder typical of New York, the ladder in San Francisco has fewer ranks and longer tenures. In San Francisco, culinary professionals skip ranks that are key in New York; half of the chefs interviewed in San Francisco moved directly from cook to executive chef, and half of them (a largely different half) were internally promoted to the executive chef position.[63] Comparing the career of a chef at an upper-middle-status restaurant in San Francisco (depicted in Figure 6) to the careers displayed in Figures 2 through 5 reveals the marked contrast between the career patterns for the two cities.

This is a typical career in San Francisco, with much longer job tenures and many fewer status fluctuations than any career in New York. The chef moved from cook to executive chef without ever having been a first cook, sous-chef, or chef de cuisine and he did so through internal promotion. Overall, this chef has held few positions and worked at few restaurants throughout his career. His career also shows the rarity of international professional experience among culinary professionals in San Francisco. If they seek international experience, it comes in the form of *stages* late in their careers, even right before opening their own restaurants.

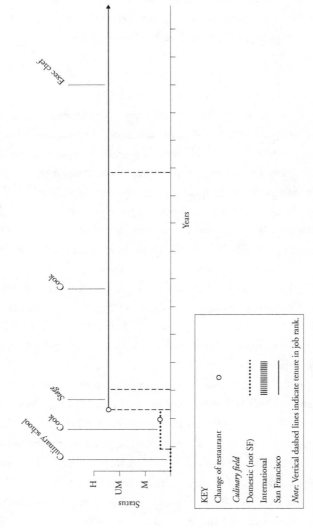

FIGURE 6. Career Path of a Chef at an Upper-Middle-Status Restaurant in San Francisco

As in New York, it is rare for culinary professionals in San Francisco to work elsewhere in the country once they have entered the field.[64] But the labor market is more localized in this city, as the majority of culinary professionals here are American and many have grown up in California. The difference between the two culinary fields stems in part from their respective global standing—New York attracts culinary professionals from all over the country and the world.[65] Also, as in New York, culinary professionals in San Francisco move primarily through internal promotion and social networks. Internal promotion is associated with length of tenure here, as a high proportion of chefs moved up in rank through internal promotion and had long tenures. Social connections are especially effective for obtaining jobs in a relatively small and closed culinary field such as this one. Either personal recommendations from well-positioned chefs or long tenures are sufficiently effective trade-offs for experience in otherwise key occupational positions on the path to executive chef. Moreover, San Francisco allows for more unusual careers than New York; some chefs came to cuisine after working in the front of the house (i.e., as service staff) for many years and with no formal training in cuisine, and a few others moved to cuisine after being in other occupations, mostly the arts.[66] Insofar as career patterns are different in New York and San Francisco, it is because individuals learn to understand and manage their careers from their environment, observing which moves send the right signals and have positive outcomes and which are not so favorable.

Career Structures and Professional Self-Concepts

Professional careers in high cuisine begin to be shaped early on, before individuals even make a conscious career choice. Whether they happened to get a job at a restaurant to make money in their youth or grew up in a food-loving family (the two common entry portals into the occupation), individuals develop a sense that their career choice "just happened." From then on, their professional self-understandings are profoundly shaped by the social organization of work in restaurant kitchens and the frequent mobility that goes with that social organization. For mobility, culinary professionals rely on internal promotion and social networks, given that these are effective means to convey information about personal trust and status, both of which are proxies for the attributes that matter in kitchen work, namely technical skills and social and psychological qualities, but are not easily assessed.

Individuals emulate the career moves that signal positive qualities and lead to professional success in their field, and thus they collectively institutionalize career patterns therein. Culinary professionals move from one job to another from early in their careers to obtain experience in multiple restaurants and acquire skills and status, strategizing to take their careers where they aspire to be. They vary in how purposeful and clear they are about their career choices— some being highly strategic right from the beginning—but do not vary in reproducing mobility patterns in their field: New York chefs move more frequently, through more ranks, and obtain more experience abroad than their San Francisco counterparts do. Insofar as this is the case, it is because the New York chefs are responding to higher pressures to differentiate themselves, as well as to the intersubjectively shared meanings associated with mobility in their field.

In careers that can unfold without regular employment in an organization within the occupation (e.g., careers in writing or music) individuals develop a salient professional identity only if they identify strongly with the occupation. With neither a guaranteed income nor an institutional affiliation to anchor a professional identity, professional self-concepts often develop early on and become especially salient—the stereotype of the self-identified "artist" is a case in point.[67] By contrast, in occupations where earning a living and an institutional affiliation can be reasonably expected, and where individuals are constantly denied responsibility during their training, professional self-concepts are typically developed later.[68] Culinary professionals should therefore not be expected to acquire a strong self-concept early in their careers. However, the apprenticeships and socializing that take place in kitchens afford them a strong *occupational* identity, a sense of membership in the trade as opposed to identification with a specific position, and this identity is reinforced by the narrow education of culinary schools. Having such an occupational identity helps individuals to endure years of hard work and little pay and to commit to a culinary career. Indeed, culinary professionals do not even experience the career path towards becoming a chef as daunting. Because careers can unfold variously, through different occupational ranks, types of restaurants, status levels, and cooking styles, culinary professionals (in successful paths) have a sense that they make their own choices and control their careers when they move from one job to another, even if they do so in response to occupational demands to acquire multiple skills and accumulate status.[69]

Frequent and seemingly easy mobility strengthens culinary professionals' sense that their careers are in their hands. To the extent that culinary professionals in New York move more often than those in San Francisco, they should be expected to have a stronger sense of control of their own careers, and indeed, they do convey this sense when they talk about their work. The perception that mobility is easy is also reinforced by the episodic nature of culinary careers. Insofar as careers are constituted by highlights and not by each and every job held (and jobs are obtained with ease), individuals can take chances because these need not be of major consequence.[70]

Culinary professionals constantly project their careers into the future, making each move as a strategy for achieving the next move—an approach that is surely associated with the sense that their careers are in their hands, and one that is therefore more salient in New York than in San Francisco.[71] Moves are never isolated, taken one by one, but rather embedded in *paths* of action, such that the ends for the present action become the means for the following actions.[72] Many chefs, even those who have recently become executive chefs at prestigious restaurants, talk about their jobs, not as accomplishments in and of themselves, but as platforms from which to build their prestige and reputation so as to move up to better establishments or open their own restaurants. Careers in cuisine are "lived forward and understood backwards,"[73] as current positions are always at the same time the product of previous career moves and a step towards future goals.

Of course, chefs have to manage their careers carefully, as these shape their status and culinary styles and effectively determine the positions they will end up occupying in a culinary field. But the positions they end up occupying are also largely determined by ratings and reviews from the media, and chefs have to consider their own understandings about their work in the light of how they are perceived by others. In the next chapter, I turn to these aspects to examine the classification of culinary styles, the role of the media, and how chefs shape their own views in response to external classifications.

CHAPTER THREE

Categories and Classifications in Cuisine

A YOUNG AND RECENTLY APPOINTED CHEF at a high-status restaurant I interviewed in New York had gained much notoriety and acclaim for his very innovative food. Planning the next step in his career, he had devised the most ambitious project I had ever heard about. Along with videographers working with NASA, he was designing a restaurant as an "immersive theater of nature," where the highest-definition videos available for public use in the world would be projected on the restaurant walls. This would create a transporting environment, where diners would feel as though they were in nature, outside the bustling city. I imagined NASA-style food in this setting or, more realistically, dishes that pushed the boundaries even more than in his current job. What kind of food was he planning to serve? "It's going to be meat and fish and pasta. Everything. It's going to be everything. No boundaries," he said. Opening a seafood restaurant would bound the dishes he could make (he could serve little red meat or poultry), as would opening a French brasserie (he could not use too many foreign foodstuffs or wild ingredient combinations). Opening a steakhouse or an English restaurant would limit how many stars his restaurant could receive because these cuisines rarely get the highest prestige. Being outside the bounds of any particular cuisine would enable him to create without constraints, attract customers, and receive four stars from the *New York Times*, his ultimate goal.

The project might have been too ambitious for the U.S. economy (it has been years since I heard about it, and the restaurant is yet to materialize), but the concept was not entirely misguided in that the chef had a very clear understanding of how classifications of foodstuffs and categories of cuisines bound creativity in the kitchen and reputation in the marketplace. First of all, ingredients and techniques are associated with particular cuisines, so choosing a given cuisine limits the elements chefs can borrow beyond the boundaries of that style. Yet all ingredients and techniques are not created equal, just as not all cuisines are created equal—some allow for more flexibility than others. Whereas someone cooking traditional Tuscan food can hardly serve spring rolls or even tortelli (ravioli-like pasta from Tuscany) filled with Peking duck without losing credibility for crossing a boundary not meant to be crossed, a chef who makes New American food—a style defined by especially loose boundaries—has more flexibility. He could safely make Pecking duck tortelli; though serving a stir-fry with stinky tofu (Chinese or Taiwanese fermented tofu with a very strong smell) would be a different story.

Cuisines are not created equal in terms of status either. In the United States, as in many other countries, French cuisine is generally afforded higher status than Italian, and Italian higher than German. As the foundation of modern Western gastronomy, French food occupies a special place at the pinnacle of high cuisine, especially in New York, even if its position has been challenged in the past few years with the ascendance of Japanese foods, modernist cuisine, the New Nordic cuisine, and customers' love for rustic Italian fare.[1] A large proportion of highly rated restaurants in New York are still French, a pattern evident in the *New York Times*, prominent magazines like *New York*, and restaurant guides such as those put out by Michelin and Zagat. In the spring of 2014, fourteen of the forty-nine restaurants (28.6%) rated with three or four stars (four being the highest) in the *New York Times* were classified as French.[2] The four-star category was dominated by French restaurants until the early 2000s, though this is no longer the case, as high-prestige cuisines such as Japanese, New American, and Italian have joined this category's ranks.

In short, choosing a cuisine, as the chef with the ambitious project knew, has significant consequences for how a restaurant will be rated as well as for the kinds of dishes the chef can put out. How and why this happens are the questions I answer in this chapter. Categories and classifications matter in any cultural endeavor and any economic market because they influence how creators understand their work, how arbiters assess it, and how consumers perceive it.[3] In cuisine, ingredients and techniques are the elements that define culinary styles and by which these are classified into regional categories (such as French, Tuscan, or New American) as well as in terms of their innovativeness. Restaurant critics and the media have a large influence on the classification of chefs and culinary styles, determining how they will be perceived, and what ingredients and techniques chefs will be able to use without breaching boundaries. Chefs are naturally quite concerned about how their styles will be classified, and develop their own understandings and narratives to control and manage their classification projects. To understand how chefs do so, one must look first at the building blocks of cuisine—ingredients and techniques—and the factors that go into restaurant ratings and reviews, because it is in light of these matters that chefs reflectively shape their understandings of culinary styles.

Techniques and Ingredients

In cities like New York and San Francisco, chefs have access to a wide range of cuisines and ingredients from all over the world. Such availability means that over time foreign foods become more familiar and symbolically less foreign, and therefore that the boundaries that separate cuisines weaken.[4] By the same token, it means that local diners have more familiarity with exotic foodstuffs and are consequently more willing to order a wider array of foods. A chef in these cities therefore has a lower risk of accruing sanctions for borrowing ingredients or ideas from other cuisines (e.g. negative reviews for making food perceived as unpleasant or "inauthentic" or loss of patrons) than do chefs in other locales.[5] Still, some foreign foods can seem more foreign than others; to most Western diners, Senegalese food is more exotic than Chinese, and even though soy sauce no longer seems exotic to most of them, stinky tofu still does. A chef at a New American or even a French restaurant can use certain Chinese or Japanese ingredients (e.g., miso, dried mushrooms, the herb shiso, or fish sauce), make Italian preparations (e.g., pasta or risotto), or draw inspiration from Middle Eastern or North African dishes (e.g., hummus, tabouleh, or tagine) and Latin American food (e.g., ceviche or tacos) without appearing "inauthentic" because these foodstuffs are familiar to many diners and are served at other New American and French restaurants.

Both techniques and ingredients demarcate the boundaries of culinary styles but to quite different degrees. Chefs can avail themselves of a wide variety of ingredients, but French techniques still reign supreme in the elite restaurant world. Chefs cooking in styles that range from New American to

Mediterranean, Austrian, and even Italian use many of the basic French techniques in their kitchens.[6]

TECHNIQUES

In many ways, techniques have a more rigid role in cuisine than ingredients.[7]
For instance, risotto is an Italian dish made with a short-grain Italian rice
(Arborio, Carnaroli, or Vialone Nano) that is cooked by gradually adding
broth to it, a specific technique that differs from the way rice is cooked in
most other cuisines. The dish is defined by the main ingredient and by the
technique, but the two do not have the same influence; one could make the
dish with another short-grain, starchy rice and still legitimately call it risotto,
as I have seen chefs do, but stir-frying, or even boiling Italian rice would not
yield the specific texture that defines a risotto.

There are far fewer techniques, of course, than there are ingredients. Countries like Germany, Portugal, and Scotland have their own typical foodstuffs,
and some of these are made with specific techniques (e.g., sauerkraut, salt cod,
or haggis), but they have not developed a distinctive and elaborate grammar
of techniques that served as the foundation of a whole new cuisine, as France
has. Techniques are typically distinguished by regional origin, and some of the
most distinctive have led to unique and complex cuisines—Japan, China, and
India are cases in point.[8] Techniques are also categorized in terms of innovativeness, so whereas French techniques are now viewed as traditional, the modernist techniques, developed in Spain, are seen as innovative.[9] French techniques
consist of all the cooking rules, including how to make basic preparations for
stocks and sauces as well as methods for cooking meats, vegetables, and desserts. Some of the traditional techniques have been adapted to be less labor intensive; whereas stocks were traditionally made by roasting bones and simmer-
ing them with meats and vegetables for hours to use as the base for any soup
or sauce, now chefs often take shortcuts and make speedier broths, or even
purchase them pre-made. Of course, chefs today also make use of electronic
equipment like food processors, blenders, and microwaves, which also shorten
preparation times.[10]

For their part, modernist techniques require extraordinarily careful and
precise work and a more advanced understanding of chemistry and physics
than any other technique, indeed more of a scientist's approach.[11] Modernist

cuisine uses chemical ingredients not typically considered food for human beings and high-tech electronic equipment that were commonly used in industrial food processing but unheard of in the world of high cuisine until recently. Many of the chemicals and techniques are used for altering food textures, turning a beet into a gelée, mayonnaise into a fried nugget, or potatoes into a foam. Some of the most commonly used chemicals are xanthan gum to thicken ingredients at either hot or cold temperatures, methylcellulose to thicken ingredients and incorporate air into them in the process, and agar to jellify hot ingredients. Some of the most frequently used electronic tools are the Pacojet, which makes ice cream, sauces, or purées in a matter of seconds; the Cryovac machine and the immersion circulator, to vacuum-seal food and cook it in a low-temperature-controlled water bath for a long time (a technique called cooking *sous-vide*, which is French for "under-vacuum"); and the Thermomix, an appliance that can delicately blend and heat foodstuffs.[12]

The sociological literature on boundaries would suggest that types of techniques should be separated by stronger boundaries than ingredients due to their smaller number, which should make it more acceptable for chefs to borrow ingredients than techniques from culinary styles other than their own.[13] In effect, classical and modernist techniques, embodying the authority of tradition and allure of the new, respectively, are separated by a strong boundary. Since modernist techniques (or the innovative trends of the day) are often seen as a source for creativity and originality, chefs who cook traditional food sometimes struggle to attract the attention and prestige that newer trends get from the media. The contentious relationship between classical and modernist techniques comes to the fore when chefs talk about their own food or the current state of high cuisine. Traditional chefs underscore the authority of history and the value of craft and emotion to justify the use of traditional, low-tech procedures. As a highly respected chef at a high-status restaurant in New York put it, modernist techniques are "bad for the soul":

> We do emulsion sauces with a hand blender, like they did in nouvelle cuisine in the 1970s. But I'm not really into like the whole chemical aspect of it, which, you know, is big now. . . . I ate at El Bulli in 1997 and I didn't particularly care for it. Not my style. And it's almost soulless. It's chemistry, it's science, for sure. . . . The short ribs [a popular dish on his menu], you eat it, and it's very soul-satisfying.

Traditional chefs rarely discuss modernist techniques without conveying how strongly they feel about the matter. The symbolic meaning of innovative techniques is also subject to contestation, especially when it comes to techniques that can cross over from innovative to traditional styles.[14] One such case is the use of a Cryovac machine and an immersion circulator. Unlike any other cooking method (including boiling, steaming, stewing, sautéing, frying, grilling, roasting, and braising), this method insulates ingredients from any liquid or air as they are cooked sous-vide. This prevents flavors from evaporating, which intensifies the taste of ingredients; in addition, the low and slow cooking makes ingredients much more tender. These qualities have made cooking sous-vide widely popular among chefs of all culinary styles, even fairly traditional ones.[15] Unlike most innovative techniques, this one does not alter the chemical state or visible appearance of foods, so an average diner cannot tell that something has been cooked sous-vide, even if she may marvel at the flavorfulness or tenderness of the food. Sous-vide cooking cannot be said to be used for gimmickry, so chefs with traditional styles may still use it without feeling that they betray their principles or risk their authenticity. Nevertheless, the strongest stalwarts of tradition, like the chef quoted previously, still reject the technique on the grounds that using such machines is not "what cooking is about."

INGREDIENTS

Like techniques, ingredients are also categorized by region and innovativeness, but the boundaries are fuzzier. Olives are typical in France as well as in Italy and Greece, sauerkraut is German and also one of the most typical foods in Alsace, and the origin of hummus is hotly debated among residents of Middle Eastern and Arabic countries—determining where any of these foodstuffs come from is a slippery task.[16] Innovative foodstuffs are rarely newly invented but rather newly introduced into a culinary field. Kale and lowbrow cuts of meat such as pork belly or offal, for instance, were rare in elite restaurants in New York and San Francisco until recently, but common in other fields. Borrowing ingredients from other cuisines is therefore a much less contentious matter than borrowing techniques. A chef at a high-status French-Mediterranean restaurant in New York discusses this practice as he describes his culinary style.

It's pretty contemporary French here. We don't do anything that's too Asian but there's no point in holding yourself back, limiting yourself to traditional cooking. People now want lighter, easier to eat dishes, less stuffy dishes. You have to move with the times as well. That's the reason why, even if it is Mediterranean, there is stuff like lemongrass and non-Mediterranean ingredients here.

This chef had recently moved to New York from abroad to work at this renowned traditional restaurant. During the interview and subsequent conversations, he emphasized the contemporary nature of his style to account for his use of ingredients that are neither typically French nor Mediterranean. Moreover, highlighting customer demand for lighter and less traditional dishes helped him to present his choices as those of necessity, thereby protecting his authenticity.[17] Chefs at Italian restaurants, for their part, point out that cooking with local ingredients is the very heart of Italian cuisine, so they use American ingredients where the Italian ones are not available (e.g., substituting striped bass for a local fish from Veneto or kale for Tuscan bitter greens). In doing so, they note, they are cooking in the Italian style. Some chefs point out that cooking in any style necessarily entails an interpretation, an argument that legitimates borrowing ingredients from other styles and allows for more freedom to cross boundaries. Even those who cook in highly traditional styles, regardless of the cuisine, can thus incorporate local foodstuffs and ingredient pairings without putting their authenticity at risk, so long as they use traditional techniques. That there is no classical American cuisine that has codified the use of local foodstuffs (what ingredients go together and which are not to be mixed, and how ingredients are to be cooked) to the extent found in a country like France likely weakens boundaries between ingredients, so chefs are better able to borrow ingredients from other cuisines without accruing penalties.[18] Indeed, I have frequently heard chefs compare the New York restaurant world favorably to Paris due to the greater freedom to innovate facilitated by these conditions.

Borrowing from foreign cuisines is also easier when cuisines are perceived as different but not opposite, because categories viewed as opposite are separated by much stronger boundaries. Even French and Italian cuisines, often contrasted for their different approaches, are not quite seen as opposite, and this is why chefs at French restaurants can have Italian preparations on their menus (e.g., risotti or pasta dishes) without appearing inauthentic and facing the risk of negative reviews or loss of patrons. Crossing the boundary between traditional and innovative styles is riskier since these are seen as opposite categories. When traditional chefs innovate, they make a point of incorporating only a few and not too innovative elements, and still underscore the traditional nature of their food. A chef who serves traditional Italian food could safely substitute pork belly for Italian sausage in a classic dish of orecchiette (small dried pasta) with sausage and broccoli rabe, but serving Italian sausage gelée with broccoli rabe foam would be more threatening to his authenticity. That is, he could more safely borrow ingredients from different cuisines than techniques viewed as opposite to his style.

When chefs serve food that falls squarely within the boundaries of their styles, they reinforce such boundaries, and increase the risks of challenging them.[19] By contrast, when they borrow extensively from a cuisine other than their own, they eventually weaken the boundaries between the two cuisines, and reposition them as complementary.[20] This is what has happened between French and Japanese food; as French chefs have borrowed ingredients, ideas, and even techniques from Japan increasingly since the nouvelle cuisine in the 1960s and 1970s, it is now easier for French chefs to introduce Japanese elements into their food.[21] French chefs often extol the virtues of combining French and Japanese foodstuffs, but one would be hard pressed to find a traditional French chef expounding on the merits of innovation.

Now, any chef may stay within the bounds of a cuisine or cross boundaries and make unusual dishes, but not all chefs have the same influence on the fate of boundaries. High-status chefs are much more influential. They weakened boundaries between highbrow and lowbrow, for instance, when they began to serve newfangled versions of hamburgers with expensive cuts of beef, foie gras, or even truffles and to cook with pork belly or offal. In doing so, they opened the doors for other chefs to follow suit and in time increased the status of such foods.[22] Analytically, this means that both chefs and foodstuffs are classified in culinary and status terms, and that both structure the social space within which they acquire meaning and prestige.[23] High-status chefs have more influence on the meaning and prestige of foodstuffs because their work attracts more attention from the media, and is therefore more visible, and because it is more likely to be emulated by other chefs.[24]

Classifications of Styles: Reviews and Ratings in the Media

When it comes to classifying elite restaurants, ratings and reviews from the media matter greatly; the stars awarded to a restaurant by the most influential publications effectively determine that restaurant's fate. In New York and San Francisco, these publications are the *New York Times* and the *San Francisco Chronicle*, respectively, with media like the Michelin Guide and *New York* and *San Francisco* magazines bearing some influence as well.[25] These publications also classify restaurants into culinary categories (e.g., German, Middle Eastern, New American), and list establishments in their print or online platforms under these categories, as well as under number of stars (one can, for instance, search for restaurants within the New American or Steakhouse category as well as within the two-star or three-star category).[26] Innovation is not a formal category, in that it is not a label under which restaurants are listed, but it is an assessment embedded in reviews that is highly consequential for ratings.[27] Sam Sifton, for example, a former *New York Times* restaurant critic, extols the innovativeness of the food in a review of Del Posto, an Italian restaurant that had recently opened.[28]

> Mr. Ladner's pastas are insanely good. After a wintry appetizer of warm, soft cotechino in a lentil vinaigrette, his spaghetti with Dungeness crab, sliced jalapeño and minced scallion arrives like the sun. It is a dish that speaks directly to Mr. Ladner's genius, to a view of Italian cooking that allows for both jalapeño and Dungeness crab. His cooking is not about recreating Italy on a luxe scale so much as it is about recreating the Italian spirit on the grandest scale imaginable.

Finding the chef's innovativeness unambiguously praiseworthy, Sifton awarded the restaurant four stars, turning it into the first Italian restaurant to be given the highest number of stars in the *New York Times* since 1974. Frank Bruni, a previous restaurant critic for this newspaper, was even more explicit about the positive valuation of innovation in a review of Perbacco.[29]

> After that we had prosciutto e melone, which may not sound unusual. But wait. At Perbacco they're not partners in an antipasto; they're partners in a pasta dish, tortelloni filled with prosciutto and mascarpone cheese

and sauced with mint, butter and cubes of cantaloupe. Another surprise. Another winner. . . . [S]omething is indeed happening here . . . since the restaurant welcomed Simone Bonelli, a 26-year-old chef brimming with ideas and ambition. But it's no longer conventional. It's experimental, Lupa meets wd-50.

Enthralled by the originality of the food, Bruni awarded this modest restaurant two stars.[30] Like him, other critics also assess innovative food more favorably than traditional fare so long as they perceive that innovation is done for the sake of flavor, but they will review such food more negatively when they think there is too much innovation and/or that innovation is used for the sake of effect. Finding innovation to be detrimental to the food at Porchetta, another Italian restaurant, Bruni imbued the entire review with a negative tone, and awarded the ambitious restaurant only one star.[31]

[Pork cracklings in a cocktail] aren't so much improvements on a winning, sturdy formula as they are cheeky curiosities, meant to prompt stares and chatter. . . . Porchetta is a restaurant that's determined—sometimes too determined—to snap you to attention, to take you by surprise. . . . Take the gnocchi. Mr. Neroni aced the potato dumplings themselves, which couldn't have been softer or lighter on the tongue. And they were elevated as high as need be by a sauce of cream, butter, crushed black truffles and truffle oil. But Mr. Neroni couldn't and didn't stop there. In a flourish too far and too abundant, he added candied lemon zest.

Given how heavily innovation weighs on critics' assessments in the current culinary world, I wanted to know if there was a strong association between innovation and ratings. Do critics generally favor innovation over traditional food? Can restaurant ratings be predicted on the basis of innovation? I conducted content analysis of the reviews of all restaurants included in this study ($N = 44$) to analyze how critics understand and assess innovation.[32] Not surprisingly, I found that there is no simple direct relationship between innovation and ratings (i.e., that more innovation leads to higher ratings). How restaurants are rated is explained by critics' evaluation of the combination of degree of innovation and type of innovation. The degree of innovation has to do with how innovative the food is and whether the innovation comes at the expense of flavor (i.e., it might be original and interesting food but not quite as tasty as desired).

The type of innovation has to do with the four forms of innovation critics write about: in ingredients, ingredient combinations, technique, and presentation.

Like most diners, restaurant critics assess the food based largely on the information that arrives on their plates—what they see and taste. They can easily comment on ingredient combinations, but not always on the selection of ingredients because that requires information that is not necessarily available (e.g., the geographic origin of ingredients or the names or locations of the farmers who grew them).[33] More significantly, critics tend to write about ingredient combinations because those are seen as the best indicator of a chef's creativity. The selection of original ingredients says more about good sourcing than creativity.[34] Presentation, while easily observable and a clear indicator of creativity, has more to do with visual aesthetics than flavor. As a result, a chef who serves dishes with highly elaborate presentations is prone to being negatively assessed for being "over the top" or "show-offish" and ultimately not so concerned with "what cooking is about." Techniques are the least visible part of the dish, except for the modernist techniques that transform the textures of foods; thus, if critics comment on techniques, it is about the modernist ones.

Overall, innovation in ingredient combinations is the most commonly mentioned type of innovation *by far* ($N = 95$) and the most positively assessed; all other factors being equal, it leads to generally more enthusiastic reviews than any other type of innovation.[35] Innovation in presentation is the (very distant) second most frequently discussed ($N = 23$), and the most likely to be negatively portrayed. Innovation in technique is referred to significantly less frequently ($N = 8$), followed by innovation in ingredient selection ($N = 6$), the least frequently and not too enthusiastically discussed. Though the four types of innovation are assessed very differently, no single type determines the review of a restaurant. The most positive reviews always combine positive comments about several types of innovation and restraint in innovativeness.

Chefs' Views on the Classification of Styles

As one might expect, chefs use the same categories as critics to talk about food and restaurants, and they focus on the factors that are central to their reputation and commercial success, namely culinary styles, originality, and status.[36] Restaurant reviews and ratings are the most effective sources for figuring out a culinary field, even for chefs, given that they convey information about all the attributes that matter in the field.[37] Furthermore, relying on reviews' classifications of restaurants means that chefs develop views that are in line with those of evaluators and customers, and this better equips them to make choices for their restaurants that stand a good chance of succeeding commercially.[38]

Now, chefs use the same categories as critics to talk about food and locate restaurants in a field, but when it comes to being categorized, that is a different story. Except for those who have a clear regional orientation (e.g., Tuscan cuisine), chefs always qualify the labels others use to categorize their culinary styles, assuming that they do accept them. Very frequently, they reject the categories altogether. A chef at a high-status restaurant in San Francisco, for instance, insisted (with sarcasm) that she does not "set herself to create French food" and that she has a range of influences. This statement was not intended to help others place her in the correct category but rather to undermine any attempt to place her in any category.

> I personally don't really like to classify [my style]. I don't really like to stick it in a box and say, "It's French," or "It's California cuisine," or "It's Asian, Pan-Asian.". . . I kind of pull my ideas from a wide variety of sources, and I usually take the ingredient, the raw ingredient itself, and draw my inspiration from that. . . . Just out of the sake of needing to call it something, people call it "French-inspired, California cuisine.". . . My foundation of cooking . . . I guess you could say that it's primarily French, stylistically. But you know, sometimes I use ingredients that are not traditionally, like, French, and sometimes I draw inspiration from different kinds of cuisines.

Why do chefs generally resist having their styles classified? It is, in part, because the categories involve *others'* preconceived ideas and expectations. Also, being placed in a category suggests that at least some of one's creative process is not really one's own at all but is generic to the category.[39] This becomes even more problematic for someone holding her first job as executive chef, as in the above case, because she is at a stage in her career when she faces strong pressures to demonstrate that she has a style of her own.[40] It is not that she is mistaken, and certainly not that she is duplicitous, in insisting that her distinctive style cannot be accurately characterized with any preexisting label. Insiders have nuanced understandings of their work and see distinctions invisible to outsiders.[41] Chefs also resist being placed in a category because it involves a forced association with others placed in that group. If we are elevated by being in good company, we are also tarred with the same brush as any fools and incompetents who happen to share our label.[42] Chefs also often purposefully seek to distance themselves from a particular category due to the social and symbolic attributes of that category. Those in San Francisco, for instance, resist having their styles classified as Italian because that label still evokes the low-quality Italian American restaurants that stock the tourist area of North Beach.[43] A chef at a high-status Italian restaurant in this city described his restaurant this way:

> What's the theme? My response always was "There was no theme." I would just say it's an Italian restaurant and we are just based in California. Everything would be with the intention of going in the direction to homage Italian food but not like a menu in a region. . . . I always eat in France too, so I want to put something more French. . . . Most Americans don't know what real Italian food was in the first place, so we would have not labeled it that. *And it would have been to my detriment too, I think.* . . . But . . . I don't think I need to get pigeonholed in, like, "This is California cuisine." What's that, you know? [Emphasis added.]

In an ideal world, one would get to choose one's peers and how one's actions are interpreted, but like everyone else, chefs cannot escape being categorized. And because culinary categories vary in prestige, chefs often prefer to be placed in a certain category as opposed to another. Once a restaurant is placed in a category, that classification will guide the attributes of the food that will stand out in reviewers' and diners' assessments and their overall perception of the food.[44] A dish of eggplant with cheese and tomato, for instance, is the very classical eggplant parmigiana in an Italian menu, but it has a different set of references and symbolic meanings in a Spanish menu.

Chefs purposefully select culinary styles when they open new restaurants with an eye to how their food will be classified and assessed.[45] Beyond formal categories, they also shape how their styles will be perceived through stories that provide a background to their food: consider the chef who opens a restaurant to serve the food his mother cooked when he was little, or the environmentally minded chef who opens a rustic carnivore restaurant serving all animal parts ("nose-to-tail eating") because it is a more conscientious way of cooking and eating. These are widely used stories, and therefore serve not only to define a restaurant's style but also to legitimate it.[46] The story of the mother's cooking never loses its appeal, and that of the return-to-the-farm restaurant, however deeply felt, resonates with issues (environmental, political, and aesthetic) that have gained attention in the past few years, as well as with a trend in carnivorous eating that has become widely popular.[47] Chefs' attempts to shape their images are much like the impression management that we all engage in to control our "presentation of self."[48] Just as we constantly fine-tune our self-presentation and adjust it to circumstances, so do chefs adjust the identities of their restaurants. If they receive lukewarm reviews and struggle economically, they tinker with the food to gradually modify the culinary style, making it simpler and more casual, using more popular ingredients, or even shifting from elaborate New American to more rustic Mediterranean food.

Innovation: The Scholarly Viewpoint

For critics, or any outsider who does not see the nuanced distinctions understood by insiders, categories are more clear-cut and, without a doubt, much less contentious. This is the case when it comes to innovation; to an observer, a product is more easily reduced to a binary option, such that it appears either innovative or not.[49] Innovation is typically characterized this way in the scholarly literature as well as in popular media. From a sociological standpoint, and building on pragmatist theories of action, Hans Joas argues that creativity arises when habitual action fades.[50] Habitual action and creativity, the exploitation of old ideas and exploration of new ones, conformity to established styles and originality, tradition and innovation, are all analogous binary categories commonly used in sociology and organizational analysis, wherein one of the components refers to the reproduction of old ways and the other is the force of change, and is as such afforded an intrinsically positive value.[51] Furthermore, innovation is often characterized as the end product of a particular kind of motivated action, a strategy (whether conscious or subconscious) to increase one's prestige.[52] That is, individuals strategize as they respond to incentives and constraints of innovating, including the economic costs and risks of innovating, how their status influences the perception of their work, and the information they obtain through social networks.

The scholarly literature explains innovation in terms of three analytical levels: individual, organizational, or interorganizational. At the individual level, a person's social position explains her likelihood to innovate, because some status positions make innovating a riskier strategy than others, and network positions differ in their potential to open access to new ideas that can help a person to innovate.[53] At the organizational level, the characteristics of an organization's size, hierarchical structure, geographic location, and communication channels influence individuals' access to different ideas and ability to apply new ideas.[54] At the interorganizational level, social relations across organizations can facilitate (or hinder) access to different ideas, depending on whether organizations are geographically close, have formal or informal communication channels with other organizations, and have individuals who tend to draw on ideas from other groups.[55] Beyond these three levels of analysis, a small body of research shows how self-understandings and social identities inform individuals' inclinations to do creative or original work.[56]

Hearing the perspective of practitioners shows the limitations of the more structural explanations of innovation. Many of these explanations—whether at the individual, organizational, or interorganizational level—entail assumptions about how individuals understand their social environment and their motives for action (e.g., if a low-status chef creates traditional dishes, it is because he knows it is too risky to innovate). But individuals differ in how they perceive their environment, approach their work, and project that work into the future, and these factors inform the goals they set for themselves and the actions they undertake, including whether they will innovate or not.[57]

Innovation: The Chef's Viewpoint

To explain how chefs understand innovation, let us take the traditional pork roast as an example. In a common technique in classical preparations, pork is wrapped in bacon to impart more flavor to this lean cut of meat. A chef could employ a modernist technique to innovate the dish: sprinkle bacon powder, made using chemicals to dehydrate bacon and turn it into a powder, on the pork. Another chef might turn to different ingredient combinations, pairing the roast of pork with salt cod. In yet another option, a chef might innovate with a new ingredient, roasting the pig's head, a part of the pig that has only recently begun to appear in elite restaurants in New York and San Francisco. Or a chef might turn to the presentation and arrange the roast pork as a brick with layers of bacon (held together with meat glue, the enzymes called transglutaminases), departing from the traditional presentation of pork slices wrapped in bacon.[58]

With the exception of the traditional preparation, one might expect chefs to view all the above dishes as innovative, even if to varying degrees. However, this is far from what would happen. Why is this the case? For a chef, a dish is not simply a combination of ingredients, techniques, and presentation, but is rather something embedded in traditions, culinary conventions, technical knowledge, fads, and creativity. How chefs understand these various factors, and which ones they prioritize to create dishes, informs their views of what is innovative and what is not.

One of the fundamental logics chefs follow is that of function: an ingredient should be included in a dish if it contributes to the overall balance of flavors.[59] From this standpoint, replacing ingredients with others that are functionally equivalent, modifying textures, or creating eye-catching presentations has no bearing on the overall dish. To return to the traditional example of roast pork, bacon adds fat and saltiness, and hence flavor, to a lean cut of meat. Turning bacon into a fine powder, and eliminating the fatty strips of bacon, makes the dish lighter. The contemporary belief is that rich foods tire the palate, so lighter preparations help people to appreciate flavors; this is especially important at high-end restaurants, where tasting menus, consisting of multiple courses, can easily tire the palate. Lighter preparations also cater to diners' preferences, given that some customers favor, and occasionally demand, a lower calorie intake. For its part, salt cod fulfills bacon's function of adding salt and fat, and a pig's head adds a more intense flavor than the typically mild-tasting pork roast. Lastly, the innovative presentation, by gluing layers of pork and bacon together, ensures that diners eat all the ingredients of the traditional recipe at the same time so that they appreciate the combination of flavors. To the extent that an innovation is made in the cause of flavor, it is not seen as an innovation by its creator.

Chefs understand and use the logic of function variously. Those who see themselves as traditional foreground this logic to think about their food. They would consider the above dishes to be minor variations on the classical recipe, arguing that there is never any real innovation because "everything has already been done." Even if diners think their food is innovative, these chefs beg to differ because they are "not reinventing the wheel." This was the reaction of a chef at a middle-status restaurant in New York, one of the first to serve comfort food in an elite restaurant in this city, indeed fostering the trend. She has gained a very good reputation (for a "fun and creative restaurant"), received numerous positive reviews, and has run a widely popular restaurant for years. I suggested that diners and critics believed her food was inventive.

> That part I haven't completely understood. I would never claim to have invented *aaaanything*, and in fact, have believed to not have to. Just like there's no story that hasn't already been told, you know, you can just write your version of it . . . So all the food here is the same thing, it's like, I'm just roasting a chicken. So I roast my chicken with a little point of view. Or, these dishes are classic, they live in a world, they are part of the traditions of world cuisines, like real food.

Chefs who foreground the logic of function push the "little point of view" in their dishes to the background, regardless of how innovative they may be. By contrast, those who *aim* to be creative foreground inventiveness and are therefore likely to view their food as original. For these chefs, adding a "little point of view" entails reinterpreting classical recipes to create dishes that are different, interesting, or original. To be sure, there is variance here; someone who "tweaks classics" is closer to tradition than someone who makes dishes that are "different" or, even more distant from tradition, "innovative." A chef at another middle-status restaurant in New York who serves relatively rustic dishes—reinterpretations of European and Mediterranean classic recipes—represents his style and himself quite differently from the chef cited above.

> And so I tried to learn both . . . by learning the classics or traditional dishes, regional and traditional dishes and classic dishes, and then start to create your own cuisine with those as the base. . . . So you'll find remnants of a classic French dish somewhere in a dish, whether it is, I hate the word, "deconstructed.". . . But there is a familiarity there that, for some reason, it makes sense. . . . There is a traditional lamb stew in Morocco that is made, stewed, made with black olives, lemons and squash and a mixture of spices, and this [a dish on the menu] is very similar to that. So it would be the same flavors in your mouth, but it is not a stew, it's a grilled lamb chop.

Over a long career in New York, this chef has worked at a few well-known restaurants, acquired renown, and developed his culinary style. He spent a good deal of time commenting on the value of tradition, classical regional dishes, and familiar flavors, but he also pointed out that, in contrast to the previous chef I quoted, he *re-creates* classical recipes, turning them into dishes that are his own. Whereas the previous chef set out to offer simple "real" food, and therefore underscored the traditional quality of her cooking, for this chef it is important to serve dishes that are *his own;* hence he foregrounds the process of the reinterpretation of traditional recipes.[60]

As important as the balance of flavors is, chefs cannot guide their actions just by this logic. In areas of cultural production where work is not necessarily for profit, creators may concern themselves solely with aesthetic qualities intrinsic to the products they create—with "pure" values.[61] But chefs cannot disregard profit, and therefore need to differentiate themselves from competitors to stand out in the market. This means that originality—the response to differentiation—is the other logic that is key for them. From this logic's standpoint, new creations are made *in the cause of* originality. The two logics are not equally important to all chefs; whereas flavor (along with tradition) matters most to some, for others originality is just as important as flavor, and for still others creating original dishes is the main goal. Those for whom differentiation is especially important always make remarks about the value of being original; focusing on the innovative elements in their food, they naturally view their styles as original. A chef at a prestigious middle-status restaurant in New York, known for a wildly creative style, explains the key to his style.

> People come to my place to be *wowed*. They want to be pleasantly surprised, a little whim. And they want to be satisfied. And you know what? You can make someone smile before they taste it. . . . To get a fifty-year-old man to smile before he ate it, a guy that eats out every day, then you hit a home run, you know. . . . You gotta start to think outside the box. If you put apple sauce with pork chops, why can't I put figs? . . . Pork is fatty, fruit helps you digest. So use any fruit, use brown sugar, use vinegar.

Over years of experience working at several prestigious restaurants in New York, this chef created a unique culinary style, characterized by ingredients reshaped to such an extent that they were hard to recognize (e.g., fish prepared with ingredients and techniques used for pork, so that it no longer looks or tastes much like fish), unusual ingredient combinations, and elaborate architectural presentations—whimsical is a word often used to describe his style. For him, creating original food matters more than anything else, a principle in line with his self-understanding as an artist—in need of being constantly stimulated and challenged—as well as with the pragmatic understanding that original dishes guarantee a steady stream of customers.

Let us imagine a perfectly plausible scenario—that each of the three chefs I have been discussing here takes the classical recipe for boeuf bourguignon and, instead of serving the traditional French stew of beef, wine, pearl onions, and mushrooms, turns it into a steak with the onions, mushrooms, and sauce on the side. The chef who serves comfort food would maintain it is still a traditional dish, the one who reinterprets European and Mediterranean dishes would view it as a creative take on a classical recipe, and the chef who makes whimsical food would characterize it as an inventive creation. If three chefs could characterize a dish so differently, it is because they understand food through different logics that lead them to focus on certain things and ignore others. The logics they follow are in line with how they see themselves as chefs: the pure traditionalist, the creative traditionalist, and the innovator.[62] I have found self-described traditionalists among chefs who combine numerous Asian and Latin American ingredients in elaborate dishes or use complex techniques in high-end New American restaurants as well as among those who make classical rustic pastas at simple Italian restaurants. Chefs go through an involved process to create a recipe, and the parts of the process they consider most significant given the principles that matter most to them (e.g., sourcing the freshest ingredients, mastering classical techniques, or making inventive ingredient combinations) will shape how they understand the dishes they create.

Classifications and Reflective Understandings over Time

Chefs work in a field with fairly rigid structures built around culinary styles, innovation, and status, that are underpinned by a system of ratings and reviews. Being classified around these categories not only shapes chefs' field positions but also bounds the kinds of foods they can put out, as this chapter showed. In particular, chefs vary in their ability to cross boundaries and borrow ingredients or techniques from other cuisines relative to their culinary styles. Because being placed in one culinary category rather than another holds so much sway in their careers, chefs carefully attempt to control how their food will be classified.

Culinary categories of regional origin are fundamental in cuisine, of course, but assessments of innovation (based on a combination of types and degree of innovation) also matter greatly for the classification and rating of restaurants. Innovation may be evaluated by means of varied criteria by critics, but it is even harder to define for creators, who understand it from within. Chefs understand innovation in ways that are associated with the main logics that guide them in cooking—either function or differentiation—and with how they see themselves as chefs along a continuum that goes from tradition to innovation as I explained in this chapter.

Like anyone, they have to find ways to negotiate external classifications of their styles with their own views so as to maintain a consistent sense of self. This is not simply because they need to project a fitting image to others but, more fundamentally, because this sense anchors their actions, helping them focus on the principles that matter most to them and make choices about their work that are in line with their styles, such that these choices "feel right" to them *and* are effective for audiences.[63] Most chefs who cook in traditional Italian styles ignore much about modernist techniques (even if the information is easily available to them) and also much of the information about new exotic products that arrive every season, and chefs who cook in simple French bistros do not necessarily follow the ups and downs of the truffles market or look out for trendy Latin American ingredients.

What is more, chefs are unlikely to cook in culinary styles that are not in line with their self-concepts, even if they have the required skills, and they rarely accept job offers from restaurants that are at odds with their normative views about what matters in cooking. When they do accept these jobs, it is only because they lack a better choice, and they stay only until they find a job that is more consistent with their views. However, just as jobs change over time, so do self-concepts, for chefs are unlikely to maintain a self-image that no longer resonates with the food they cook.[64] Culinary styles and self-concepts are adjusted vis-à-vis one another in an ongoing process, a typical example of which is evidenced when chefs move to downscale establishments after years of working at high-end restaurants and become critical of the elaborate and intricate cooking they had once wholeheartedly embraced. It is a common transition because the expectations of excellence at high-end restaurants introduce exceptionally high pressures, and chefs grow tired of working under such conditions; they also choose to open lower-status establishments because high-end restaurants are not so profitable.[65] A chef who worked at a few high-status restaurants in New York during his training, before becoming a chef at a celebrated middle-status restaurant serving traditional rustic Italian food, talked about the transition from one extreme of the culinary spectrum to the other.

> I don't believe in a lot of the Escoffier style, you know, everything from zero, homemade stocks and shit. . . . So I decided to have an alternative cuisine for that matter. . . . And then [a chef and business-partner] really helped me how to adapt a lot of those ideas into a more Italian aesthetic. Discipline is very different in Italian food, it's more, it's more based on shopping, product, and then also with restraint and knowing when to leave the food alone. . . . And there's nothing wrong with that [elaborate high-end food]. In fact, when I am off, I love to eat that food, because I do miss it. I just don't want to cook it everyday, that's all.

That this chef left the world of composed French food behind to cook simple Italian food was certainly not due to lack of opportunities or skill; his choice was consistent with his views on cooking and the kind of chef he wanted to be. He recounted that his first restaurant job as a teenager was at an Italian American restaurant that, as his first exposure to professional cooking, captured his heart, so when he had an opportunity to cook simple Italian food again, he seized it. This does not mean that his early experience was the *cause* of his career choice. For one thing, a large proportion of chefs in the United States begin their careers in (generally low-quality) Italian American restaurants and never long to make this kind of food—quite the contrary. Instead, this chef reaches back to his early experience to anchor his narrative and formulate a coherent self-concept that is in line with his recent career choice. Furthermore, his rejection of the high-end world and praise of simple Italian cooking is not a case of making virtue out of necessity. Given his experience at high-status restaurants, the recognition he had from peers and the press, and the social networks that come along with this career path, he could have easily obtained a job at a high-end restaurant. Indeed, after a few years of cooking in this rustic establishment, he left for a position as the chef at a high-end restaurant that was just opening, where he still makes Italian food but much more elaborate and composed.

Working at one type of restaurant or another has a profound impact on how chefs are classified and consequently on how their careers will unfold. In view of this, chefs make career choices that entail a working out of opportunities and self-projects. Far from passively reacting to their environment and just accepting what is offered to them, they try to work out options that are in line with their past and their vision for the future. If at some point those options no longer work for their self-projects, they look for other opportunities and resort to other parts of themselves—which may have been temporarily pushed to the background—to anchor the new opportunities and new ways in which they will be classified.

Making adjustments between their self-understandings and the categories of cuisine within which they are placed is a more gradual and subtle task when chefs remain at the same restaurant than when they change jobs. When they are at a restaurant that is far from their ideal choice, chefs often engage in two strategies at the same time: they try to change the restaurant's menu towards their views of cuisine, and they foreground the aspects of their self-concepts that are in line with the restaurant's style so as to focus on what the job can bring to their self-projects.[66] They also modify their views over time as they gain experience, solidify their reputation, and go through the palate changes that come with aging (most notably, an increasing desire for simpler foods and stronger and more acidic flavors). In this case, they tweak their food to find a compromise between the styles that customers expect at their restaurants, given how these are classified, and their changing inclinations. A chef who has run a high-end restaurant in New York for years saw the evolution of his culinary style as the result of having matured and become more accommodating in life. He explains the transformation:

> But I have always been a minimalist, really, sometimes too much of a mini-malist. . . . Like, to cook a fish, and serve it in its own juice [*laughter*]. And say, "You know what? It's so beautiful, that fish and that juice, I'm not put-ting *anything* with it." You know? It's actually very Japanese thinking, you

know, very. But I know it was too extreme. . . . You have to find a middle
way in between what you would *love* to do or what you would *hate* to do.

This chef has transformed his culinary style more than once during his tenure
at the same restaurant. Though the changes in the kind of chef he wanted
to be drove some of the transformations of his culinary style, other factors
also contributed. Traveling and learning about new cuisines, he remarked,
influenced his menus significantly; trips to Japan and other Asian countries
marked his minimalist menus of past years, and visits to Spain and Latin
America inspired his "middle way" menus. These changes are also in line with
trends that have swept the New York culinary field, in particular the fascina-
tion with Japanese food and the fusion of French and Japanese styles that
marked the late 1900s and early 2000s, and the growing interest in Iberian
and Latin American cuisines that has followed those trends.

The kind of food he makes has not changed radically because he is bound
by the way his restaurant is classified. He cannot be too minimalist, because
diners expect artistry at high-end restaurants, and neither can he serve purely
Japanese, Iberian, or Latin American food because his restaurant is not categorized within any of these cuisines. In short, the subtle changes in his culinary style are a product of a confluence of factors, including his remaining at
the same restaurant, general trends in dining, his own changing interests and
inclinations, and the confidence that comes after a long tenure at one of the
most prestigious restaurants in the country. This *confidence* amounts to much
more than reputation and self-esteem. It is the outcome of the internalization
of knowledge acquired over years on the job, which enables him to experience
his choices for his restaurant as being less subject to external pressures to remain competitive and within the same exclusive high-end category and more
subject to his own taste—the latter of which is ultimately the embodiment of
professional experience.

To varying degrees, all chefs need to constantly obtain new ideas to keep
up with dining trends and attract customers in order to remain competitive
and maintain their positions in the field. This is not an easy task, not only because chefs are bound by how their restaurants are classified but also because
they need to look at what peers are doing to come up with new ideas, while
being careful that they do not end up serving food that is too derivative. This
complex scenario is what I turn to in the next chapter.

CHAPTER FOUR

Managing a Culinary Style

SHOCKING AUDIENCES with highly unusual creations is a strategy that works well in the arts to attract attention and acquire renown—Andy Warhol and Marcel Duchamp are but iconic examples of the case. For chefs, however, this strategy is a path towards bankruptcy. Like artists, chefs stand out among competitors only when they offer something different, but they cannot serve a dish that is just shocking. Food has to please the palate, of course, and what pleases the palate for most diners is familiar food. This means that chefs cannot stray too far from the canon, so there is a narrow range within which they can create dishes and develop distinctive styles. In other words, culinary creation is, of necessity, closely derivative.

Like creators in any cultural field, chefs get inspiration and borrow ideas from contemporaries and predecessors, but unlike creators in many other cultural fields, they have no means to publicly acknowledge that they borrowed an idea. In academia, for instance, scholars regularly use references to give credit to colleagues upon whose work they build, and in doing so, they make relations between their work and that of colleagues explicit. In cuisine, the exchange of ideas is not legally regulated. Recipes cannot be copyrighted; cookbooks are copyrighted, but copyrights protect cookbooks as combinations of recipes along with descriptions and explanations, not the individual recipes insofar as they are listings of ingredients. Recipes can be patented only when they involve complex technical procedures, but even when chefs could resort to this legal tool, they almost never do. They similarly almost never try to obtain trademarks or treat recipes as trade secrets, two other forms of intellectual property available to them.[1] And they almost never seek legal punishment of those who transgress shared norms about knowledge exchange, by, for instance, copying an entire dish. They do, however, use other mechanisms to regulate transgressions, namely spreading critiques or gossip through social networks, which effectively damages transgressors' reputations.[2]

Developing a style that is not too derivative and managing relations with peers is particularly hard in occupations where creativity needs to occur through minor changes and the relationship between one's own and somebody else's ideas is fuzzy.[3] Chefs engage in different strategies—culinary, cognitive, and rhetorical—to avoid the impression that they are too closely derivative. Differentiating from others is key to surviving in a market with steep costs and high volatility, and chefs learn to highlight their distance from, rather than their similarity to, other chefs, which they accomplish through the dishes they put out and the reflective ways in which they understand and represent their styles. In this chapter, I show how chefs strategize to differentiate from others by looking for new ideas with which they can navigate the balance between conformity to established styles and originality, and by managing a fitting distance from other chefs.

Conformity and Originality

Chefs have to give an impression of authenticity through the dishes they put out, which requires a balance between being consistent with their own style (whether a regional cuisine or their own signature style) and showing some originality.[4] Constantly changing styles makes chefs appear inauthentic, yet being loyal to a style without any element of novelty makes chefs appear to have no ideas of their own. Conformity to established styles and originality are obviously in tension with one another, so chefs must prioritize either one or the other. Like any activity that entails a personal investment, culinary creation is partially purposeful (i.e., chefs follow instrumental-rational logic to make choices) and partially informed by chefs' reflective self-understandings, in particular how they understand their work and see themselves vis-à-vis others. Whether chefs consider themselves traditional or innovative, advocates of simple or complex food, champions of local produce, masters of presentation, or devoted to customer service, such conceptions profoundly inform their choices.

Innovation is of course an important force for differentiating oneself from others in any field of cultural production. In high cuisine, every season brings new ingredients, ingredient combinations, techniques, and presentation styles. One chef will introduce new elements into his menu, and others will learn about these ideas and go on to adopt them, spreading these innovations through the field. However, any innovation chefs adopt must be consistent with their culinary styles and the kinds of restaurants where they work. For instance, nori, a dried seaweed used in Japanese cooking, might fit in a modern French restaurant but not a Tuscan trattoria, and matzo balls are out of place in either establishment. Chefs talk about the pressures and constraints on their creativity frequently, including the need to adhere to their styles, serve dishes that are familiar to customers, and write menus that appeal to a variety of diners. They view having to serve familiar dishes as the most limiting of these constraints. They often complain about customers' limited palates and conservative preferences: customers tend to order the same dishes over and over again and to prefer a small range of staple ingredients (i.e., chicken breast, steak, and salmon or tuna), which chefs find bland and intrinsically boring; diners are not adventurous when it comes to trying new ingredients (such as rare cuts of meat or offal) or innovative ingredient combinations (e.g., they might order pork with sweet potatoes but not pork with monkfish). Chefs cannot take staples off the menu, and neither can they take off their "signature dishes," because those are what most customers want.

Customers also impose other demands that chefs find constraining. Dietary restrictions, changing with each new diet fad, are chief among them. High-calorie foods and high-fat dairy products are among the most common things customers want to avoid, as are, in more recent times, carbohydrates and gluten. Chefs are especially weary of allergies they believe are made up, the most typical of which are claimed allergies to cream or butter or to onions or garlic (the former are related to weight concerns, and the latter to perceived digestive discomfort after eating allium species). These restrictions are burdensome not only because they put constraints on chefs' creativity, but also because they force chefs to modify well-thought-out dishes and serve food that they consider subpar. They are also problematic for kitchen operations during service; organized as an assembly line, kitchen operations are slowed down or disrupted with any special request to eliminate or substitute an ingredient in a dish.

Not all chefs are equally vocal about customers' demands, in part because they are not all equally constrained by them. Recently appointed chefs are more constrained, given their more limited reputation and experience. The demands limit their capacity to distinguish themselves from others and establish a reputation, and these chefs also feel such demands especially acutely because it is harder for them to distance themselves from the creative aspirations they consider central to their job. A young chef at a high-status restaurant in New York expressed this sentiment clearly:

> The only thing I don't have, obviously, is a green salad, and that's pretty much the most recommended thing that I don't have. I get a lot of people coming here for a green salad. And, not that I, I eat green salad when I go out, but you know, I also eat Chinese food when I go out, and I don't make Chinese food in my restaurant. You know, there's places that are more suited. . . . This restaurant, my vision was to offer people an experience, for people to come and experience my restaurant, not come and tell me "make me this and make me that.". . . . When someone asks for something, I don't know, it becomes a little aggravating.

This chef had opened his own establishment only about a year before I interviewed him, after working at high-end restaurants during his training. Making distinctive food was critical to attract attention and ensure the restaurant would survive its first, and riskiest, years in business. That strategy was indeed successful, as the restaurant received excellent reviews and tables were always booked. It is easier for chefs with an established reputation and secure restaurant to embrace the fact that, being in the service industry, their job is to cater to customers. A chef at one of the most elite restaurants in New York willingly makes spaghetti and meatballs when customers request it (at a cost of about $100). Another chef who owns a successful and highly regarded middle-status restaurant in New York talked about the transition towards this perspective:

> You're not going to take the . . . [signature dish] off the menu because people come and enjoy it. Who I am to stand in their way? When I was younger I was less willing to endure disappointments . . . It's one of those things where you come up with this, like, new creation. . . . You think it sounds fabulous; you taste it and you think it's fabulous. Nobody wants to eat it. "Why the hell doesn't anybody want to eat it? It's wonderful." Well, after a while it's like, people are real creatures of habit. And the sooner you understand that the less you'll be hurt. 'Cause it's all ego at that point.

A celebrity chef with a secure restaurant and experience running several successful restaurants in New York, he does not need to attract new attention but rather to maintain his clientele. Experiencing less pressure to differentiate from others allows him to have a more complacent view of customers' preferences. This and the above examples show that the tension between conformity and originality is a balancing act, and that there is variance in which of the two poles exerts more pressure and how difficult it is to manage the balance. A young chef who had recently obtained a job as executive chef at a high-status restaurant in New York faced strong pressures and incentives to attract attention with his food. Like the young chef cited previously, he also had a personal inclination to create highly innovative food:

> And for me, I like to kind of incorporate these new techniques with things that taste very good. . . . I put these subtle changes in the techniques, things that I've learned, things that I've come up with myself, but the *main* thing is that the food tastes good, and that people want to return for it. . . . It's like walking the balance, you have to stay balanced, you know. . . . I try to balance safe with things that are a little bit more out there. So I think people like to take chances with appetizers and not so much with entrées, so they'll be a little bit more dangerous in the beginning. . . . Most of the dishes on the menu, a good deal of, like 60 percent, are things that I've never seen before.

In response to external pressures, as well as to his personal inclinations, this chef leans towards originality in his quest for his own balancing act, adopting a strategy common among junior chefs, who still need to carve out a position in the field.

Monitoring Colleagues

The pressure to offer novelty and renew menus in elite restaurants is constant. Chefs read culinary magazines and trade publications, search the web, eat out, and travel in search of new ideas, ingredients, flavor combinations, and techniques. And they monitor culinary trends, noteworthy new dishes, restaurant openings, and what chefs in their city are doing to be up-to-date with new and ever-changing trends. For a chef in New York or San Francisco, chefs in France, Italy, Spain, or Norway can be good sources of ideas, but emulating their work is risky because they cook for different audiences, and habits and preferences vary across countries, and they may also have access to different ingredients. In contrast to foreign peers, local chefs are more accessible. High-status local chefs, whose work is especially likely to be followed and emulated by virtue of their status alone, are also more visible, as they frequently appear at events and in the media.[5] This renders information about their work easily available and facilitates monitoring and emulating it, which is a sensible strategy because those chefs are often the first to have access to new produce and rare ingredients so they are a good source of ideas. They have connections with the best purveyors in domestic and international markets and receive preferential service, so they are informed first when a new ingredient arrives in the season. They also have more connections with chefs in other fields, as they travel more than lower-status chefs (whether to eat for work, pleasure, or because they are invited to events), which gives them better access to information and therefore to new ideas that they can import.[6]

For instance, when an elite chef begins to use pomegranate syrup—a Mediterranean product not traditionally used in elite restaurants in the United States—many other chefs go on to incorporate it into their food. In the next season, another elite chef might incorporate yuzu juice—from the Japanese citrus fruit—into his food, and soon multiple menus will feature yuzu. Menus also show the same ingredient pairings; when a chef breaks culinary traditions by combining foodstuffs not typically paired together, soon thereafter the innovation turns up in many restaurant menus. The use of savory ingredients in desserts (e.g., herbs like thyme or rosemary, vegetables such as parsnips or beets, and fats such as olive oil or bacon) is a recent popular example of this tendency. Olive oil ice cream, bacon donuts, and chocolate cake with sea salt no longer look as odd as they did only a few years ago. Menus also display use of the same techniques by many chefs. If a chef begins to use chemicals and special equipment for turning potatoes into foam or thyme into gelée, subsequently many menus, even at fairly traditional restaurants, incorporate these items.

Menus are also structured around similar categories; traditionally organized around the categories of appetizer, entrée, and dessert, they then turned to the structure of tasting menus—a fixed succession of several small courses—after the fashion of high-end restaurants. More recently, menus have moved on to a "small plates" format, a selection of small dishes meant to be shared.

Menus also exhibit a similar writing style. Names of dishes with proper nouns, particularly common in traditional French cuisine (e.g., Beef Chateaubriand, Pommes Duchesse) and geographic references (e.g., Niçoise Salad, Gratin Dauphinois) have been replaced with titles with no proper names. Contemporary dishes are typically named with succinct lists of ingredients (e.g., ham, plums, kale, and walnuts), sometimes including the specific source of foodstuffs down to the farm where the ingredient was grown or the fisherman who caught the fish (e.g., "Dingo Farms Pork," "Rodney's Halibut"). This change reflects a contemporary trend to highlight the quality of ingredients, as well as ethical concerns regarding the production of foodstuffs and the environment.[7] When a prestigious chef began to use metaphoric names for dishes, or quotation marks for components of dishes that are not what they appear, other chefs followed suit (e.g., "couscous" for a dish of cauliflower chopped into small pieces to resemble couscous, or "tiramisu" for a dessert delivered as a cream broth, cocoa ice cream, a coffee cookie, and ladyfinger dust, instead of the traditional Italian layers of ladyfingers and creamy filling). In short, as chefs regularly showcase new elements to stand out, others attend to and emulate their actions, and still others go on to introduce yet newer elements to distinguish themselves, they all collectively maintain a rapidly changing cycle of fads and fashions in a culinary field.[8]

Chefs need a good understanding of where they fit vis-à-vis others—including close competitors and chefs with whom they are likely to be associated given their career paths and similarities in culinary styles—so that they can orient their actions towards those from whom they need to differentiate and towards those from whom they can more or less safely borrow ideas. Having a sense that they are different, as well as how they differ, is key because it gives them the understanding they require to make choices and manage their restaurants and careers successfully.[9] But because it is not so easy to get a sense that they are very different from peers, chefs engage in various strategies to foster this feeling. While they constantly monitor peers, eat out, and read cookbooks to obtain new ideas, they cognitively disattend to the fact that they do any of this for work purposes. Without question, following certain strategies regularly turns them into habitual actions, such that individuals may lose consciousness of undertaking those actions. But chefs convey an active disattention to particular practices when they talk about their work. This allows them to obtain the resources they require to distinguish themselves, and at the same time reflectively minimize their channels of influence and similarity to other chefs. In particular, chefs often ignore or deny that they look into the food of other chefs in the field, and especially of competitors. In doing so, they obscure how close they are to certain other chefs, and who their competitors are. And when they deny that they look into other chefs' work by eating out or reading cookbooks, they imply they do not require that information to be competitive.

Eating Out

With their lives devoted to food, elite chefs obviously enjoy eating out and do it often, both in their own city and during travel, for pleasure and work. Sometimes the two goals are combined (i.e., some work-driven eating is enjoyable), but at other times they are not, because much of the pleasurable eating chefs do has little work value, and some work-related eating feels very much like work. High-end chefs love eating lowbrow foods (e.g., hamburgers or pizza), or *ethnic* foods (e.g., Chinese fare or sushi), neither of which may offer much input to their cooking, and they also have to visit restaurants in their market niche for work, but do not always enjoy them.[10] Chefs at the most prestigious restaurants in the country remark that they do not like high-end food and would rather eat simple fare; innovative chefs express a preference for traditional restaurants; chefs of French cuisine favor Italian food. A change of style appears desirable given the tedium of cooking and eating the same foods over and over again, as do "simple" flavors and dishes with little culinary complexity, few ingredients, and limited sauces, garnishes, or flourishes. "Comfort food" and food from peasant traditions offer simple flavors, hence chefs often favor Italian restaurants, French bistros or brasseries, or establishments specializing in roast chicken or steak. Chefs also need "clean" flavors, a category associated with simplicity and lean foodstuffs. Simple and clean flavors also offer a welcome break from the rich and complex dishes they try daily, a characteristic that accounts for their unqualified preference for sushi—many of them love it and eat it regularly.

Simple and clean flavors allow for a mental break as well, because they liberate elite chefs from the disposition to analyze food developed over years of culinary work and from dining companions' expectations that they will deliver expert reports on the food (i.e., there is not much to analyze in a burger or a roast chicken with mashed potatoes). In addition, restaurants that serve simple and clean fare are often low key, which chefs appreciate because they minimize the pressures of celebrity. Most renowned chefs do not enjoy eating where they are recognized and given special treatment, because they then feel compelled to perform in the role of celebrity chef. Neither do they necessarily want to be sent several dishes compliments of the chef, something that typically happens when they are recognized. Ethnic foods offer an even better break from routine and the disposition to be analytical because they are based on culinary principles that are beyond elite chefs' expertise.[11] Lastly, because ethnic or simple Western foods are generally so dissimilar to what elite chefs cook, they do not bring about the disappointment that restaurants similar to theirs invariably do.[12]

When chefs go to restaurants that are similar to their own, it is in general at least partly for work. Few claim to enjoy it; if they do, they point out that this reaction is due only to an omnivorous nature that allows them to find pleasure in anything.[13] Chefs distance themselves from competitors in their market niche, and from the very act of surveying restaurants for work, through these claims, as they convey the impression that they have no need for information about competitors or trends in the field.[14] Some, however, do admit to checking out restaurants, and make a point of visiting recently opened establishments to learn about the new players in the field. This is such an important part of their jobs that many restaurants have formal systems in place to ensure that the staff go out to eat. Whether they have formalized systems or not, all restaurants expect chefs and cooks to check out new openings in the city. A chef at an upper-middle-status restaurant in New York that is part of a corporate group commented:

> We are expected by the corporate to go around, see what's going on, see what's, you know, what are hot restaurants. If something's reviewed in the *New York Times* and it sounds really good, they want us to go down there. . . . It's a good experience, to go around, and see what somebody else is doing.

Corporate groups have formal policies to standardize regulations across restaurants in the group, so chefs have less freedom of action; indeed, going out to eat is not voluntary for this chef. But a large number of independent restaurants also have structured systems to send chefs and cooks out to eat, all paid for. Some restaurants send staff to check out new restaurants on an ad hoc basis, and others send them out at specific intervals (such as monthly). Some restaurants also send their chefs on trips to renowned culinary destinations, typically in France, Italy, or Spain, and more recently Denmark or possibly Chicago. During these trips, chefs eat in multiple restaurants every day (often eating several lunches and dinners per day), all paid for by the restaurant. Some restaurants with relatively informal methods have a monthly budget for the staff's restaurant visits, others reimburse the staff when they go out to eat, and still others encourage them to go out but do not cover the cost. Some chef-owners take the staff out to eat on occasion, covering the expense.[15] Culinary professionals also often check out new restaurants out of their own interest or volition.

When chefs eat out, they look into the food, service, tableware, décor, beverage program, and pricing. They order numerous dishes to sample as much food as possible (even if they eat only a little of each), and take note of the quality of ingredients, ingredient pairings, and presentation. Some chefs are more open about these common practices than others, but the apprehension about discussing the topic (at least with an outsider, as I am) is consistent. Chefs could invoke many reasons to account for why they go out to eat, but there is no randomness in the reasons they actually cite. When asked, they often deny they go out to eat for work purposes, and when they acknowledge that they *have* to go to a restaurant for work, they remark that it is never *just* for work. In those cases when they comment on work purposes in eating out, they tend to mention all aspects of the restaurant business that they look into, such as the service, décor, and beverage program, but not the food.[16] A middle-status chef in New York responded this way to a question about whether he goes out to eat:

> I go out to eat with different people for different reasons to different
> places. I mean, I could go with my wife or my children or my family and
> we'll go where the food is, it's okay. . . . And it's mostly because I am *not*
> going there as [a famous chef]. . . . But then you want to go out to dinner
> to see what other people are doing, just like a moviemaker would go to
> the movies. But I'll go with [David] Burke or I'll go with Charlie Palmer
> [other elite New York chef-owners], or I'll go with Mike [the sous-chef]

or my chefs. . . . We go see what other people are doing from a décor, service, wine list, beverage program, just to, because it's your business. It's your field. You almost *have* to do it.

As a chef-owner, he is especially concerned with all the elements that make restaurants succeed, down to décor, service, and pricing, but this does not mean that food is not an important element as well. There is a common reluctance to discuss this topic that is conveyed through nonverbal communication, with changes in the tone of voice, a speeding up of speech, or attitudes and facial expressions that show unease. The discomfort indicates that looking into the food served by colleagues is a practice collectively perceived to be morally dubious. Because chefs have no way to publicly acknowledge they borrow ideas from others, doing so can look like plagiarism. Their concern is not just about what others might think; they have internalized this moral understanding to such an extent that their caution around borrowing ideas is inherently associated with how they see themselves and their projections about the chefs they want to be (moral understandings themselves). Chefs' expressive behavior around the issue is part of the individually experienced but socially shared set of norms and values that regulate the occupation.[17] Nonetheless, like any expressive behavior, this one is not merely a reaction to a moral issue; by being ill at ease chefs cue their interlocutor to stop asking morally difficult questions and change topics, and thereby allow social interaction to proceed smoothly.[18]

Knowledge Exchange in Restaurants

In contrast to how they discuss restaurants in their city, chefs are quite comfortable about borrowing ideas from restaurants in other locations. They overtly state the importance of traveling—especially abroad—for obtaining new ideas. Here, they exhibit the opposite kind of cognitive asymmetry: they talk only about the food and never mention the décor, service, or wine program.[19] A chef at a high-status restaurant in San Francisco talks about traveling in search of inspiration for his food:

I definitely get inspiration from any place that . . . I spent some time in Florence, outside of Florence and in Florence, and I was in Sienna, you know. . . . I try to go to six different restaurants in one day, and I try to eat two courses in each one. . . . So really it's like, you know, when I spent time in the Piedmont, definitely that influenced me a lot. In Tuscany, that influenced me a lot. . . . I'm usually going back, inspired by that area. I have it in the memory thing to, like, dip into.

It makes sense for someone who cooks Italian food to travel to Italy for inspiration, but this chef could, at least in principle, also obtain ideas from good Italian restaurants in San Francisco or elsewhere in the United States. He commented that, in addition to Italy, he often travels to France to eat, but he never mentioned eating out in his own country to obtain ideas. Below are the comments of a high-status chef in New York who has gained great prestige for making refined traditional French food. He similarly begins by stating that one could get inspiration from many sources, but goes on to identify only one: traveling abroad.

> There's many ways you can do it [get inspiration]. There's one way, you go someplace, you're traveling, you go into another restaurant, you enjoy what you're eating. That gives you an idea . . . then you go to the market, or in a specific region, France or South America, Japan, or whatever. And you really, you get an idea because you're in a country, to get your brain working, you get your ingredient, you get *what you like to eat* also. . . . That's about it.

Without question, visiting faraway locations is a more effective strategy for designing dishes different from those of competitors than is eating in the neighborhood. This strategy is also informed by an intersubjective understanding that food is better abroad, where cuisines with long traditions and high-quality ingredients abound. This does not mean, of course, that chefs could not get *any* idea from eating out in their own city, and this is why their single-minded attention to traveling as a source of ideas is significant. In a field where competitors exist only in one's city and where the exchange of ideas is regulated by norms, which are valid within and maintained by the group, borrowing from peers in one's city entails breaking a norm, but this norm does not apply to the same extent when borrowing from individuals in other locations.[20]

It could be argued that borrowing from field members is more risky, for it is easier to get caught, given that information about the work of field members is widely available within the field. While this factor may come into play, purely rational, self-interested calculations do not suffice to explain chefs' actions, because instrumental motives and moral principles are deeply intertwined.[21] Intersubjectively shared moral understandings of acceptable practices guide actions within a group, especially in fields where knowledge exchange is regulated by norms and status is a central organizing principle, such that reputations matter greatly.[22] Furthermore, moral understandings are especially effective for controlling behavior where individuals are in close proximity and embedded in a tight network, because misbehavior is easier to catch and punish.[23]

Disattention to Knowledge Exchange

Rather than the practices they acknowledge, the habitual practices chefs leave out, play down, or deny engaging in, such as checking out restaurants in their city to remain competitive, convey the most meaningful information.[24] The systematic apprehension about discussing these practices is not the product of a psychological inclination for denial, but a social organization of disattention.[25] Attending to and ignoring given phenomena become socio-cognitive patterns in a group to the extent that group members share an understanding that the practices are beneficial (for the group and/or the individual) and collectively uphold them.[26] These practices are context-specific, even within a conversation. Chefs disregard that they eat out for work when the topic of conversation is knowledge exchange, but readily talk about it when the dialogue revolves around something else. What is more, they talk at length about the restaurants they believe they need to check out when the formal interview is over.[27] Attempts at differentiation are so critical but difficult in cuisine that chefs' most accessible means is to disattend to their knowledge-exchange practices, and thereby blur the distance between them and others in the field. A young, highly innovative chef working at an expensive high-status restaurant in New York pointed out he is not too keen on eating out, and especially not for work:

> I don't like to be influenced. I don't want to go to a restaurant and eat something and say, "Oh, that's cool, let me try that." I have my experience. You're only as good as what you're exposed to. . . . I worked for two three-star Michelin chefs and three four-star restaurants in New York. Very few chefs have that on their resume because it's hard to work in those

places. . . . I don't go to be exposed to these restaurants. First, I don't like to pay money . . . for me it's a sin to spend that much money on food. . . . I don't really eat out. If I go out to eat, I'll eat pizza, or I'll eat sushi, or I'll eat good, tasty, simple food.

This chef built a prominent career early on thanks to a distinctive and original style, something he could not have accomplished without information about similar restaurants in the city, for such information is a requirement to achieve the fine balance between conformity to the kinds of foods served in other restaurants and differentiation from them that is the key to success. In the following comment, a more senior chef, owner of a middle-status restaurant in New York, discusses his stance on going out to eat for work.

Absolutely, sure, sure. Absolutely. You *have* to. I don't as much as I should. And I'll tell you, some years ago I stopped. We used to go out a lot. Every day. After a while it became too much information that you found your tendencies to be more somebody else's and less your own . . . and you get influenced by brilliant people. And there's a lot of them here.

Well-established, with a successful restaurant and a culinary style recognized as his own, this chef has a secure place in the field and thus a lesser need to check out other restaurants than his junior counterparts. Years of experience and successes also give well-established chefs more confidence, which lowers the subjectively experienced urge to monitor competitors to ensure they themselves are keeping up. Less threatened by competition, these chefs can be more candid about knowledge exchange and, moreover, can experience more concordial relations with peers in the field. Chefs at the beginning of their careers, by contrast, still having to establish their own culinary styles, have more need for information about the food served at other restaurants in order to develop their styles and differentiate, and therefore a stronger tendency to rhetorically obscure any possible channel of influence.

When chefs make no comments about competitors (whether about the need to know what they are doing or curiosity about the food), they blur the distance between themselves and competitors. When they invoke concerns about unwanted influence to explain why they do not eat out (however reasonable these concerns are), they disattend to the many reasons why it is important to visit restaurants in their city. In short, disattention to knowledge exchange helps them manage relations with peers and avoid adversarial or tense interactions, an especially valuable practice in a field where individuals form a tight social network and are bound by social proximity such that they see each other frequently and/or are connected through third parties.[28]

Cookbooks

It is sensible to think that cookbooks are a good source of ideas for chefs and, in many ways, more convenient than eating out—they are available at one's fingertips, and perusing them requires little time or money. Not surprisingly, chefs have large cookbook collections and often talk proudly about them. However, when asked about cookbooks, they assert they find them of little use. Naturally, culinary professionals would not use cookbooks as a home cook might, as they have the expertise that makes reading recipes closely often unnecessary and, in fact, they remark they rarely read recipes. Also, being cuisine insiders, they know the realities of the cookbook business that escape gullible home cooks. For one thing, recipes can be inaccurate, a common flaw because not all chefs test all the dishes that go into a book. Moreover, cookbooks are often written largely by professional cookbook writers or food testers, rather than by the chefs whose names grace cookbook covers.[29] The inaccuracy is also sometimes a purposeful strategy, because it allows chefs to keep some key information secret.[30]

Despite all their limitations, cookbooks could still offer inspiration, as do travels, dinners at friends' houses, or food markets, but chefs tend to deny it. Like borrowing ideas from restaurants, taking ideas from books for which one cannot give public credit entails crossing a moral boundary. As with any issue with strong moral implications, chefs become uncomfortable around this one; they change their tone of voice and attitude and become less consistent or articulate in their discourses. A young chef at a high-status restaurant in New York explained:

> I like cookbooks. Yeah. I have cookbooks. I have lots of cookbooks. And I'll buy them for ideas, but I buy them for, mostly for visual, and a lot of [a] cookbook is set up for, you know, for visual. . . . I could never copy somebody. Just not what I do. At least, not intentionally. . . . But I definitely don't go on record saying, "I nor my staff don't read cookbooks purposely." I heard that stuff before and I think that's kind of very untrue.

You have to draw inspiration. We all know that it's been written. You know, there isn't anything that hasn't been done before. . . . Whether or not you directly took it from somebody is a different story, but, yeah. I read cookbooks for inspiration, you know, for inspiration essentially, but not to copy.

If he stumbles, hesitates, goes back and forth, and repeats his words, it is because, like his peers, he has internalized the moral norms of the community and struggles to discuss how he creates a dish when demarcating the boundary between his own dish and somebody else's is a fuzzy and thorny issue. Chefs' expressive behavior shows that, as sources of ideas, cookbooks present a stronger moral boundary than visiting restaurants. This is partly because eating out can be said to be motivated by the pleasure of dining or going out, but cookbooks are more restricted in the functions they can serve—other than acting as sources of ideas they can afford cultural capital, and this is indeed why chefs talk proudly about their cookbook collections. Chefs often point out that they only look at the pictures and, what is more, that if cookbooks consisted only of pictures, they would actually use them. Another young chef at a high-status restaurant in New York, well regarded for his personal and innovative culinary style, commented:

I don't look much into cookbooks. I like to look at books that are beautiful, and look at the pictures, I think it's a wonderful thing to do. But I do not look at books, at a book, to make my dish. *Ever. Never do that.* I don't. I can get inspired by certain things, I look at pictures and so forth but I do not take virtually a recipe. *Never do that.*

Highlighting pictures minimizes the value of the recipes, and emphasizes that the speaker does not engage in the morally wrong practice of borrowing ideas from cookbooks. Similar to their behavior when discussing eating out, recently appointed chefs tend to dismiss the value of cookbooks, whereas chefs with longer careers and well-established culinary styles are more likely to remark that they use cookbooks for ideas that they can adapt to their styles, and even that they may check technical information about how to cook a piece of meat or make a sauce. If these chefs are more prone to making these comments, it is undoubtedly not because they are in more need of know-how than their junior counterparts, but because they feel less threatened by acknowledging that they draw on others for ideas. However, even well-established chefs have to manage the inability to give credit for their knowledge exchange, so they are also likely to qualify the claim that they read cookbooks. Chefs resort to an array of reasons, including moral, ethical, practical, and cognitive explanations, to justify why they do not look at cookbooks. The most common arguments are that pictures are the only inspiring part of these books, that cookbooks are nothing but publicity for chefs, that recipes are not reliable because chefs rarely test them, that using somebody else's recipes is not feasible because they can never represent one's own culinary style, that copying a recipe is not proper, that they have no time to read recipes, that they have a short attention span and recipes are too long, or that they do not like reading.

The lack of legal regulation makes cuisine look like an information commons to outsiders, wherein knowledge can be easily borrowed and ideas flow freely, but it is treated by insiders as a space organized by normative fences, with clear regulations about which borrowing practices are acceptable and which are unacceptable.[31] Articles in newspapers and magazines substantiate the outsiders' view. Writing about the issue of intellectual property rights in cuisine, Pete Wells, the current *New York Times* restaurant critic and a regular contributor to food columns in other media prior to this job, has likened chefs' work to an open-source model, because chefs have always engaged in "freely borrowing and expanding on each other's ideas and, yes, sometimes even stealing them outright."[32] Yet chefs unambiguously demonstrate an intersubjectively shared understanding that borrowing is not to be done freely and that some borrowing practices may be acceptable (i.e., emulating restaurants in other locations) but others are not (i.e., taking ideas from local restaurants or cookbooks).[33] Given how difficult it is to demonstrate that they have ideas of their own, as well as unfeasible to give public credit for borrowed ideas, chefs' easiest coping mechanism is to insulate themselves (at least in ideality) from the channels that might appear as conduits of information.

Professional Lineage

Chefs borrow ideas from contemporaries as well as predecessors, whether friends with whom they openly exchange information, chefs for whom they worked during their training, or chefs they have never met or even whose food they have never eaten. Together these contemporaries and predecessors form a chef's *professional lineage*, a kind of genealogical tree constituted by relations that transfer social capital, ideas, and reputation.[34] Unlike a genealogical tree, though, a professional lineage consists of both actual social connections—made through work or informal social ties—and figurative relations built through a perception of one's similarities with others' culinary styles or approaches to the job. In this sense, a professional lineage goes beyond a career path.

To learn about their professional lineage, I asked chefs whom they admire and whom they would have wanted to work with if they were to start their careers over again. Just as genealogies are not merely historical records, but narratives that *create* relations of ancestry, so do chefs' professional lineages result from endeavors to establish certain connections and erase others.[35] Chefs' discussions of their professional lineage therefore provide information about their struggles to obscure conduits of influence, differentiate from peers, and assert their positions in the field. Thus the most telling information comes from what is omitted, namely chefs who may be seen as conduits of influence, whether due to past employment or strong similarities between culinary styles. While professional genealogies serve personal interests, they represent socially shared understandings of relatedness, and principles of inclusion and exclusion.[36] In particular, they are the product of moral understandings of the relations that are most relevant (i.e., chefs for whom one worked, peers with especially similar styles) and those that can be omitted, and of the values that matter in a professional lineage (i.e., culinary styles, status, and work ethics).

Choosing chefs one admires and selecting those one would have liked to work with are not quite the same, a distinction that clearly transpired in conversations with interviewees. Admiration is often wider-ranging, since one could admire individuals for a host of reasons, some of which one may consider central to one's job or self-concept, but others not so much. By contrast, wishing to have worked with someone else is more bounded, as one would choose a person with the qualities one considers key. A chef may admire peers for their encyclopedic knowledge of cuisine, kitchen skills, delicate palates, eye for new products, or creativity. This chef would have a long list of peers he admires, but he would value some of these attributes more than others and would wish he had worked with chefs with those attributes—a far shorter list that says more about what matters most to him.

Chefs do not have much respect for peers who, in their eyes, turned into businesspeople, with multiple restaurants in their portfolio, or engaged in commercial endeavors such as a catering company, line of kitchenware, or television show. These chefs can spend only a little time in any kitchen, so instead they delegate and manage, which makes them appear not committed to cooking but "only after the money" in the eyes of others. This is an issue with strong moral implications, given that cooking is so central to chefs' professional identity, and chefs distance themselves from the identity of the chef-turned-into-businessperson and underscore they are *working* chefs. What is more, most chefs I have talked with claimed that they spend much more time behind the stoves than their peers. At the same time, they express admiration for chefs-turned-into-businesspeople, and precisely for their business acumen. This seeming contradiction should not be surprising, not only because admiration can encompass a wide-ranging spectrum of attributes but also because the context of conversation—that is, the perception of what the conversation is about—will lead individuals to focus on varying attributes that matter to them.[37] Below, a chef who owns one middle-status restaurant in New York that serves rustic Italian food highlights the contrast between business-oriented chefs and himself. He does spend all his time in the kitchen during service and cooking rather than expediting.

> And most of the times the chefs aren't there . . . you can feel it. I can feel it. I can feel the difference. If you're lucky enough to have Mario Batali cooking dinner, it will probably be the best thing you've ever had in your life, but that's not going to happen. Unless you're sleeping with him or investing a few million dollars on the next project, it's not going to happen. . . . All my energy goes to those five hours a night. That's why this restaurant is what it is. But that's my world, it's a *completely* different world.

This sentiment is echoed by a very different kind of chef, someone who earned a very high reputation due to a distinctive and elaborate culinary style and who had recently opened a high-profile upper-middle-status restaurant in New York.

> What I miss the most of it today is that, because of the ownership, I'm probably a little bit less in the kitchen than I would like to be, but I'm a *lot* in comparison to a lot of my colleagues, because that's who I am, that's

what I want to do. I know that's the nucleus for everything else, if that part is working, everything else can be.

As widespread as the moral understanding is that being in the kitchen is what matters most, admiration for chefs who spend little time in the kitchen but are enterprise builders, good managers, or economically astute (all important attributes in the restaurant industry) is not uncommon. It is far less common, however, to express a wish to have worked for them. That is why claims about the peers chefs would have wanted to work with provide a stronger indicator of a conduit of influence—these are the peers chefs would wish to emulate in some significant way. Selections of admired chefs and chefs with whom interviewees would have wanted to work differ in three central aspects, as I explain below, especially in New York, so I begin with this city and then compare it to San Francisco.

Establishing a Professional Lineage in New York and San Francisco

On average, New York chefs chose twice as many chefs they admire as chefs they would have wanted to work with, though there was a wide variance in the number of individuals each selected, from some who cited countless names to others who were hard pressed to come up with a single name.[38] Of a total of about thirty New York chefs who answered the question about whom they admire, twelve selected Daniel Boulud (likely among others), a chef who owns multiple high-status (as well as lower-status) French restaurants in New York City and in other domestic and international locations. Seven chefs named Thomas Keller (also likely among others), another chef who owns several restaurants—both new American-style and French-style—in the city and across the United States, a few of which are very high status. The third and fourth most often cited admired chefs were each selected by five individuals: Wylie Dufresne, a high-profile, innovative modernist chef, and Mario Batali, an exceptionally successful chef-entrepreneur who owns several acclaimed restaurants in New York and other U.S. cities, only few of which are high status, as well as numerous related businesses, in addition to hosting television food shows.[39] Boulud and Keller, while both owners of multiple restaurants and other food businesses (e.g., a catering company, a bakery) are admired for their refined culinary styles. Dufresne is often admired for his audacity, since not all individuals who claim to admire him appreciate modernist cuisine, and Batali is admired for his business skills.

In contrast to admired chefs, nobody was selected by more than four respondents as a person they would have wanted to work with. When it comes to admiration, chefs think mostly of peers in their city; when it comes to individuals they would have wanted to work with, they think of chefs in Europe, France in particular—not a surprising choice given this country's place in the world of high cuisine.[40] The three most popular choices of chefs with whom respondents would have wanted to work (selected by four respondents each) were Frédy Girardet, a Swiss chef coming from the French nouvelle cuisine tradition and generally considered one of the greatest chefs; Alain Ducasse, a French chef with numerous high-status (and lower-status) restaurants in France and across the globe, including New York and other locations in the United States; and Batali, who was also one of the most admired. The next two most frequently mentioned chefs (selected by three individuals each) are also French: Joël Robuchon and Alain Chapel. It should not go unnoticed that the only New York chef respondents would have wanted to work with is the businessperson; this choice has little to do with his culinary expertise but much to do with learning from his business acumen, as well as with obscuring any possible conduit of influence in their own field.

The organizational literature and field theory indicate that individuals orient their actions to those who are in their field, particularly in their market niche.[41] Yet chefs do not mention many peers in their field, and especially not in their market niche, as professionals they would have wanted to work with. Even those who recently became chefs, with plenty of colleagues in New York they could reasonably look up to, generally think of names abroad. Of all the chefs with whom interviewees would have wanted to work (a total of 66 responses—not 66 different names), only 44 percent are in New York, with most of the others in Europe, whereas of the chefs they claim to admire (116 responses—not 116 different names), 72 percent are in New York, with most of the others in Europe as well.[42] This shows, again, that obscuring the channels that may be seen as conduits of influence is the most easily accessible means for chefs to convey the impression that their styles are not derived from those of other field members.

Chefs in San Francisco differ significantly from their New York counterparts in the selections of peers they admire and those with whom they would have wanted to work, in particular in that they make similar selections in both categories. They gave, in total, about the same number of responses in the two categories (twenty and twenty-two, respectively), with each interviewee selecting an average of three chefs in each of the two categories.[43] They selected as varied a sample of admired chefs as those they would have wanted to work with, and in their own field as much as in other locations—of the chefs they named about 35 percent were in San Francisco, 30 percent were in Europe and a similar number in New York, and the remainder were in other domestic cities, for both categories equally.

If the nature of work is similar in the two cities, what explains the variance in the answers? First, the culinary field is much smaller in San Francisco, and it is not a culinary destination with the prestige of New York; thus, if San Francisco chefs claim they admire and would have wanted to work with chefs in New York, but the opposite is not the case, it is because chefs only select peers in locations with a higher status than their own. In addition, the culinary field in New York entails a more highly volatile market and more intense competition, conditions that intensify the need to differentiate to stand out. Experiencing more pressure to assert the distinctiveness of their styles in order to carve out a position in the field, chefs in New York are more likely to obscure connections with local colleagues who may be taken to be conduits of influence.

This practice is not "just" discourse, a rhetorical strategy typically considered part of the power play inherent to a field.[44] Rhetorical representations develop from how individuals understand their work and see themselves vis-à-vis others in their environment, and these are meaningful reflective understandings that guide action. Individuals are more likely to perceive differences from others than similarities; this affords them a stronger sense of individuality, and therefore a more solid standpoint from which to delineate paths of action.[45] A good understanding of how they differ from others, along with the perception that they are noticeably different, equips chefs with an effective compass for orienting their actions and responding to the environment.[46] Given the varying pressures for differentiation in New York and San Francisco, chefs in New York should be expected to engage in more strategies, discursive as well as practical, to distance themselves from local peers, especially those in their market niche. That chefs in San Francisco are likely to choose local peers as chefs they admire *and* as chefs with whom they would have wanted to work puts the different conditions found in the two fields in high relief.

Managing Culinary Styles and Social Relations

Differentiation—driven by both external pressures and reflective understandings—is key to explaining how chefs manage their work and relations with peers. Creating a distinctive style is as critical as is elusive for elite chefs, given the derivative nature of culinary creation and the limited room for innovating. Chefs require a fine balance between conformity to established styles and originality, and in order to achieve it, they monitor peers to both borrow ideas and differentiate from those peers. But because it is so difficult to demonstrate that one's ideas are distinctive and also not possible to give credit for borrowed ideas, knowledge exchange is a delicate practice in cuisine. Such conditions, as I showed in this chapter, profoundly inform how chefs manage their culinary styles and relations with others so as to give the impression that they are not copying peers in their field and are not too similar to any of them.

Chefs differ in how they manage their styles and relations with peers. Those with longer tenures and well-established restaurants, having more secure positions in the field, experience fewer pressures to differentiate and demonstrate that they have a distinctive style, so they engage in fewer strategies to obscure their conduits of influence. Tendencies towards differentiation also differ across culinary fields. Chefs in New York are more likely to emphasize that they have distinctive culinary styles and to obscure their conduits of influence so as to blur their proximity to others and establish their own field positions. Their discussions of knowledge exchange—in particular when they talk about whether they eat out or read cookbooks to obtain ideas—show evidence of these attempts, as do their selections of peers they admire and those they would have wanted to work with.

The different patterns in New York and San Francisco are explained to a large extent by the level of competition in each field, but also by another element of cultural fields: the means of cultural production. Thanks to its geographic location, San Francisco has greater access to local, high-quality ingredients year-round, and this leads to de-emphasizing technique in cooking because—as one of the fundamental culinary principles goes—pristine ingredients ought not to be tampered with but served simply, so as to high-light their qualities.[47] Relative to ingredients, techniques and the culinary artistry associated with them travel through social channels that are easier to identify; that is, two chefs who serve a bacon gelée will be more readily associated than two chefs who source tomatoes from the same farmer. The de-emphasis of technique thus lowers the pressure for chefs to sever ties from peers who may be perceived to be conduits of influence. In turn, this allows for more concordial relations among individuals in a field.

Chefs in San Francisco foster concordial relations when they talk openly about local peers as chefs they admire or would have wanted to work with, even when these other chefs may be seen as conduits of influence. They gener-ally convey a much more concordial disposition than their New York counter-parts. In particular, they are less bound to be critical of colleagues in the city or dismissive of their food, but instead tend to bestow praise on the merits of many local peers. In doing so, they convey information that is not about individual psychological traits and also not a product of *culture*, in the sense of a broad set of norms, values, and established forms of expression and be-havior (in this case, the allegedly "laid-back nature" of Californians) that are independent of material, organizational, or institutional conditions.[48] Rather, the disposition to be more concordial is an attitude that grows as a concrete response to the pressures and incentives of the environment, which individu-als incorporate by observing and interacting with their peers, and figuring out which behaviors are greeted as acceptable and which as unacceptable.

Chefs manage their knowledge exchange and relations with peers in re-sponse to what they perceive their environment calls on them to do. In turn, through the ways in which they manage their knowledge exchange and rela-tions with peers—emulating some and distancing themselves from others—they collectively maintain particular pressures for differentiation, as well as a set of acceptable ways of responding to these pressures.[49] Given the condi-tions of the culinary field in New York, chefs in this city experience a more pressing need to have information about restaurant openings, chefs' moves, and the latest culinary trends—they spend much time talking about all this during interviews and even more in informal conversations. By contrast, chefs in San Francisco talk little about new trends, the food served at other restaurants, or restaurant openings in the city, and even less about *having* to visit recently opened establishments. In general, they have a lower orientation towards the latest trends in cuisine, whether local or global.[50] Whereas virtually no New York chef discussed culinary matters without expounding on modernist cuisine, many San Francisco chefs had little information and only a vague interest in it.

Moreover, the conditions of the culinary field in San Francisco better enable chefs there to see peers less as competitors than as colleagues with whom they can exchange ideas and cooperate. In turn, through their concordial relations, chefs maintain the social and organizational conditions that allow such approaches and social relations.[51] In short, the different patterning of relations in the San Francisco and New York fields is produced neither simply by *culture*, in the sense of widely shared attitudes, nor by *structure*, as a fixed arrangement of conditions that regulate action, but rather by the patterning of relations that chefs constitute, which constitutes them as chefs in turn.

But chefs do not come to occupy positions vis-à-vis peers in the field only through the ways in which they manage their knowledge exchange and social relations. The dishes they create are, of course, key for the positions they occupy in the field, their relations with others, and their self-understandings. It is therefore the creation of dishes that I turn to in the next chapter.

CHAPTER FIVE

Cognitive Patterns and Work Processes in Cooking

RUNNING A HIGH-END RESTAURANT is not an easy job. There is an incessant expectation of excellence in everything from the food to the wine program, décor, and service. The food must be not just flawless but also creative, and chefs need to keep their menus looking novel. This is not so easily done because chefs typically do not have a lot of time to develop new dishes, and because they do not always have the inspiration. There is no one way to manage these pressures and constraints, and chefs vary greatly in how they deal with them. A chef at one of the most elite restaurants in New York described the special conditions he requires to create dishes:

> But I am inspired always at night; never during the day, almost never during the day. During the day for me is more like action, and at night is more obviously of reflection. . . . I need an environment which is very peaceful . . . I need something which is the right lighting, the right silence around me, the right energy, the right, everything has to be like, something to bring me down. Here, all day long, you are . . . basically, managing a team all day. And then at night is when you can *really* focus on an onion [*laughter*].

With his days taken up with meetings and constant requests for attention from the kitchen and service staff, purveyors, public relations professionals, and the media, and his evenings dedicated to overseeing a large kitchen staff, this chef rarely cooks and hardly finds the time to conceive of new dishes when he is at the restaurant. A chef at a recently opened high-status restaurant in New York expressed a similar sentiment about the conditions required to create dishes. But, with a new restaurant and limited experience as a chef, he still does some cooking in the kitchen every evening, which brings to the foreground the sharp contrast between the creative side of the job and the routine and "robotic" nature of kitchen work.

> Our job is mundane. I mean, we create stuff and we just repeat it, over and over and over and get exactly the same dish. . . . My artistic side is when I go home and I'm creating this stuff and I'm thinking about things and stuff, and trying to be introspective. But I turn into a robot during service, where each motion's gotta be . . . It's more like business, it's almost like military. . . . So it changes, it goes from artistic to robotic, almost.

It is common for chefs to resolve the tension between the routine side of the job and the creative side by physically and temporally separating *action* from *creation*. Ironically, though the creation of dishes is a fundamental part of their professional identity, they commonly create dishes when *not* at work, and not so frequently either. Many chefs choose a special context that allows them to be quiet and relaxed so they can switch to a deliberative cognitive mode conducive to playing with ideas to create new dishes. Other chefs are more improvisational and create dishes at random times and places, without much deliberative thought about how they assemble ingredients to make a new dish.

How chefs go about creating dishes is tightly associated with their views on cooking and their culinary styles, and in particular with the cognitive patterns through which they think about food and work on new ideas. Specifically, chefs approach cuisine as either a *conceptual* or a *practical* activity, and this profoundly informs how they conceive of new ideas and create new dishes. In this chapter, I describe the processes whereby they design dishes—from the moment when they come up with a new idea for a dish until the dish goes on the menu—and look closely at cognitive patterns and practices.

Culinary Principles

In designing dishes, chefs are guided by three culinary principles. First, a dish should have a balance of tastes, comprising the four basic tastes: salty, sweet, sour, and bitter.[1] Second, a dish should have a balance of textures, including soft, smooth, crispy, and crunchy.[2] And third, a dish should be made of ingredients that "go well" together, a notion that revolves around two possible logics—geographic or gustatory.[3] According to geographic logic, ingredients from the same region belong together, where region can be understood as narrowly as, say, Tuscany, or more commonly as a whole country, or even as broadly as a global region, such as the Mediterranean or Southeast Asia. In this logic, the Italian Arborio rice used for risotto belongs with sage, a common herb in Italian cuisine, but not with the South Asian herb lemongrass. Gustatory logic is based purely on taste. Here, insofar as lemongrass goes well with Thai jasmine rice, there is no reason why it would not pair well with Arborio rice as well. This kind of thinking undoubtedly leads to more innovative dishes, for it allows for combinations of ingredients not typically paired together.

After relying on the same principles to design dishes for years, chefs come to understand and use the principles intuitively; they have a deeply incorporated sense of what is required for a well-balanced dish, without necessarily being able to articulate the criteria. This is especially evident when they discuss how they assess whether a dish is good. A chef who runs a high-end restaurant in New York explained how he knows when a dish is good:

> It's when you don't have to explain. You don't have to say, "Try that. And you know, this is the salmon, by the way, and it's wonderful because . . ." If I have to explain to you why it's good, something's wrong.

Having been at the helm of one of the most prominent restaurants in the country for many years, this chef has the knowledge and confidence that are gained only through experience. His career path and his culinary style, characterized by a restrained use of ingredients meant to showcase the main component in a dish, partly explain his answer (i.e., the salmon he mentions would be paired only with a delicate broth and a garnish of a vegetable or two). Beyond the specifics of his style, his answer is revealing of his intuitive understanding of cuisine, an approach shared by many other chefs. Few chefs are able to articulate how they assess when a dish is good enough to be added to the menu beyond saying that a good dish is one that "makes sense," or that a dish is good "when it works," or that "you just know."[4] Through years of experience, what was once explicit knowledge—the codified knowledge of culinary conventions—that was grappled with through extensive, deliberative cognitive processes becomes internalized as a deep intuition.[5] That is, culinary conventions become practical logic, an everyday kind of reasoning that requires no deliberative thought and helps chefs process information, generate ideas, and assess the quality of dishes.[6]

Experience—nothing but the accumulation of habitual action—enables chefs to combine ingredients, conceive sauces, or decide on cooking methods in ways that are apprehended as intuitive, which in turn makes rules and conventions seem much more flexible.[7] This is indeed what a practical logic consists of, the ability to create dishes through processes that are experienced as more intuitive than rule-following.[8] Over time, chefs require less checking and tasting when they make a dish, so those with more experience can make new preparations (so long as they use familiar ingredients and techniques) with less trial and error.[9] The incorporation of a practical logic explains why chefs represent culinary categories as guidelines (as opposed to rules), and recognize some prescriptions that guide their work but not so much proscriptions that constrain it. They are more likely to discuss cooking rules that have to do with the chemical properties of ingredients (e.g., the starch content of a type of potato, the burning point of peanut oil, or how sugar reacts to heat) than culinary conventions about ingredient pairings (e.g., lamb "goes well" with mint or rosemary, but it is not paired with basil). They often take an especially strong stance against the implication that they might be bound by rules. A chef at a middle-status restaurant in New York was exceptionally expressive in arguing for the flexibility of cooking rules:

> People say that baking is so uncreative, it's so scientific . . . it's really untrue. Once you understand the rules, you can fuck with them all you want. . . . Same as writing. Once you know your grammar, you can be E. E. Cummings. Once you understand what's going on in a dish, you can play around.

Surely, if cooking rules appear less constraining to those who have mastered them, it is at least in part because experience teaches them that rules can be played around with. Further, chefs do not even agree on what the right rules are (even about such basic procedures as whether it is advisable to blanch vegetables or salt a steak before cooking), just as they vary in how rigidly they treat rules. To the extent that rules vary, new entrants to the occupation receive varied information and do not necessarily become "socialized" into any one given way of doing things.[10] The multiplicity of information facilitates viewing prescriptions and proscriptions as flexible, and enables chefs to develop their own views from the range of knowledge to which they have been exposed.[11]

Exploring New Ideas and Exploiting Old Ones

Introducing new ideas provides a competitive edge, but chefs can maintain standards of quality only when they serve dishes that are well thought out and when they have a kitchen staff well trained to cook them. Chefs vary in the degree to which they either innovate or reproduce their old ideas, a variance associated with both their approaches to cooking and characteristics of their restaurants.[12] However innovative he may be, though, no chef creates dishes devoid of past influences, whether those influences come from his own earlier creations or the socially shared culinary canon.

Chefs develop the ability to find a good balance between innovating and relying on established ideas over time. Recently appointed chefs are more likely to prioritize the new and novel, which often manifests itself in dishes that have "too much going on," as in a dish of foie gras seared with lardo (cured pig fat) cut in strips, with a pine nut crust, cherries roasted in balsamic vinegar, the herb anise hyssop, and shaved fennel—a dish made early in his career by a chef I interviewed in San Francisco. In other words, too many flavors and ingredients result in an underdeveloped dish. The chef was now at a high-status restaurant in San Francisco and, though he expressed pride in the artistry behind this creation, he admitted that it had foodstuffs that should not be combined (most notably two highly fatty ingredients, foie gras and lardo), and an obscure combination of ingredients. He described the kinds of dishes he designed during those early years in his career:

> [T]hat kind of food . . . in conjunction with [a] lamb dish—it was to-
> gether in the menu. And I started to get this very esoteric style. . . . That's
> a really good example of how the cuisine was really pushing.

Why are new chefs the ones most likely to create dishes with "too much going on"? For one thing, more limited experience with creating dishes means that they are less competent in assessing their ideas. More significantly, they have more pressures to design original dishes to make a name for themselves, and they generally feel personally compelled to serve dishes with unusual foodstuffs or ingredient combinations to signal creativity. Chefs with more experience, especially those with longer tenures in the same restaurant, face the opposite risk, namely overreliance on ideas they came up with long ago. Having a deeper well of ideas on which to draw, these chefs can easily bring back old dishes when they need to renew their menus. Yet reproducing old ideas brings with it the perils of losing a competitive position in the market, and chefs are aware of that. It also has the risk of becoming habitual practice, because regularly resorting to one's repertoire of dishes to change the menu can eventually turn this routine into a disposition.[13]

Being in a restaurant that has been around for a long time also limits chefs' ability to explore new ideas because the restaurant has a large repertoire of dishes, a solidly defined culinary style, and established ideas about how to do things.[14] Large restaurants add even more constraints due to a high volume of production, as this demands more standardized operations and therefore allows less room for the exploration of new ideas. Any new dish requires that many staff members must learn to cook it properly and the purchase of a large quantity of ingredients, which can lead to significant economic loss if the dish turns out to be unpopular. Large restaurants are also likely to belong to corporate groups, and such groups exercise comparatively tight control over chefs' work—including their dishes, the management of food costs, and profitability—and this introduces even more constraints on the exploration of new ideas. A chef at a large upper-middle-status restaurant in New York that belongs to a group of about a dozen restaurants and hotels, for instance, participates in a weekly meeting with all the other chefs in the group and a daily conference call wherein they discuss business, review the previous night's specials, and suggest specials for the evening. Corporate chefs and senior chefs are expected to try new dishes and give feedback before these are added to the menu.

Whether chefs explore new ideas or fall back on proven successes is also explained by their perceptions of market pressures. The organizational literature shows that being in a highly competitive market encourages individuals to actively develop new ideas to gain an edge, but the degree to which individuals will be inclined to innovate is related to how much pressure they perceive is needed to be competitive.[15] Their inclinations to innovate are also inherently associated with their dispositions to take a passive or active role in response to their perceptions of the market.

Intuitive Knowledge and Deliberative Thinking

Chefs create dishes through particular approaches, even though these vary according to contextual circumstances.[16] Chefs are more deliberative when they work on something they deem important (e.g., a special event) or when they create a complex dish, and they are more likely to follow routine procedures automatically on ordinary occasions, when they work on simple dishes or with familiar components. In general, they have inclinations to think about food either explicitly or implicitly, inclinations that are associated with their views on cooking and culinary styles. Those who approach cooking intuitively, having incorporated culinary principles to the degree that these are now second nature, no longer apprehend and apply those principles as explicit knowledge. For them, the process of creation is typically experienced as an idea that suddenly hits them, and they are rarely able to explain how the idea arrived or why they knew it would result in a good dish. A chef at a high-status Californian restaurant in San Francisco who approaches cooking intuitively explains how she combines ingredients to make a dish:

> You sort of put pieces together. . . . Sometimes you're never satisfied, and you know you just need to leave it alone because you've touched it too much and it's . . . And other times it's just okay: "I really like this, it feels right."
>
> Q: How do you know when a dish doesn't work?
>
> Maybe if I feel like it doesn't quite connect, like I'm forcing something to work and it doesn't quite fit. . . . Sometimes something might not work, and I'm horrible at the scientific ideas in my cooking, it's not my thing . . . I don't have a solid idea, understanding of . . . basic things, yeah. Other than that, I just do what I feel is right. I got instincts.

This chef does not lack formal knowledge about the classical composition of dishes, tastes, and textures, especially given that she attended culinary school, where this information is taught. But after years of applying formal knowledge to practical tasks, the knowledge has become tacit.[17] Formal culinary knowledge (at least some of it) is less likely to remain tacit for chefs who make innovative food because these chefs seek to challenge the ideas that are implicit to most others, and this requires thinking analytically about those ideas. To be sure, these chefs also draw on information intuitively when they create dishes with familiar elements and, not aware that they are processing information, they experience the creation of a new idea as a "spark."[18] A new, innovative chef at a high-status restaurant in New York discusses how he finds inspiration:

> Everywhere. Anything. Walk through a grocery store and see things and it's just, "Oh, wow, that'd be pretty cool." . . . You know, you see things, just by seeing something. You kind of, it sparks an idea. . . . Usually I get fixated on a product. I, like, one vegetable, like I get fixated on something. And it kind of, that sticks like that, always just like sits in the back of my mind until I see or smell or eat something that triggers, like, "Oh, wow, that'd be good together," and then kind of, then the idea kind of unravels.

Discussing particular examples of that spark, he describes how he came up with an idea for a dish of smoked duck egg scented with truffles and cinnamon:

> When I was home one day, I had a bottle of truffle oil in my cabinet. And my wife and I had gone out to Curry Row, and I went to Kalustyan's and I bought a bunch of spices and everything 'cause I needed to make stuff at home. So I put cinnamon in there, cinnamon sticks and, like after two days, I went in the next day, opened up, "Oh, it smells like truffles and cinnamon." It kicked me in the face. "Oh, wow," I was like, "that smells good together, that's pretty interesting."

This is a common story of how chefs conceive of new combinations of ingredients: a sudden event triggers the thought of using an ingredient, recalls another ingredient that was stored in the person's memory, and sparks the idea of combining the two foodstuffs. Even though chefs recollect the spark that triggered the novel idea, they cannot trace all the information—largely tacit—that actually made the novel idea possible. When they work on a special event, experiment with unfamiliar ingredients, or try to improve a flawed dish, they are more deliberative throughout, and experience the creation of the dish as a *process*. The chef in the previous example had to create a menu for a unique lunch organized around a collection of the best wines of the twentieth century, with a cost of $25,000 per person. Not surprisingly, he was exceptionally purposeful and deliberative in designing dishes for the event.

> So we made roast barley, and we'll make a tuile [a thin, crisp wafer] out of it. So roasted barley was on my brain. I didn't want to make a barley

risotto really. . . . Some stuff carried over. . . . The salmon was, I don't remember what the salmon dish I had originally was. So I wanted to put a leafy green on there, braised green, stuff like kale and crab. And I was thinking maybe what sauce I would serve with the salmon. "What would work, what would work, what would work?" I put mushrooms on it, and I used the consommé in my tortelloni. So I was there, picking up one day, and tasting the consommé and I was plating it: "Oh, I'm not going to make a consommé. I already have it. What if I fry barley and put it into the thing?" And I just melted it with a little bit of olive oil, and then buzzed it [pureed and blended it] and I did it and it became the sauce.

Contingent elements trigger an idea but, in contrast to the previous example, here the chef recalls all the steps between the initial idea—not recognized as a spark—and the final dish. Exceptionally attentive to flavors and their combinations, he brought together ideas and knowledge that are part of his repertoire with new thoughts to create special dishes.[19] This turned the creation of the dish into what was phenomenologically experienced as a *process*.[20] Another new chef at a high-status restaurant in New York, who acquired much notoriety for an innovative and sophisticated culinary style, shows the extent to which chefs can go in their deliberative thinking when motivated to do so. He explains how he creates dishes:

I try to imagine, this sounds kind of weird, I'm coming to this world and there was nobody in the world and I'm trying to use what this world has to apply heat, to apply salt . . . I'm thinking about how I can come at it from a different way. And I try to create my mind, like a blank slate, starting from the point where I haven't seen anything before. And it's difficult to do that, it really is. And it takes a *long* time to come up with something where I'm happy with it. So I'll think about all the different parts of the tongue, then I'll think about the textures that I want. And I like contrast in my food. I like, you know, balance with acid, with sweet, with spice. . . . I think about the feeling of how it's going to feel being put in your mouth. . . . I'm thinking about a thousand different things at one time. And then it all has to balance.

This is a highly deliberative consideration of a whole set of categories, a common pattern among chefs who make innovative food because they require an analytical understanding of the codified knowledge that constitutes the foundation of cuisine. For these chefs, cooking is a conceptual endeavor, one that involves an intellectual engagement with ideas. This kind of cooking requires purposeful and fastidious work to design dishes, which can only be accomplished outside the restaurant, in a setting conducive to a contemplative mode of thinking.

Motivations and Processes of Culinary Creation

Chefs who cook in traditional styles, with little to no experimentation with new ingredients or techniques, create dishes through more intuitive habitual processes, which are well suited to styles that strive for flawless cooking but no innovation. A chef who ran a number of high-end French restaurants in New York, and acquired great prestige due to his refined, traditional French style, described his approach to cooking, one that is intrinsically associated with his views of cuisine:

> My style, you know, I think my style is very, everybody's going to tell you, it's very simple. My style is based on the ingredients. And my style is based on where I'm coming from. And my style is based on what I'm feeling about myself as a chef, to be very down to earth. My style is based also in classic. . . . Things never change. It's basics. . . . Classic is very important. With classic is, you gotta cook that pea [*he points to the peas in one of his recipes*], you gotta cook them to be just right.

His style may be simple, but this should not be taken to mean that it is built on few ingredients, inexpensive foodstuffs, or little technique. His dishes often involve multiple and elaborate techniques to cook each ingredient (e.g., truffles, foie gras, and caviar) separately. From his perspective, his style is simple in that it is inspired by and faithful to the ingredients and classical recipes of his region, and the cooking is phenomenologically experienced to be simple because, after years of working with the same foods and techniques, it has become second nature.

Like this chef, many approach cooking from the belief that food is about basic, sensorial pleasures. A chef who makes rustic Italian dishes built on few ingredients, none of which costly or rarefied, and cooked with straightforward methods (e.g., grilled fish with nothing but salt and olive oil) at a middle-

status restaurant in New York, expressed these same views. The whole restaurant—from the food and wine to the tableware and décor—was designed
to be rustic and simple, down to the wood-fired oven in the kitchen, where
much of the food is cooked. The chef describes his approach to cooking:

> I could be doing any cooking I wanted in that kitchen, but it's more or
> less thinking, having an idea. Well, the reason I cook as simplistic as I
> do is because the fire becomes the main ingredient in the dishes. I'm not
> going to disguise the fire by too many herbs, too many things going on in
> the plate, too many spices, where you don't know really what you're tast-
> ing anymore . . . it's not natural anymore. So if you go back to cooking
> with fire, cooking with charcoal and wood, to me, there's only one way to
> do it, and that's by keeping it as simplistic as you can.

This is simple food taken to an extreme in a restaurant context; the chef rarely
uses any spice other than pepper, and if he adds herbs, it is never more than
one per dish. With a strong belief that food should be connected to nature
(and not polluted by modern techniques or fads), habitual practices formed
over years of cooking the same food, and a full restaurant every night, he has
no motivations to experiment with new ideas and no well-honed skills in innovating.

Chefs who seek to regularly renew their dishes are motivated by a few
different forces. Some have a *personal* motivation to make new dishes, due
to an intensely experienced creative drive, a desire to distinguish themselves
from others, or a need to fight the tediousness of the job. Others make regular
changes to their menus in response to *external* pressures—that is, their perception of the need to differentiate themselves from competitors. Chefs inclined
to regularly renew their food value originality. If the motivation to innovate
was not originally present, it is present now because they have internalized
the pressures to differentiate from competitors and have developed skills and
habitual practices for innovating. Motivations are not prior to—much less
dissociated from—action. Individuals set goals in response to their perceptions of the environment, but these perceptions are intrinsically associated
with action in that the environment appears as a realm of possible actions, so
what individuals perceive is informed by the kinds of actions they are capable
of undertaking.[21]

Even when the motivation to renew their food is due largely to a perceived need to respond to external pressures, chefs develop enduring skills and methods to create original dishes. A chef at a renowned New American upper-middle-status restaurant in New York, which has been around for years, had an especially well-developed and efficient method for responding to the pressures to differentiate from competitors. He discussed the creative elements in his style:

> So I always try to use something different that nobody else is using. . . . Like one ingredient, I have this guy in Italy who will ship it to me, and these are little peaches, baby peaches, that are cured like capers. . . . No one has them anywhere. . . . I try to do stuff like that, find something that's just unique to me or different. . . . When somebody has something new to sell you, you get tons of phone calls, so, and usually I think, we are one of the first few restaurants, if something new comes out, we get approached first. . . . Or, I mean, because I always try to, like if something like that comes by, I would try to use it before it ends up in the *New York Times,* which it always happens in the food section, you know, within a week.

Not having a strong personal motivation to be innovative or stand out, the best strategy for dealing with the external pressures to differentiate for this chef was to develop an effective method for the creation of dishes that does not require cognitively onerous and time-consuming procedures. Instead of approaching each dish as a blank slate, like the most innovative chefs, he follows a process of bricolage.[22] He meticulously created an archive with all the dishes he has made, along with indexes of the seasonal produce expected to be available each week of the year, notes about good ingredient combinations, and ideas for dishes. This system allows him to easily recombine elements from different dishes or substitute new ingredients in old recipes to make novel dishes. The approach is both effective for responding to the forces the chef perceives in the environment and in line with his motivations and views on cooking.

Those with *internally experienced* motivations to be creative and distinguish themselves have approaches in keeping with their motivations, with elaborate work processes, skills, and habitual practices—developed over time—that facilitate the creation of innovative dishes. For the new, highly innovative chef at a high-status restaurant in New York cited earlier, the creation of dishes is primarily guided by a desire to be creative and original:

> Most of the dishes on the menu, a good deal of, like 60 percent, are things that I've never seen before. And it's not like, for me it takes a long time to create a dish, an original one. . . . Some of these items, most of these items, I've never seen before.

When he talks about his work, he tells of a need for stimulation, tightly associated with an artistic self-perception, that leads him to search for new ideas constantly. His dishes, in the modernist style and heavily reliant on complex techniques, are made with numerous and unusual ingredients (e.g., Asian herbs, spices, tropical fruits, dried foodstuffs), even more unusual ingredient combinations (e.g., all of the above combined in one dish), varied textures, and striking presentations. One of his dishes, for instance, combined pork belly with salsify purée, butterscotch candy, pineapple vinegar, and ramps. His emphasis on the value of originality, as the following excerpt shows, also suggests that he has internalized the pressures to differentiate. Indeed, he remarked several times during the interview on the importance of innovating if one wished to succeed in the New York restaurant world.

> The dishes on the menu, I don't ever go back and repeat a dish. I always try to keep going further. A lot of the chefs I worked for were, "Let's do the old dish," and it gets boring, you know? I like to be stimulated, and I like to keep things *forward*. . . . So I came up with the idea of putting the sauce on the plate like this. *Again, something I hadn't seen before.* So I was thinking, I'm thinking in art, I'm thinking of all different ways to apply paint to the canvas . . . trying to think of different ways, different utensils. And how I can get the paint in essence on the plate. [Emphasis added.]

Only a few chefs (with similarly innovative styles) make so many remarks about a need for stimulation and constant change.[23] Now, the academic literature generally equates habitual practice or dispositions with the reproduction of established ways of doing things, but in listening to this chef talk about food and observing him work, it is clear that his predilection for imaginative, forward-looking action is itself now a disposition.[24] He deliberately ponders about how to assemble ingredients to challenge established ideas and create something novel when he approaches each dish, but there is no deliberative thinking about the decision to create something novel or about how to do so. The inclination to innovate, and the ways of thinking and work processes through which he approaches every new dish, have become all but second nature. His sense of self, much like a visionary artist equipped with great business acumen, is tightly associated with his culinary style and approach to cooking, and in line with his perception of the environment.

Improvising in the Kitchen

Even if they are profoundly stimulated to innovate, most chefs change only a few dishes at a time, typically every two or four months, in line with sub-seasons or seasons, respectively. Some others change a few dishes every day, others every week, and still others almost never change their menus. Most chefs keep some items on the menu forever, either "signature" dishes or simple preparations popular among customers (e.g., steak or grilled salmon).[25] Changing many dishes at a time is rare not just because chefs may not have the time or inspiration, but because new dishes put more pressure on the kitchen staff and threaten their ability to prepare the food flawlessly.

Chefs vary not only in the frequency with which they renew their menus and the degree to which they rely on old dishes to do so but also in the ways that they use their repertoire of dishes to devise new creations. Whereas some see their repertoires as archives of finished dishes, not to be fiddled with, others treat them as toolboxes from which to take individual ideas and re-combine or modify them to make new creations. These repertoires are not just recipes stored in files; they also consist of information, stories, images, and other ideas stored in chefs' minds, the residue of foods eaten in the past. Some of these memories are well defined and can be easily retrieved, whereas others are more vague and blurry and may be triggered by a sudden event (with or without awareness of what the trigger was). Like the cultural toolkits theorized by Ann Swidler, chefs' repertoires amount to more information than they know they have and normally use.[26]

Chefs regularly pull out ideas from their repertoires when they create dishes, even when they improvise, which they do often. Sometimes they improvise to respond to an unexpected problem (e.g., running out of an ingredient for a preparation), and at other times they do so because they are suddenly hit by a new idea (e.g. an unusual combination of ingredients). A chef at a middle-status restaurant in New York that makes traditional, rustic Italian food, but occasionally strays from the canon, once served a panna cotta (a traditional Italian pudding) garnished with dried apricots and whole pink peppercorns, the latter garnish being a clear deviation from any Italian tradition and an innovation in its own right. Asked about how he thought of assembling these ingredients together, he said:

> Hm . . . I don't know. It was just sort of an accident. We had been doing a condiment for a cheese, with apricots and mustard and somehow, I don't know how, it just happened.
>
> Q: How did you think it would work well?
>
> Because I am not a pastry chef, I don't have the training, so all the desserts here are with some sort of fruit and I try not to get too creative with them because I don't have the skill, I don't want to embarrass myself [*laughter*]. I do have . . . and this has become very popular, it's a sort of sweet-savory in the dessert. . . . So I like the idea of savory herbs in desserts but I thought that the black peppercorn would be too strong. Certainly you can't eat a whole black peppercorn but a pink you can. And also they are pretty.

If he is not quite able to explain how he came up with the idea for the dessert, it is because the idea was not the result of a purposeful and deliberative creational process, but rather a thought sparked contingently, in-practice, while he was doing something else. This is the kind of insight phenomenologically experienced as an "aha" moment, an idea that seems to appear suddenly and effortlessly (because it is the product of information so well known that it is engaged with implicitly), which, in turn, triggers positive feelings and confidence in the idea.[27] Chefs who improvise as a response to a problem are of course more purposeful and therefore experience the process differently. Below is an example of one such case, described by someone at a high-status restaurant in New York who makes intricately composed and sophisticated dishes.

> We always have an agnolotti [a type of pasta] on the menu. . . . The previous agnolotti was stuffed with cranberries . . . a late summer dish, early fall. And then, it's a Sunday, and the kid comes to me and says that he doesn't have any more filling for the agnolotti and there's no more cranberry beans

in the house so, "shit, what do I do now?" That weekend, that Friday, the chef sent us a big box of chestnuts. . . . It's Sunday, I can't pick up the phone and get more cranberry beans . . . it's getting colder, we have the chestnuts in the house, so "Why don't we think about doing chestnut agnolotti?". . . . OK, now we have the agnolotti, and "What are we going to do with it?" We have these beautiful little pumpkins, so we'll clean those, and dice them and caramelize, and it evolves to sage, and in the chain of events is brown butter.

This improvisational strategy, triggered by a purposeful attempt to solve a problem, is phenomenologically experienced as a deliberative cognitive process.[28] The chef looked at his options—the ingredients he had in house—and deliberatively thought about the foodstuffs he could assemble to make a new dish, consciously drawing on his repertoire of ideas and on widely shared notions about what ingredients go well together. This is why he is able to trace every step in the creation of the dish, unlike the chef who comes up with an idea suddenly through a more implicit cognitive process.

Not only do exceptional problems, such as running out of an ingredient, lead chefs to improvise; a change in the flavor of foodstuffs is a regular contingency that also forces them to make changes in-practice. Carrots differ in their sugar levels, onions vary in their pungency, and halibut is not always as fresh as it could be. This means that even the most habitual of practices are susceptible to needing changes. Sometimes only subtle tweaking is required (e.g., the overly pungent onion can be cooked a little longer), but at other times the whole preparation has to be changed (e.g., the less fresh halibut will be better off with a strongly flavored sauce than simply grilled). Everyday adaptation to contingencies in routine tasks can therefore lead to innovation just as purposeful strategies do. This means that conceiving of creativity as opposite to habitual action, as is typically the case, is misleading because it fails to capture the whole range of processes through which cultural creation actually works.[29] This dichotomy effectively conflates the motivation of creators—namely, seeking to "be creative"—with the actual processes of action, as when novelty unfolds through happenstance.

Trial and Error in the Kitchen

Whether dishes are designed through elaborate processes or happenstance, recipes often need to be tweaked, so engaging in trial and error to improve dishes until they can be added to the menu is a common course of action. Chefs use and understand trial and error variously. They either view it as a regular step in the creation of any dish, involving minor tweaks in the preparation of food (e.g., adding more acidity to a sauce or a crunchy element for texture) or as an exceptional measure to be used only when a dish is seriously flawed, such that major changes in the conception of the dish are required (e.g., substituting a light broth for a rich sauce to pair with a fish). Whether chefs view trial and error in one way or the other is not random but tightly associated with approaches to culinary creation. For those who see cuisine as a *practical* endeavor and experiment with ingredients in-practice to make a new dish, trial and error is a standard procedure that results in regular changes in cooking. By contrast, for those who take cuisine to be a *conceptual* activity, trial and error cannot be a regular part of cooking because a dish is created in its conception, so changes made to a preparation result in an altogether different dish.[30] Of course, trial and error is used differently depending on the circumstances; a chef may spend a year fine-tuning one dish but put another dish on the menu right away, without any tweaking. An eloquent chef at a high-status restaurant in New York who takes cuisine to be a practical activity explained how he uses trial and error:

> Sometimes you're very lucky, and it's like, boom, boom [*snapping his fingers*], it's done, immediate, in one shot. And sometimes, it takes a few days. And sometimes, it's a few weeks. And sometimes, it's a work in progress for a long time . . . sometimes, you never, I mean, sometimes, you're not able to finish. . . . You can make an analogy. It's like working on an engine of a car, but not Ford Taurus; let's say, Ferrari, you know, which is very delicate. At that level, you know, five yards of altitude will change the engine, or the cold. So it's like tuning, you know, and you're tuning *all the time*. You know? It's what it is. And you have to tune it all the time because never a recipe is perfect because the quality of the ingredients change every day.

As exacting as all chefs are at the most elite restaurants, he is particularly sensitive to the most subtle changes in the flavor and quality of ingredients, and tastes preparations in the kitchen constantly to ensure that the flavors are impeccable, especially when they involve ingredients he does not know so well. That cuisine is for him primarily a practical endeavor does not mean that he creates dishes through improvisation, or intuitively, without a conscious consideration of flavors and culinary conventions. His words clearly denote a cognitively deliberative approach to cooking. He is extremely analytical when he designs new preparations, an approach that is required to create the complex dishes with multiple ingredients and intricate layers of flavors that characterize his style. If other chefs for whom cuisine is a practical activity tend to be more improvisational, it is largely because they cook in styles that make this approach possible. A more rustic style, with dishes made with fewer ingredients and simpler preparations, served at lower-status restaurants, facilitates a more casual approach to cooking wherein new dishes can be added to the menu without much tweaking. A chef at a middle-status restaurant in New York who uses familiar ingredients and cooks many of them on a grill is an example of such a case. He explains how he goes about creating a new dish:

> Usually I, realistically, I use my sous-chefs. And with them, we'll hash, we'll talk about it a little bit, and I'm very open with them. . . . I mean, sometimes I put stuff on the menu and we don't even make it until the first order comes [*laughter*]. But that's because we know the combination is right. . . . But, like, if we are doing a menu, yes, we'll do, we'll try one the day before, we'll run it as a special for a while and it gets on the menu or something like that. And do you tweak it? Yes, you tweak it. But if you have to overhaul it, then there's probably something wrong with it.
>
> Q: What would be tweaking and what would be overhauling?
>
> Tweaking would be cutting it differently. Plating it slightly differently. Maybe adding a component or even better would be that we remove a component. . . . But if you have to change . . . like, okay. We had it originally with potatoes and now potatoes don't work with it. We are going to change it to turnips or carrots. And the sauce we did it with red wine and now we are going to do the sauce with white wine and vinegar, and that's changing it. That's like overhauling it. Start over.

For this chef, trial and error does not go beyond minor changes such as adjusting the balance of a sauce; the substitution of an ingredient in the sauce would make an altogether different dish. In an approach to cooking that unfolds largely in-practice, trial and error entails (minor) adjustments in the execution of the dish. The substitution of an ingredient is not a modification in the process of cooking but in the conception of the dish, hence it entails a new dish. By contrast, when cooking is taken as a conceptual activity, trial and error is a step in the conception of a dish. Innovative chefs who meticulously design dishes late at night, when alone at home, are a paradigmatic example of this approach. Below, one of the recently appointed, innovative chefs at a high-status restaurant in New York discusses whether he uses trial and error.

> Always. Always. I always. Everything is. Honestly, 50 percent of the dishes, they never see the restaurant at all, you know. It's only, it's a gut feeling with me. Sometimes I create a dish, and it's like, "It's perfect, let's do it." Sometimes, the sous-chefs will create a special and I say, "That's nice, let's do something like that." And usually they don't like it but I change it completely around.

For those who view cooking as an eminently conceptual matter, trial and error has to do with the *ideas* that go into a dish. This does not mean, of course, that these chefs do not adjust their preparations just as anyone else would, but this is not trial and error for them because it is not what defines a dish. In short, to the extent that cuisine can be approached as a primarily conceptual or primarily practical activity, the outcome of that activity (i.e., a dish) will be viewed as either a concept or an executed product.[31]

Duality in Cognition and Action, and Beyond

It is tempting to see a neat dual picture, wherein chefs are either conceptual or practical, cerebral or intuitive, or fully deliberative while working on certain tasks and completely automatic when performing others, but such a picture would be misleading. For one thing, individuals are unlikely to rely consistently on either one mode of thinking or the other. Even single actions are unlikely to be either thoroughly cognitively controlled and explicit or completely outside of conscious awareness. Separating one form of cognition from the other in actual practice is not so easy or even advisable.[32] Nonetheless, a dual view of cognition and action has been greatly (and increasingly) influential, not only in cognitive research but also in the sociology of culture.

Research into cognition shows that the mental schemas whereby individuals process incoming information develop from experiences that have occurred repeatedly. Experimental data provide evidence that mental structures entail strong expectations about what goes together with what, and a predisposition to lump together those things that are thought to go together in order to form a holistic image. This view of thinking as something that unfolds through network connections is called the connectionist model of cognition, and it has been argued that it represents much of human cognition.[33] From this model, it follows that cognitive schemas are not static mental representations, but well-organized processors of information, frequently activated and fairly unchanging. Schemas make connections among bits of information and fill in for information that is missing, so they can create interpretations even from minimal inputs. That they develop from experience and adapt to circumstances means that mental structures are more flexible than they were once thought to be.[34]

In contrast to automatic thinking, deliberative cognition works through symbolic processing. In this case, individuals encode inputs as symbols to form a representation, and follow rules of logic serially to process the symbols and make decisions.[35] Rule following demands slower thinking than pattern recognition does. Whereas we follow rules to handle formally learned information, we process knowledge learned informally—typically from everyday experience—through connectionist networks. Serial symbolic processing and connectionist networks together make up the dual-process model of cognition, which has become a standard model for understanding cognition.[36] From the perspective of the dual-process model, individuals tend to rely on automatic associations between things (based on their sense of what goes together with what) to guide their actions because deliberative thinking is cognitively uneconomical, so only exceptional conditions lead to the latter type of thinking. Some of the conditions that lead to deliberative thinking are inputs from the environment that elicit individuals' attention, or what is called schema failure, when a cognitive schema proves ineffective in a particular circumstance. Individuals' cognitive capacities to engage in analytical thinking, their dispositions to do so, their emotions, and their motivations to think analytically are also conditions that lead them to think deliberatively.[37]

When it comes to chefs, plenty of factors lead them to think both automatically and deliberatively, inside as well as outside the kitchen. They certainly engage in much automatic cognition and action during service, and think deliberatively when they look for and evaluate ideas to create new dishes, but even during the most hectic dinner service, they respond to contingencies deliberatively, and even when they deliberatively consider ideas for dishes, they rely on information implicitly to assemble ingredients or decide on cooking methods. For instance, they may strategically decide to put duck breast on the menu because it is a popular item; they may automatically pair it with fruit because that is how it has always been done (i.e., duck breast with fruit is a classic pairing); or they may follow intuitive reactions, with a sense of "what feels right," and pair the duck breast with carrots because, being sweet, they could serve the same function as fruit.

Here I am pointing to three paths of action. One path relies on deliberative thinking to accomplish a purposeful action; another is automatic, involving little to no deliberative thinking or conscious experience of the action; and the third is phenomenologically experienced as motivated action (therefore not automatic), though not driven by deliberation but by intuitions experienced as a sense of what feels right.[38] There is an important distinction in this tripartite model that is absent from the sociological literature on culture and cognition, which has been built on the dichotomous understanding of action—as either automatic or deliberative—of dual-process models.[39] It is not theoretical musing but rather observation of how chefs create new recipes that suggests going beyond dual-process models for an accurate understanding of cognition and action. Even when chefs do not experience any conscious thought in creating a dish, they often experience their actions as motivated by intuitions, the embodied sense of what feels right. What is more, this type of action is phenomenologically experienced as motivated *and* creative.[40]

The chef who reported that the idea of pairing panna cotta with dried apricots and pink peppercorns "just happened," for instance, experienced the process of creation in just this way. The idea for the dessert was *sparked* by a contingent event, but it was not an automatic outcome of that event; rather, it was the result of a set of motivated and creative actions, led by an intuitive, embodied sense that it would make a good dessert.[41] The chef at the Californian high-status restaurant in San Francisco who characterized her approach to cooking as intuitive (and thought she was "horrible at the scientific ideas") is another example of the quick and unreflective use of know-how that has been learned through lived-in experience (therefore likely stored in connectionist networks) and has become embodied over time.

Just as having a random event spark an idea for a dish does not mean that the whole creative process is automatic, a purposeful decision to make a new dish does not mean that the dish is created largely through deliberative cognition either. After years of kitchen work, chefs develop plenty of patterns of information on which they rely automatically or intuitively to design recipes. When they decide to showcase a new ingredient, and pair it with other foodstuffs without giving much thought to it, or following a sense that it feels right, they are relying on a culinary convention so deeply incorporated that it is no longer experienced as a convention. Even when keenly purposeful, they rely on skills and conventions unthinkingly, and when largely unreflective, they engage with information explicitly.

Imaginative Action and Dispositions

In a job that involves conceptual and practical work, chefs create dishes through different approaches, ranging from highly purposeful to improvisational, and from cognitively analytical to more intuitive and automatic. I showed in this chapter that approaches to cooking are associated with how chefs understand cuisine. Whereas a conceptual approach entails an understanding of cooking as (at least partly) an intellectual activity and is associated with innovative culinary styles, a practical approach typically develops from the view that cuisine is about sensorial pleasure and is therefore more reliant on intuition and associated with traditional styles.

To the extent that motivations and actions unfold in response to one's perceptions of the environment, chefs' approaches to cooking are going to vary in ways related to their perceptions of the field and their positions in it. This explains why recently appointed chefs at high-status restaurants often adopt innovative styles and have similar conceptual views on cooking and deliberative and meticulous work processes, and more senior chefs at middle-status restaurants often have more traditional styles and the more practical and improvisational approaches that develop through experience and security in one's position. In other words, chefs with similar career paths, culinary styles, and status face (some) homologous conditions in their work, and develop thought patterns, ideas, and actions in response to those conditions that are also (somewhat) analogous. They in turn interpret their environment and make choices to respond to it guided by the thought patterns and habitual practices shaped through prior responses.

Inclinations to approach cooking in one way or another are also associated with how individuals see themselves as chefs.[42] Those who see themselves as innovative engage in more deliberative thinking and, as earlier examples showed, look for contexts with no competing demands on their attention—which can deplete cognitive resources—where they are better able to think analytically and create dishes.[43] Self-concepts guide chefs not simply because they provide a compass for making choices, but also because they shape cognitive patterns themselves. When chefs attempt to challenge a convention or think of an ingredient pairing, they activate particular neuronal connections, and if they repeat the thought, they strengthen the connections.[44] This means that these connections will be easily activated and will therefore shape the ideas chefs go on to contemplate, and also that it will take more effortful cognitive processes to undo or modify the connections.[45]

Of course, chefs do not consistently rely on a given cognitive mode, just as they do not consistently have inclinations to create novel dishes or keep serving the same old food. They often remark that they have periods when they want to explore new culinary territories, and phases when they have no motivation to be inventive.[46] Sometimes they want to create novel dishes but cannot do it because they lack inspiration. Even a chef at one of the most elite restaurants in New York pointed out that there are periods when he changes the menu often but that he can also go for months without touching the menu because he lacks inspiration.[47] At other times, chefs are not inspired but accidentally come up with an idea that leads to a novel dish. In other words, the deep-seated tendency (whether in the scholarly literature or popular accounts) to equate innovation with deliberativeness and forward-looking actions, and the reproduction of established practices with automatic cognition and habitual practices, becomes problematic in the face of actual practices.[48] That there is an association between innovative cooking and certain forms of cognition and also between traditional cooking and other forms of cognition does not mean that any particular innovative dish is created through deliberative thinking or that all traditional dishes are the product of automatic cognition. As I have shown, chefs sometimes innovate without being reflective about it, or even by mistake. Indeed, many famous dishes were created by mistake—the molten chocolate cake being one of the most renowned examples.[49] By the same token, some chefs are very purposeful in the creation of dishes and make traditional food.

The duality between dispositional and more imaginative and forward-looking actions that is common in the literature is, to a large extent, the product of a misleading conceptualization of dispositions. Dispositions are normally understood to be automatic behavior, the unreflective reproduction of ingrained habits.[50] But a disposition is not equivalent to unreflective action; although it is acquired through prior actions, it is not the actions themselves, and neither is it necessarily unreflective. Disposition refers to an acquired *predisposition* to act in a particular way under given conditions.[51] It should not be conceptualized as the repetition of acts because it does not belong to the realm of the *actual* but to that of the *potential*.[52] Accurately understood, the analytical concept of disposition helps to explain why there are robust forms of behavior—whether such behavior unfolds with or without individuals' consciousness—and where such behavior should be expected to arise.

Individuals may have dispositions to engage in imaginative action and be forward-looking and yet not effect change. Without question, to the extent that dispositions are built on past behavior, ingrained in associative networks or embodied, they are more likely to be actualized than are actions that require the more cognitively onerous serial symbolic processing and speculation that is tied to the future rather than to the past.[53] Moreover, desires to undertake one given action or another are more fleeting than dispositions, and they may be present yet lack sufficient force or the right conditions to be actualized. In short, in contrast to dispositions, desires or forward-looking actions are not axiomatic.

Just as dispositions and forward-looking actions are always in flux, constantly shaped by the choices chefs make in their work, so are self-understandings. Chefs develop patterns of cognition and action that shape their culinary styles and self-concepts as they create dishes, in an ongoing process.[54] Of course, they do not do any of this in a social vacuum. They create dishes and shape their culinary styles as they strategically attempt to position themselves vis-à-vis others in the field and struggle to gain recognition and legitimation, so it is to this that I turn in the next chapter.

CHAPTER SIX

Culinary Styles and Principles of Creation

EARLY IN 2013, Dominique Ansel, a French pastry chef with experience working in high-end restaurants in New York, opened a bakery in Soho. He had a very good reputation in the restaurant world built on his traditional French pastry, but he attracted an outsized amount of attention when he created the *cronut*, a cross between a croissant and a donut. People form long lines outside his shop by seven in the morning every day, waiting for the chance to get a cronut when the store opens. There have been countless newspaper and magazine articles, numerous television shows, and constant internet chatter about the cronut and its inventor. Ansel now has a reputation that is unusually widespread for a pastry chef, but even then, the cronut receives much more media attention than he does. As a result, many who have heard of the cronut would be unable to name its creator.

A chef may become tightly coupled with a culinary creation that attains fame, but once knockoffs of the product proliferate—as has happened with the cronut—the association between the chef and the product loosens until it is lost altogether, such that it is not known to most persons. Even more than the cronut, the molten chocolate cake—a warm individual cake with a liquid chocolate center—is a paradigmatic example of this phenomenon. The cake is generally claimed to have been created (accidentally, as described in Chapter Five) by the chef Jean-Georges Vongerichten, a high-status French chef in New York, but it is so ubiquitous that few associate it with him.[1] The cronut and the molten chocolate cake have been decoupled from their creators to the point of no longer being perceived with the attributes of their creators, whether French or high-status.

These examples raise a few related questions that are important for understanding the work of elite chefs and, more broadly, the process of cultural innovation. What is the nature of the relationship between the reputations of chefs and of their dishes (i.e., do their reputations co-vary?)? Why do chefs innovate on culinary traditions to produce new dishes? What leads them to turn away from the food they were trained to cook early in their careers? And how do they earn legitimacy and reputation? Chefs sometimes innovate by mistake (e.g., the error in baking that led to the molten chocolate cake) but at other times strategize to create original dishes. Chefs come to understand dishes and culinary styles by learning what they mean to others, and make choices about them in view of how they will be classified by others. In particular, chefs often strategize in the culinary styles they adopt and the ways they represent them (e.g., Modern French or New American? Italian or Mediterranean?), with an eye to where in the field the styles will place them.

In this chapter, I explain how chefs use culinary styles to position themselves vis-à-vis others in their field, and struggle to gain legitimation and recognition through the food they put out and the ways in which they represent their styles. Culinary styles are means for chefs to position themselves in a field in terms of status (e.g., New American cuisine has higher status than German food) and also to associate or dissociate themselves from other chefs (e.g., making Asian-inflected French food dramatically increases one's chances of being associated with Vongerichten, renowned for this style; making Spanish food exponentially decreases them). Culinary styles associate (or dissociate) chefs, and encourage (or discourage) relations among them; this is why chefs use them strategically in view of where in the field they want to be and where they want to take their careers.

Principles of Culinary Fields

Cultural fields are typically conceptualized as hierarchical structures with social positions occupied by individuals based on their unequal possession of relevant resources (i.e., the different forms of capital, in field theoretical language).[2] To understand culinary fields, it is important to bear in mind that chefs occupy positions based on their culinary styles and status, and so do dishes. Put differently, the structure of a culinary field consists of relations among chefs as well as relations among dishes. This is not to be taken to mean that dishes have agency, along the lines of Bruno Latour's actor-network theory, but rather that dishes are imbued with social relations—with the chefs who created the dishes and those who borrow them.[3] Chefs and dishes are bundles of relations of *both* chefs and dishes, and therefore the two have distinct but analytically inseparable trajectories in a field. Like chefs, dishes have career paths, styles, and status.

Creating a complex dish can increase a chef's reputation, but the chef's reputation will also inform how the dish is perceived. The cronut, for instance, would have had quite a different reception had it been created by a cook at a bakery chain in Staten Island instead of by an elite pastry chef in Soho. In more analytical terms, chefs and dishes influence one another's standing in a field.[4] Chefs increase their reputation when they serve dishes that attract attention and gain visibility (to the extent that this happens for positive reasons) and when they make dishes with high-status ingredients (e.g., foie gras or truffles). By the same token, lowly foodstuffs acquire prestige when served in elite restaurants (e.g., tacos, once seen as lowbrow, are now a staple in elite restaurants). Associations among individuals and products are constantly in flux, embedded in a dynamic patterning of mutual relations.

If chefs and dishes both have careers that unfold over time, the structure of a field is then constituted by chefs' actions and their dishes, as well as by past chefs and dishes, because they are all embedded in dynamic relations of interdependence.[5] Chefs borrow ideas from past and contemporary dishes and, in doing so, establish associations with those dishes and the chefs who created them, and thus with the styles and status of both. Offering a dish closely inspired by René Redzepi's food at Noma (a restaurant in Copenhagen considered the leader in the New Nordic style and rated as the best in the world in several consecutive years in the 2010s by the influential *Restaurant* magazine) establishes an explicit association with him and the style and status he represents. Such association influences the standing of the chef who borrows the ideas and, over time, also the perception of the dish that was the source of the inspiration and of Redzepi himself. At first, the borrowing will increase Redzepi's reputation, but repeated and expanded borrowings will eventually lower the allure and standing of his dish. This is what happened with the molten chocolate cake, a dessert born in the high-end confines of French cuisine that, after years of borrowing by chefs at lower-status establishments of all styles, is now perceived as a relatively pedestrian and not necessarily French dessert.

Chefs' understandings of their styles are shaped by the established perceptions of culinary styles that already exist in their field. Like individuals in any field, chefs develop embodied knowledge of the work they do, but acquire a full understanding of what they do only when they know what their actions mean for others. This gives them an appreciation of their actions in a context of meaning, and allows them to understand their actions vis-à-vis those of others.[6] They require these intersubjective and relational perceptions to understand their work, articulate their ideas (for themselves as well as for others), and strategize.

Heteronomy in a Field

The ways of thinking and doing things that are intrinsic to a cultural field shape the logics that guide action therein, but no field is entirely autonomous in relation to the larger social world. Social, cultural, and economic forces external to a field impinge upon its internal dynamics.[7] However, some fields have a higher degree of autonomy than others. Academia is a paradigmatic example of a field with a relatively high degree of autonomy. Much of what drives academic research is internal to the world of scholarship and universities, including factors such as scholars' specialized interests, theoretical and methodological trends, and incentives for research agendas. Moreover, scholars produce work largely aimed at other scholars.[8] At the opposite end of the spectrum, the movie industry constitutes a highly heteronomous field, much more closely dependent on forces external to it. The production, distribution, and consumption of movies are tied to persons, interests, events, institutions, and audiences that are not internal to the movie industry.[9]

In line with Pierre Bourdieu's work, research on cultural fields generally assumes all these fields are structured by the coexistence of two impulses, namely commercial success and artistic reputation, and a trade-off between them that is well understood by field members.[10] However, only one of these impulses is present in some fields. In some largely autonomous fields, products are very rarely turned into money (e.g., in academic philosophy), and in many highly heteronomous fields, commercial success is what ultimately matters (e.g., in the advertising industry).[11] In contrast to fields organized around *either* artistic reputation *or* commercial success, in the culinary field these two impulses are largely fused. As in literature, music, or the fine arts, artistic creativity is important in high cuisine, but as in the corporate world or biotechnological industry, work is necessarily done for profit. Artists can make paintings regardless of whether they have a dealer or gallery that represents them, but chefs cannot do their work without a restaurant job.[12] Poets could go to a café or park to write or present their work to others, but elite chefs can hardly prepare meals without a restaurant kitchen or serve them without a proper setting.[13] Put differently, while painters or poets can, in theory, claim devotion to *art for art's sake*, chefs cannot possibly disregard audiences. Given that their jobs involve kitchen work as well as managing the business, disattending to economic concerns is hardly possible.

Management constrains chefs, not only by limiting the amount of time they can devote to food but also by making them keenly attuned to food and labor costs. Being responsible for creative *and* administrative tasks significantly informs chefs' self-understandings and the means through which they legitimate their work. In areas of cultural production where administrative tasks and artistic tasks are assigned to two distinct roles, each occupational group relies on either economic or artistic values, respectively, to represent and legitimate its work, but both sets of values are critical to elite chefs' reputation.[14] Serving creative and flavorful food at an unprofitable restaurant does not build a chef's reputation and neither does running a profitable business with subpar food.

That chefs work in a heteronomous field also means that audiences are outsiders to the field and, as such, are not experts in cuisine. This introduces more constraints on the dishes chefs create because the food cannot be too obscure or unusual but has to appear familiar to customers.[15] Without question, chefs respond to market pressures and cater to outside audiences, but they do so by relying on a distinct set of principles that guide their actions and define excellence that are internal to their field. This means, in other words, that there is *some* degree of autonomy in the field, and therefore that chefs gain recognition and attain field positions (at least partly) through values that are central to the logics of action in the field. Flavor is one such value, but elite chefs also need to create original dishes and develop distinctive culinary styles. Indeed, when it comes to field positioning, culinary styles are key.

Culinary Styles and Social Associations

To the extent that chefs have the ability to select a cuisine when they open a new restaurant, how do they make a choice? They select cuisines strategically,

in view of the field positions they aim to occupy (e.g., high-end Mediterranean food will place them in a higher-status position than gastropub fare),
though their choices are always made within constraints.[16] For one thing,
chefs can only cook in styles they master, so they typically choose cuisines
with which they have worked before, particularly during their training. However, because cooking in given styles or making certain dishes makes connections with chefs who are associated with those styles and/or dishes explicit,
chefs who open their first restaurants have especially strong incentives to move
away from the styles of the chefs for whom they worked, to shun associations
with them and demonstrate that they have ideas of their own.

Culinary styles are thus not just the *outcome* of chefs' career paths or reputation, but also *means* for action that can be used strategically for field positioning. Being strategic about culinary styles is especially important for those
who have worked for high-profile personalities because they face the highest
risks of being associated with their former employers; choosing a different
style from the chefs for whom they have worked makes it easier to demonstrate that their styles are not closely derivative.[17] Plenty of chefs who worked
at renowned French restaurants during their training have gone on to open
establishments serving Italian food, others who worked at innovative restaurants fusing Western and Asian foods have deliberately restricted themselves
to Western ingredients when they opened their own establishments, and still
others with thorough training in high-end food have chosen to cook only
with low-end foodstuffs.

Adopting a style entails an association with an established culinary category and its attendant prestige, as well as with individuals who cook in that
style.[18] A chef who works in the New Nordic style, for instance, is likely to
attain relatively high prestige (i.e., higher than if he cooked Brazilian food),
and will be lumped together with, and compared to, others at New Nordic
restaurants. Common membership in a culinary category also increases the
chances of meeting others in the category at professional or social events. Just
as academic subdisciplines or specializations in the practice of law bring individuals together at conferences, meetings, or social occasions, so do subareas in cuisine.[19] Chefs meet peers with similar culinary styles at specialized
conferences, workshops, or dinners. Of course, just as academics and lawyers
do, chefs also meet peers who work in very different styles at industry events,

award ceremonies, and social gatherings, and engage in social interactions that foster social ties and information exchange.

They typically talk about food whenever they get together, even ad nauseam, as several remarked in conversations with me. They draw on one another for ideas, sometimes explicitly (e.g., asking for advice on how best to cook a squab, what to do with seasonal morels, or how to get hold of truffles) and at other times contingently (e.g., finding inspiration from random comments made by others during a get-together). Through their face-to-face interactions and by looking to one another to orient their actions and ensure they stay in the game, chefs strengthen the web of interdependence that structures the culinary field in their city.

Conduits of Information: Social Connections

Though chefs exchange ideas when they get together, they are reluctant to talk about it (at least with a field outsider, as I was) given their inability to give public credit for information exchange in cuisine, so tracking the diffusion of ideas is not easy.[20] The ideas that travel in the field, the channels through which they travel, and the strategies chefs follow to distance themselves from connections that may appear as conduits of influence can be inferred by combining three sorts of data: the dishes chefs put on their menus, which indicate, among other things, the ideas that are influential across a field; chefs' career paths, as they offer information about who worked with whom and therefore about conduits of influence; and chefs' comments about peers, which give evidence of sources of inspiration and ideas that chefs recognize and acknowledge (and those they ignore or deny).

When chefs comment on seeking out help from friends, they are often referring to technical requests such as how to cook an unfamiliar ingredient or source a foodstuff that is not readily available. Those who belong to a corporate group have especially advantageous access to direct conduits of information because they have regular meetings and teleconferences with colleagues at partner restaurants, as well as corporate newsletters and listservs, and they can discuss information about new products, techniques, or ideas for dishes through all these channels. As a result, these chefs can more easily acknowledge such conduits of information because the other chefs in the company are not competitors but part of a team.[21] Kitchen staff (chefs de cuisine and sous-chefs in particular) constitute another easily available conduit of information, and chefs do often draw on them for ideas. These individuals work for the chefs, so they are not competitors nor a threat to the impression chefs strive to maintain that their styles are not derivative. A renowned chef at a middle-status restaurant in New York discussed his channels of information exchange with unusual candidness:

> I pick up the phone, as I have done for many, many years. "You know, I have this piece of bass, and I don't know what the hell to do with it." "You know, I did it with lentils and . . ." "Oh, cool, thanks." The fact is that if I set about absolutely replicating what a friend of mine just said, it's not going to have the same translation anyway. If you look back to the relationship between Picasso and Georges Braque as an example, I mean . . . they looked the same but they obviously were not the same. That's cool; it's the only, it's a way for us to learn, you know. Because once you step up and you're the big cheese, you don't always learn as much from the people working *for* you. . . . So consequently, we have to lean on each other as the old daddies and get help from there.

Few others were as open about information exchange, especially regarding advice about ideas for dishes. Well-established in the New York culinary scene for a long time, with a recognized personal style and a restaurant in an economically secure position, this chef is able to talk more candidly about the diffusion of ideas.[22] As a celebrity chef, he has close social ties with others with similar seniority and status (and even similar culinary styles), and having built a good camaraderie over the years, they can all share information. He does not rely on his staff for ideas, he explained during the interview, because he believes it would challenge the hierarchical relationship between them.[23] It is significant, though, that even with the most candid chef, the specifics of the diffusion of ideas remain vague. For one thing, to make a point about knowledge exchange, he resorts to the fine arts, and thereby distances himself from the risky territory of cuisine. And when asked about the types of ideas he might exchange with friends, he explained that they mostly discuss issues related to business ownership and management.

By and large, chefs mention conduits of information between peers with direct social connections (friends or staff) and (likely, but not necessarily) with similar culinary styles and status. Sharing styles or status is especially likely among members of a corporate group, given that restaurants in a conglomerate have some common characteristics, but the "old daddies" in the above example are also quite homologous, as they are all high-profile chefs, restaurant owners, and middle-range in status, and a good number of them also cook relatively traditional food, whether New American, Mediterranean, French, or Italian. Like these established chefs, the young and innovative chefs in New York also tend to socialize with one another. In contrast to the "old daddies," they have fewer years of experience at the helm of a restaurant, work in restaurants of relatively high status, and experiment with modernist techniques and other innovative trends. These chefs form especially tight networks; being part of the most avant-garde movements in cuisine, they come together in specialized conferences and workshops, both locally and globally, and also get together through more informal means.[24] Social connections among them are especially valuable conduits of information because the skills, techniques, ingredients, and knowledge required for their styles are highly complex and so not widely known, so relying on peers for information and products is more critical.[25] To be sure, chefs also socialize with others with different culinary styles, status levels, or seniority, including former employers, former colleagues who took different paths, and staff, but also with peers met through informal means.

Sources of Information: Dining Out

Chefs also seek out ideas by dining out, especially during their travels. They generally look for cuisines homologous to their own, either visiting the countries on whose cuisines they draw and/or going to establishments with styles similar to their own. This makes sense, of course, because it allows them to find ideas that they can more readily adapt to their restaurants. However, one might expect that foods that are very different from theirs, and even products that have nothing to do with food, could spark the most creative ideas. This is what research on innovation would suggest, for it shows that access to objects, actions, and ways of thinking that are different from one's own are critical for the creation of novel ideas.[26] For one thing, an idea borrowed from another group, even one that is old in that group, will be novel in a new context. More significantly, exposure to different ideas, practices, or cognitive styles can encourage innovative thinking by altering how individuals understand the objects of their work or how they go about doing things.[27]

Nonetheless, there is no strong evidence that these factors lead to innovation in cuisine. Chefs rarely make comments that indicate that they came up with new ideas from restaurants with dissimilar styles, and rarely mention any activity or area unrelated to food as a source of new ideas. Neither does diversity in social connections appear to be a source of innovation; for one thing, social connections with individuals outside the restaurant world are relatively rare for most chefs, given that their schedules make such socializing difficult.[28] I have heard chef after chef describe how he comes up with ideas for dishes in detail, and go through all the steps whereby he turns the initial ideas into finished dishes, and have almost never heard any comment that might suggest—explicitly or by inference—that he found inspiration outside of cuisine, whether as a result of purposeful strategies (e.g., looking at art to obtain ideas for dishes) or by accident (e.g., having an idea sparked from a description in a novel). In addition, in conversations about their work and lives, chefs in New York and San Francisco do not make many comments about social connections outside of cuisine, either because they do not have them or because those connections do not function as sources of ideas.[29] If there is any diversity in sources of innovation, it is in status levels, as chefs look to peers and culinary fields with different (generally higher) status levels for ideas.

Chefs look to what others in their field are doing to obtain information and to identify competitors in order to adjust their cooking to what their customers are eating in restaurants in their market niche.[30] They select ingredients, ingredient pairings, techniques, and presentations based on their information or assumptions about who their customers are and what they are likely to order.[31] They also look to chefs who are not competitors for new ideas, even if they take precautions due to the deeply incorporated moral boundary that separates acceptable from unacceptable borrowing practices.[32] As a result, like fiction writers who stay away from literature when they are writing a book to avoid inadvertent influence, some chefs do not go out to eat or read cookbooks when they are designing a new menu for fear of unintentionally copying others. A chef at a middle-status restaurant in New York commented on the practice of going out to eat:

> You do that [go out to eat] for creative reasons and you, not that you emulate or copy, but you see what other people are doing. But actually sometimes when I am doing a menu I intentionally *don't* go out to eat because I

don't want it to influence, and it can, subconsciously. . . . You know, like, I'll go out and all of a sudden, you know, I'll do the special the next day, and you realize you're looking at it the third time. . . . And you go, "That's *very* like what I had two weeks ago over at whatshisname's place," or something, you know, or something like that. So I do. I try to isolate that sometimes.

Purposefully insulating themselves from influence is easier for chefs who are well established in the field, with a personal culinary style and a restaurant in a secure position, like the chef in the above example. Yet, avoiding eating out is not a foolproof strategy, because chefs are constantly picking up information from the environment—whether purposefully or not—and certainly cannot prevent drawing on ideas that are stored in their brains, especially given that this often happens subconsciously. For one thing, memories of food eaten long ago are often blurry, and may also be modified with the passing of time so that they bear little resemblance to the original experience. For example, a chef may design a stew of lamb and prunes inspired by a tagine (a traditional Moroccan preparation for braised or stewed meats) with only a fuzzy image of a lamb tagine with prunes he once ate or, worse, with no recollection of having eaten this dish. In short, chefs are not, and could not possibly be, always conscious of the sources that inspire them.

Capitalizing on Social Connections

Chefs regularly talk about the work of higher-status peers and, what is more, make frequent and lengthy comments about their social ties with these peers. Social ties with high-status chefs serve various purposes beyond being conduits of influence, including opening access to jobs or work opportunities such as food festivals or special events and helping chefs to recruit staff or source rare products. They also serve as symbolic capital, the prestige that comes with being friends with certain persons.[33] Social connections are not created equal, of course, and ties with high-status chefs are more instrumental for most purposes. Indeed, chefs rarely mention connections with lower-status peers. In the midst of a conversation about an unrelated topic, a chef at a middle-status restaurant in New York commented on his social ties:

I love wd-50, I love eating there. And it's so opposite of what I do. But I really love it. Because he's doing it right. He really does it right. Flavors are

always right on. His textures are right on. Wiley's cooking's brilliant. . . .
There's a perfect contrast, my mentality and what I believe in, and what he
does. We're friends, him and I.

Another chef at an upper-middle-status restaurant in New York similarly remarked on his social ties with the same chef in the midst of talking about
something else:

> And as a matter of fact, I was looking at wd-50 too. He's a good friend of
> ours, and he's a good guy. He's using a lot of stuff that's far out.

The two chefs cited above cook in very different styles from one another (and
from the chef with whom they claim to be friends); the former makes rustic,
traditional Italian food and the latter uses some modernist techniques to make
composed, innovative French fare broadly inspired by other cuisines. Both
highlight their friendship with Dufresne, the chef who earned a great reputation after opening wd-50 in 2003, the first modernist restaurant in New York
and considered among the most innovative in the city until its closure in late
2014. Beyond these two persons, a large number of New York chefs, across
culinary styles and status, claim to be friends with him and, similarly to these
two, express pride when they report on this social tie, taking time to convey
the strength of the connection, thus showing evidence that the social tie serves
as a proxy for their own reputation. Modernist chefs in particular talked longer and more enthusiastically about this tie, as would be expected given that
they accrue more advantages from a connection with this chef.[34]

Chefs also talk about other social connections with colleagues, including
those in foreign countries, but no social tie was invoked nearly as frequently
as this one. To be sure, there will be more variance in social connections with
peers in other countries, because chefs travel to different locations—related
to their culinary styles—and will develop more ties in those locations, but
this does not explain why friendship ties with other local chefs were not mentioned more frequently. The remarkable frequency with which individuals
claimed to be good friends with this high-profile chef recalls Kurt Vonnegut's insight that "[a] New York friendship is a friendship with a person you
have met at least once. If you have met a person only once, and you are a
New Yorker, you are entitled to say, whenever that person's name comes up
in conversation, 'Yes—so-and-so is a friend of mine.'"[35] Claims about strong

ties with a chef who occupies an important position in the field are not to be taken as an indicator of that chef's sociability (and I have not heard any comment that would indicate that this may be the case), but as a proxy for the speaker's own qualities and social standing in the field.[36] Moreover, chefs' comments about their social ties with peers show evidence that they actively monitor these ties. Such ties matter because they help chefs advance their careers, attain positions in the field, and control their positions. Ultimately, however, what matter most for field positioning are culinary styles.

Culinary Styles and Field Positions

If social ties allow room for interpretation (e.g., is someone I run into every once in a while a friend?), culinary styles allow even more interpretation. Is a menu with many Italian dishes and some Mediterranean influences Italian or Mediterranean? Modern Italian or traditional Mediterranean? Because culinary styles combine a range of characteristics (such as regional origin, innovativeness, cooking techniques, and ingredients), they can be defined differently given the salience of any particular characteristic and the criteria that matter most to the chefs. Of course, not all culinary styles are equally susceptible to interpretation; a traditional Spanish tapas bar can be defined in no way other than Spanish and traditional, but a style may be, for instance, a combination of Spanish and Mediterranean, somewhere between rustic and elaborate, or somewhat traditional but with innovative influences.

Some chefs are devoted to a cuisine's regional origin, others are particularly committed to the source of ingredients, and still others are invested in keeping to tradition or crossing boundaries. Thus, for instance, a menu with many pasta dishes crafted with a nose-to-tail approach to cooking may be defined as Italian by a traditionalist chef, as nose-to-tail by a chef concerned with environmental and animal rights, or as New American by a chef not bound by regional conventions. How chefs classify their styles is not mere subjectivity, though, but rather emerges out of field positions, because chefs choose and understand their styles from these positions, and strategize about the classification of their styles from there.[37] Through their classifications they position themselves closer to some peers and further from others.

A New York chef who had recently opened his first restaurant, a high-status establishment that promptly acquired a good reputation, had several

Italian and French dishes on his menu, including numerous pastas and risotti, a foie gras appetizer, and a Provençal stew. When he described the food, he explained that it was strongly influenced by Italian cuisine but created within a French framework. This was not surprising, given his reliance on French culinary principles and techniques, but he could have represented the food differently, and indeed he did later in the interview, when asked to define his style. He knew well that by highlighting the French framework he was bound to be associated with French restaurants and dissociated from Italian ones. Just as foregrounding certain attributes leads to associations with peers who share those attributes, backgrounding other attributes blurs resemblances with other particular styles and therefore associations with chefs with those styles. The chef in this example had worked for a renowned Italian chef for a long time, right before opening his own restaurant, so it was in his interest to dissociate himself from that style; he had also worked for a prestigious chef who cooked French food earlier in his training. In the interview, he noted that his foundation and techniques came from the two famous restaurants where he had worked, but that they were combined with his own ideas. When it came down to the key task of defining his style, this is how he proceeded:

> That's why, whenever I'm asked, "What is it?" I say, "It's kind of European cuisine." It's a mix of, you know, a lot of the avant-garde Spanish technique and idea, and philosophy behind, you know. I'm on board with a lot of that stuff too, to a certain point. I think it offers excitement and a new way of dining. I don't think it's very trendy, I think. I like to take, to do the more stable of them. Only what's going to make the dish taste better.

To define his style, the chef stays away not only from Italian cooking but also the French framework. He represents his food as "kind of European cuisine" and highlights the use of modernist techniques, even if French techniques are dominant in his kitchen, and Italy has a significant influence on his menu with a special section with eight homemade pastas, an uncommon feature outside of Italian restaurants. His food was not the prototypical example of modernist cuisine, since he relied on some of the techniques but many of his dishes were served in more traditional styles, something he indeed pointed out during the interview. However, defining his food as he did allowed him to distance himself from the two renowned chefs with whom he was likely to be associated. At the same time, culinary innovation matters deeply to him, and therefore foregrounding this attribute is not a mere strategic move, given the position he occupies in the field and where he wants to be, but a reflection of where his cognitive attention is, given his interests and values.

Chefs associate or dissociate themselves from others and attain field positions by means of the identities they shape for themselves in an active, ongoing process as they move from one position to another, their cooking changes, and the field itself goes through transformations.[38] The following comment is from someone at an upper-middle-status restaurant in New York, who has had a long and highly regarded career, having run some of the most elite restaurants in the city, and had only recently opened his first restaurant as chef-owner.

> One of the big changes that I have felt, maybe not related to cooking, but my palate has changed. I feel that my palate has changed in the sense of longing [for] more acidity versus sweet. The palate has changed also in [liking] more potent flavors, stronger flavors because your palate gets tired after a while. . . . And the cooking has changed. . . . I think it has changed in the sense of the complicated things that you put on the menu that are too difficult to execute. . . . That has changed *a lot.* When I was at . . . [a high-end restaurant] I had an army of people, five, six people working on one plate. First of all, I don't think that's necessary anymore. I also don't think it's a good thing, it's very expensive labor-wise. But I think that's evolved for the better, in my opinion, in trying to stick to two or three main things and try to focus on them.

With his renown and well-established culinary style, this chef no longer needed to struggle to gain a name for himself, like the chef in the earlier example, but he faced other pressures as an owner of a new restaurant that was costly to build and maintain. He was now more concerned with economic matters than he had ever been, and this influenced the style he sought to develop, and his whole thinking about food. Simplifying his style was driven by economic pressures, but it was also made possible by his reputation, since he no longer needed to "wow" diners with many unusual items or flourishes to prove his creativity or lure customers to his restaurant. The simplification of his style is in line with a change in trends away from the more formal and ornate dining customs of the

1990s, when he gained a reputation for his extraordinarily elaborate and refined food. His current style was thus the product of his own career path and standing in the field, and of the monitoring of chefs in the city. Along with changing work conditions, new culinary trends, and even physical changes (the palate changes, which are nothing but the embodied crystallization of a long career), his understanding of cuisine and his role as chef were transformed and materialized in his new approach to cooking.[39]

Chefs are constrained in the styles they select for their restaurants by their present work conditions and standing in the field, the choices they made in the past (in particular, the restaurants where they worked and skills they learned), and the actions of other chefs in the field. The latter cannot always be anticipated, but chefs must respond to them to stay in the game—that is why they constantly monitor the actions of peers. The narratives they delineate to understand and represent their work are intrinsically associated with their perceptions of what others are doing, as well as with their own career paths and projections to the future. Such narratives thus have a critical role in forming the careers they outline for themselves.[40]

Against Innovation

Of all the narratives that guide chefs in their work, none are more central than the two main logics they follow to create dishes, namely flavor (i.e., the function of ingredients in attaining a balance of flavors in a dish) and originality (i.e., the response to the pressures to differentiate). Flavor is the principle of excellence in a culinary field and, as such, the logic that affords chefs legitimacy and prestige. This follows the notion that every field has its own principles of perception and appreciation whereby individuals delineate their actions and gain reputation, paradigmatically formulated in Bourdieu's concept of the *enjeu*, the specific value that is at stake in a field.[41] The other main logic can lead chefs away from the goal of flavor, and indeed undermine it if chefs are too focused on creating new flavor combinations for the sake of originality (i.e., a dish may be original but not so pleasant to eat if it has overly odd flavor combinations or unpleasant textures).

The two main logics encompass several normative standards. The logic of flavor is often bound by the norms of regional cuisines (e.g., the established ways of cooking Tuscan, Mediterranean, or Mexican foods). Even if some chefs do not constrain their styles to any one region, regional standards are there in the background when they design dishes. The notion of balance of flavors is tightly associated with the composition of dishes, a norm that comprises the kinds of nutrients and proportions that should constitute a dish (e.g., proteins, carbohydrates, and vegetables in a main dish).[42] This notion changes with culinary fads, which may affect the use of ingredients, ingredient combinations, textures, and presentations (e.g., dietary fads can reduce the amount of carbohydrates deemed desirable in a dish, the faddish love for animal fat can increase the proportion of fat deemed acceptable, and trendy pickles can draw attention to the role of acids in food). Lastly, the logic of originality leads chefs to try to distinguish themselves and deliver innovation through rare or exotic ingredients (e.g., high-quality fish flown in from Japan, seafood from Australia, white truffles from Italy, or a rare cut of venison from the best local farm), intricate ingredient combinations, delicate and complex techniques that may involve days of work and several kitchen staff, and stylized presentations.

If one did not know better, one would expect chefs who are at the pinnacle of high cuisine on a national (and even international) level to draw attention to the creativity, originality, and complexity of their food. After all, these are the attributes that earned them reputation and brought them to their top positions. However, these chefs, and especially those at the most elite restaurants in the United States, describe their food as simple. Moreover, they reject any suggestion that they might be creative or innovative, and even that they strive to create complex or original dishes in the first place. Instead, they maintain that their goal is to deliver good flavor, and that the quality of ingredients is what matters most for the culinary excellence expected at their restaurants.

Elite chefs must undoubtedly showcase high-quality ingredients and impeccable flavor, all the more at high-end restaurants, where expectations about excellence are not forgiving. But they are also expected to deliver complexity and originality. In focusing on flavor and the quality of ingredients to describe their culinary styles, they obscure the centrality of originality—that is to say, the pressures of differentiation—as one of the main logics that guide them in their work. Consider a chef at one of the most elite restaurants in New York who has been portrayed as someone who has transformed the approach to ingredients. A review of his restaurant in the *New York Times* praises the originality and complexity in the layering of flavors, and highlights the balance of textures, colors, appearance, and flavor present in many dishes. I asked the chef what constituted the innovativeness in his food.[43]

> Innovation? . . . Hmm. Well [*laughter*] . . . I don't know. I really, seriously, it's something that I cannot answer because I'm not into the foams. I'm not into the sous-vide. . . . My approach, I think, is very traditional. . . . So I'm not innovative in that way in terms of technologies or playing with gelatin. I'm not a fashionable chef in that sense. . . . So I don't know how I am innovative. I don't. Actually, I do not care about being innovative or not. It's seriously the least of my concerns. I am in my trip, and whatever happens. . . . And I don't know what is the perception out there, if people believe I am innovative or not. But being in my trip, I cannot care about that, you know?

This chef was genuinely surprised to hear that his food was innovative. If modernist cuisine is the standard by which innovativeness is measured, as his words imply, his style is undoubtedly not innovative because he does not use any modernist techniques.[44] Chefs commonly take an almost ideal typical version of modernist cuisine (i.e., multiple technical flourishes in every single dish) as the standard by which to assess their own innovativeness. Consequently, even if they use some modernist techniques, they are bound to conclude that their food is traditional—there is always someone more heavily reliant on modernist cuisine than they are.[45] Chefs typically frame their culinary styles through an oppositional logic, a tendency resulting from a few factors. For one thing, modernist cuisine has been so tightly associated with innovation (especially in the early 2000s), and particularly in New York, that it has become synonymous with it. Ironically, this ends up conflating innovation with fads (a not uncommon occurrence), even though for a fad to exist, it requires widespread emulation, such that what may have been an innovation can no longer be technically considered as such. This is in effect what the chef in the above example claims, that he is not innovative because he does not follow fads.

Using an oppositional logic also follows common cognitive patterns. First, it is in line with the principle of cognitive economy, because relying on a single category provides maximum information with the least cognitive effort.[46] Second, it is in line with the cognitive tendency to code phenomena into binary categories.[47] Establishing an opposition between two categories also allows individuals to do boundary work, casting the other side in a negative light, and themselves positively.[48] To the extent that modernist techniques can seem faddish, gimmicky, or devoid of "soul," and can therefore be seen as instrumental strategies used for the sake of differentiation, representing themselves in opposition to modernist cuisine makes chefs appear devoted to the principle of excellence in their occupation, and thus places them in a more desirable symbolic position in the field.

The *Sens Pratique*

In line with the principle of excellence in cuisine, the chef in the above example developed his own tenet for creating dishes, namely that the main ingredient in a dish is "the star of the plate," to be elevated and not hindered by other elements or flourishes, so that any extra ingredient is to be included in a dish only if it serves an important function for the overall balance. If he considers this principle key to his culinary style and the chef he has become, it is because doing it any differently would clash with the value he deems essential, that is, being single-mindedly devoted to flavor ("in my trip"). Listening to chefs talk about their food makes it clear that claiming devotion to the principle of excellence in their occupation is not merely a strategy to attain legitimacy and increase their reputation but a value they have internalized to the extent that it has become a core moral component of their self-understandings.

Now, although they typically invoke the principle of excellence to describe their approaches to cooking, they bring up the incentives to make complex and innovative dishes to attract attention and customers when they explain the motivations and success of others. Adopting faddish ingredients, new techniques that alter the textures of foods, or intricate presentations, *for the sake of* complexity and originality, amounts to working for the "wow factor," which implies an instrumental pursuit of attention and success, and a morally impure goal in chefs' eyes. The wow factor therefore encompasses others' shameful strategies to gain recognition from critics and diners. Claiming disregard for complexity and originality, along with a single-minded pursuit of flavor, by contrast, conveys commitment to morally pure motives in one's own work.[49]

If chefs talk about their styles in ways that may seem inconsistent to outsiders, it is in part because styles are not one-dimensional, so they can be variously defined, and in part because chefs cannot possibly foreground two competing logics of action equally (i.e., flavor and originality), so they invariably emphasize one dimension over the other in defining their styles. Without question, chefs strategize through their representations, because these are means for legitimation and field positioning, but their representations are not pure instrumental strategy. In particular, chefs represent their food differently in response to the context of conversation; the context calls on them to think about specific aspects of their work, and this leads them to foreground the principles that are most relevant for those aspects.[50] The conversation may remind them of their passion for cooking, the values that matter to them, or the pressures to survive in the market, and any of these issues would bring to the foreground particular characteristics (e.g., the quality of ingredients, French technique, or the complex layering of flavors), leading to a representation of their food in line with those characteristics. The context of conversation may, in other cases, trigger a subjectively experienced need to legitimate themselves, so chefs will emphasize the attributes of their styles that convey a commitment to flavor (e.g., culinary traditions and high-quality ingredients). In still other cases, the conversation may elicit a subjective need to differentiate their styles from those of former employers or competitors, leading chefs to think about the qualities of their food that are distinctive.

That chefs represent their styles in ways that do not always resonate with outsiders' perceptions is also explained by the fact that they draw on ideas and criteria that pertain to the perspective of the practitioner. In addition, some of them lack the vocabulary or cognitive dispositions to describe the motives, impulses, and ideas behind their dishes, so they end up with somewhat odd descriptions and explanations. It is not unusual for chefs to struggle to explain the reasons why they put certain ingredients together to make a dish. This is not because they do not know what they are doing. If they generally make the right choices when they assemble ingredients to make a dish (the choices that enable them to stay in the game), that is only because they know how to combine ingredients to attain an overall balance of flavors, and also how to make complex and original dishes.

Chefs are able to make the right choices because they have an embodied understanding of the institutionalized criteria that matter, which, put differently, means they can make the right choices because their understandings are in line with the core principles that structure the field itself.[51] When they explain how they created a dish by stating that the dish "makes sense," they show a coherent response to the principle of excellence in cuisine, because they demonstrate the priority of flavor (i.e., a dish that "makes sense" is consistent with the established notion of balance of flavors). Dishes that "make sense" enable chefs to both earn legitimacy and ensure commercial success (i.e., a dish only "makes sense" if it is easily recognizable, hence familiar, and thus responds to customers' preferences), which in other words means that they fit the principles that organize the field. There is no better evidence of a *sens pratique*, or the internalization of the principles that organize the field, than chefs' typical inability to articulate what makes a dish good beyond the succinct formulation that it is one that "makes sense."[52] Working towards the wow factor, chefs' coherent response to the other principle that structures the field, breaks with the core internalization of what is at stake in the field (i.e., the principle of excellence), and this is why chefs identify it more often as others' orientation of action, and why it is verbalizable in a more substantive formulation than the *sens pratique*. If there were no differentiation of chefs in the field, and therefore no more than one strategy of action, all that anyone could do to explain his logic of action would be to shrug his shoulders and say that he does what he does because it just "makes sense."

The principles that guide action in any well-established field are, in general, not easily formalized—formalizing them would cut against the endogenous social definitions that guide action—that is why chefs sometimes represent their work in vague and inchoate terms. Just as the nobility would not have had a book of manners intended to define etiquette in their midst, so chefs do not have a fleshed-out formulation of excellence in cuisine. Thus, when asked to talk about their work, they find themselves expected to articulate principles they know well but cannot quite verbalize. They have local understandings that are embedded in larger cognitive schemas (institutionalized ideas about how to prepare and combine ingredients, and knowledge of market forces), which take specific instantiations given the variations and improvisations that arise when individuals outline narratives to justify and legitimate what they do.[53]

The Logic of the Field

In line with the emphasis on constraint over creative action, sociological and organizational research typically analyzes creative styles as the outcome of given social forces, whether established cognitive schemas, status, or network constraints.[54] In addition to discussing the significant influence of these social forces on creative styles, in this chapter I showed that culinary styles are also means for action, as chefs select styles strategically with an eye to the positions they want to occupy vis-à-vis peers. This chapter offered a close examination of the logics of action that guide chefs in making choices about their styles, and showed the inherent relationship between phenomenological understandings and the structural organization of a field. Looking at the role of social connections as conduits of information and sources of symbolic capital provided further insight into the phenomenological understandings and structural factors that together shape dynamics in a field.

In particular, the two central logics that guide action in cuisine—flavor and originality—manifest themselves, at the individual level, in how chefs approach each dish and, at the organizational level, in the creation of normative standards and trends that drive cuisine forward. These logics are the basic coordinates that structure a culinary field, determining where chefs, dishes, and culinary styles will be placed in the organizational space. In short, flavor and originality are not just abstract principles that guide chefs in their actions, or available narratives to justify or legitimate culinary styles, but structural properties that constitute the very outlines of a culinary field.

The notion that individuals are embedded in a field that precedes them—wherein there are established cognitive schemas and a set of principles, values, and hierarchies that structure the social space—all too often leads to an image of constraint, and little room for creative action, diversity, or change.[55] What underlies this image is the assumption that the organizational environment exerts an unmediated effect on individuals because individuals subconsciously incorporate the cognitive schemas institutionalized in the environment and/or because field positions determine actions. However, organizational structures are configurations of multiple cognitive patterns with varied principles and ideas that guide perceptions and actions, and with networks of attention and disattention.[56] Different contexts will encourage individuals to focus on diverse criteria, and to adjust their attention and actions in response to circumstances. Individuals will sometimes respond to circumstances routinely, while at other times they will improvise, react to contingencies intuitively, or strategize purposefully.[57]

I have shown that chefs select which principles to prioritize to guide their actions from their field positions, and struggle for the meaning and prestige afforded to their actions from those positions.[58] Indeed, insofar as a field is organized around individuals who endow their work with value, there is going to be a struggle around that value.[59] In a culinary field, chefs struggle for the definition of what it means to be a good chef, what makes a good dish, and what it means to be innovative. When they claim that they work towards the principle of excellence, and that others work for the wow factor, they are struggling for the meaning and value of what they do.

This chapter outlined critical analytical tools to explain the logic of creation in cuisine, but the dynamics of any particular culinary field are not just the product of general principles. Culinary fields are social structures shaped by local conditions, and organized around social positions that bring particular pressures, incentives, and constraints along with them. Chefs apprehend the logic of creation from their field positions, given the particular conditions of their field, and make choices about their food and how to represent it from this standpoint. The final chapter looks closely at how this manifests itself in New York and San Francisco.

CHAPTER SEVEN

Mapping Out Creative Patterns

A CHEF who cooks rustic Italian food at a highly regarded middle-status restaurant in New York passionately advocated for the value of peasant cooking. He expressed strong opinions against the fads and fashions that, in his view, are ruining cuisine, and remarked that he and his friend Dufresne (the chef generally considered to be the most innovative in the city at the time), both "have the same idea that we stay in the kitchen, we care about what we are doing." That is, *in contrast to* most chefs, they are not devoted to fame and success but to the craft of cooking. He noted:

> I cook from my heart, and I cook what I want to cook. Where all of these chefs, not all of them, but a lot of them are gearing what they are producing to please Frank Bruni [the restaurant critic for the *New York Times* at the time] or the *New York Times* or the people who eat out in New York. You know, you live, and you die—unless you're doing something you believe in, for me it's . . . I don't read the reviews . . . they're frustrating for me.

Unlike most of his peers, he cooks on the line during service and hires someone else to expedite. This is a rare kitchen arrangement, only possible because his dishes have few ingredients and a rustic aesthetic with no presentational flourishes (e.g., a grilled whole fish placed on a terracotta plate with nothing but a slice of lemon and a thyme sprig), so checking them before sending them to the dining room is not highly demanding and can be delegated without risk.[1] This chef's stand on his work is not an illusion and certainly not mere rhetoric; he is devoted to the kind of cooking he believes in, and spends his time on the tasks that matter to him, namely cooking and sourcing good ingredients.

Chefs' actions cannot be explained without according independent analytical weight to self-understandings, in particular moral views on cooking. But to the extent that individuals acquire understandings, values, and ideas from their social positions, culinary styles and self-concepts must be placed in their field to be analyzed. If the chef in the above example underscores his dedication to making simple and flavorful food, it is because he is in a middle-status position in the culinary field in New York. Were he at an upper-middle-status restaurant in either New York or San Francisco, he would not emphasize these values, and if he was in San Francisco he would not draw attention to his ties to the most innovative and one of the highest-profile chefs in the field.

Individuals develop a sense of who they are as chefs, where they are coming from, and where they want to go from their place in the field. Their theories of their current direction in and through the field guide them in navigating the social space and making choices about their culinary styles and how to represent them. In previous chapters, I have shown how chefs come to understand their work and make choices about it in view of their career paths, current work conditions, and positions vis-à-vis others. In this concluding chapter, I place chefs in their field to explain the patterning of relations between culinary styles, self-concepts, and field positions. Through analysis of the distribution of culinary styles and self-concepts in the culinary fields of New York and San Francisco, I describe the choices chefs make about their styles and representations, and compare the internal logics and social organization of the two fields. This analysis is followed, in the second half of the chapter, by a discussion of the analytical and theoretical implications of the study of culinary fields laid out in this book.

The Patterning of Culinary Styles and Self-Representations in New York

Previous chapters have shown that chefs uphold different values, follow diverse strategies of action, and disagree about the purpose of cuisine and the meaning of innovation. In particular, they invoke different principles to represent and legitimate their culinary styles, but they do so in ways that map onto culinary styles with predictable patterns related to status. Figure 7 maps chefs' self-representations and status in the New York culinary field. Chefs are placed in the figure on the basis of how they characterize their culinary styles and the principles of culinary creation they claim are most important.

The figure shows that chefs who characterize their styles as traditional tend to underscore principles of creation that signal moral purity (e.g., "Flavor is number one. Flavor and the taste. . . . Number one is flavor."), and those who characterize their styles as innovative tend to highlight more morally impure principles of creation (e.g., "The visual appeal has to be perfect. . . . I am always trying to find unique plates that nobody else has or different styles."). The figure puts in high relief the differing views of traditionalists and innovators, in that those who see themselves as traditional—critical of the use of novel techniques or ingredients for the wow factor—emphasize a

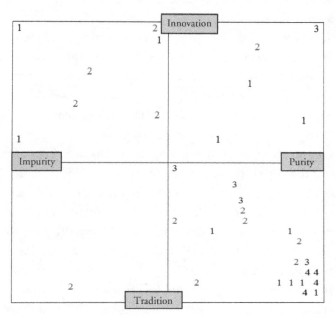

KEY
New York Chefs
1 = Middle-status chef
2 = Upper-middle-status chef
3 = Three-star high-status chef
4 = Four-star high-status chef

FIGURE 7. New York Chefs' Self-Representations of Their Styles
NOTE: I have divided the high-status category into two categories to distinguish chefs who received three stars in the *New York Times* from those who received four stars, a meaningful distinction here. For information on how I located chefs in the figure, see the Methodological Appendix.

single-minded devotion to flavor, simplicity, or ingredients, and those who characterize their food as innovative foreground originality, the look of dishes, or even the wow factor.

The relationship between innovation and impurity (the upper-left quadrant in Figure 7) is weaker than that between tradition and purity (the lower-right quadrant in Figure 7), because elite chefs are not quite as likely to claim that they are willing to trade devotion to the principle of excellence in their creative work for success in the market. In general, they invoke morally impure values only if they can counterbalance them with remarks that entail something more positive (e.g., "For me . . . it was about just . . . discovering new techniques and new ingredients and new processes. . . . But that being said, it wouldn't work if we weren't all classically trained. . . . Otherwise, it's just, it seems hollow.").

Though innovation is linked to the moral impurity of the wow factor, it is also tightly associated with creativity, which means that it can signal something positive, so chefs who represent their styles as innovative have some degrees of freedom to invoke morally pure or impure values in their approaches to cooking without the risk of a delegitimizing self-presentation. This is why these chefs are distributed across the two top quadrants in Figure 7 (e.g., "For me it's not just about innovation or originality. The most important thing is flavor. And then I go back from there," in the right quadrant, versus "Innovation, as a chef . . . There are 21,000 restaurants in NYC . . . you have to be different, you *have* to," in the left quadrant). By contrast, those who represent their styles as traditional can almost only invoke morally pure values (e.g., "While everybody's going forward, looking for the next cuisine, I'm going back. It's all about the pit, and the fire."). Since traditional styles can be perceived as not so creative, chefs would be left with little of positive value to represent and legitimate their work if they claimed their approaches to cooking were led by morally impure values. If their food is not the most creative, they can highlight a positive value by emphasizing their dedication to the principle of excellence in their work. This should not be taken to mean that chefs are calculating, duplicitous, or delusional in their characterizations. That they represent their styles as traditional and claim devotion to morally pure values is logical; if they wanted to wow diners, serving simple and traditional dishes would most certainly not be an effective strategy.

Status introduces different incentives and constraints, not only on the food chefs serve but also on how they understand and legitimate it. Both middle- and high-status chefs are highly constrained in their self-representations, but in different ways. Middle-status chefs have comparatively little freedom. First, their relatively low status introduces more constraints to be loyal to a well-established and therefore easily recognizable culinary style, be it a traditional regional cuisine or a restaurant's signature style.[2] Innovative dishes, being unfamiliar, are more prone to negative perceptions, and if they fail to be appreciated as innovations, they may be perceived to be poorly conceived or improperly cooked, a risk with serious economic consequences for a restaurant.

Second, middle-status chefs have more economic constraints than their higher-status counterparts. They often have tighter budgets and therefore more poorly equipped kitchens, fewer kitchen staff (relative to the number of covers served per day), and more restrictions in the ingredients they can use (a constraint also due to the prices they can charge given their market niche). Third, limited reputation introduces more pressures to attain legitimacy but at the same time constrains middle-status chefs in their reflective self-perceptions and, consequently, in how they can mobilize these to legitimate themselves. Middle-status chefs thus shy away from claims that evoke spurious interests (i.e., working towards the wow factor), and tend to claim instead devotion to flavor and tradition. In doing so, they also align themselves with high-status peers, who profess devotion to the same values, and this can help increase their reputation and, in turn, their commercial success.[3]

High-status chefs are actually more highly constrained than those with middle levels of status, but for opposite reasons. They are constrained to present themselves in ways that are in keeping with their status. With the highest prestige, they are the bastions of excellence in the field, so they are likely to claim dedication to the most morally pure principles of creation. All but one of the high-status New York chefs are in the lower-right quadrant in Figure 7, where traditionalism and moral purity meet. The small group of four-star chefs is more constrained than the chefs with three stars are, and indeed, these elite chefs profess the most single-minded devotion to flavor and simplicity, and claim they do not innovate at all but make the same food that has been made for decades, or even centuries. Four-star chefs are *all* to be found at the lower-right corner of the lower-right quadrant in Figure 7, the location for the highest degree of moral purity and traditionalism.

When it comes to cooking, high-status chefs have fewer constraints to innovate on established styles than their middle-status counterparts do. They face fewer risks when making dishes that look unfamiliar because, due to their reputation, they have diners' trust in their mastery of cooking. Nonetheless, they are more constrained to be loyal to their own culinary styles. They are more likely to have distinctive styles and more visibility than lower-status peers, given their careers, renown, and frequent appearances in newspapers and magazines and on television and the Internet. Customers who go to their restaurants are therefore more likely to have especially clear expectations about the food.[4]

Upper-middle-status chefs have a few more degrees of freedom than those with lower or higher status. They have acquired enough prestige to be able to make innovative food and to count on diners' trust in their culinary competence. And with a lower profile than their high-status counterparts, they have relatively weaker pressures to be loyal to their styles.[5] They also have fewer constraints to admit morally impure interests because they have enough legitimacy to be able to make claims that convey morally impure values, but not so much status that they *must* show devotion to the principle of excellence in their work. At the same time, upper-middle-status chefs face more pressures to differentiate than higher- or lower-status peers do. Unlike high-status peers, they are not in a small and secure group at the pinnacle of the field, and their culinary styles are not as easily recognizable, so they still need to distinguish themselves from others to stand out and ensure recognition and economic success. Relative to middle-status peers, they have fewer constraints to innovate but more pressures to differentiate because, being placed in between middle- and high-status individuals, they must distinguish themselves, not just from their plentiful upper-middle-status competitors but also from lower- and higher-status chefs. Cooking traditional dishes (insofar as they are also served at other restaurants) is not an especially effective means to attract attention. Therefore these chefs are more likely to invoke morally impure values (e.g., claiming they purposefully seek to be original, or consider presentation of major importance), because they have more incentives to create original dishes and serve them in eye-catching presentations, and also have fewer constraints pressuring them to claim morally pure motivations in their work.

Comparing chefs across status categories, there is much more consistency in the values invoked by high-status chefs (as indicated in their clustering in the bottom right corner in Figure 7). From the perspective of social networks analysis, it may be argued that this consistency is the outcome of the tight communities typical of elites, wherein shared values are transmitted and re-inforced.[6] High-status chefs have strong connections with one another, but they also have meaningful ties with lower-status culinary professionals, includ-ing chefs and lower-ranked kitchen staff working for them. In short, there is not enough evidence to suggest that a tight community among high-status chefs is what explains the consistency in values among them. The narratives chefs use to represent and legitimate what they do are certainly informed by social relations with peers, but through a process that is mediated by their re-flective understandings of their field positions and career paths. Chefs will be more drawn to narratives that capture their experiences (i.e., the culinary styles they have learned and types of restaurants where they have worked), and more likely to adopt those that are more fitting with their current positions, which better represent their phenomenological experiences. Self-representations are not merely strategic responses (whether conscious, semiconscious, or subcon-scious) to the pressures and constraints introduced by field positions, and nei-ther are they just the *outcomes* of social positions or processes, for they are means for action that guide chefs in making choices about their work.[7]

Comparing the Culinary Fields of New York and San Francisco

The patterning of culinary styles and self-representations in New York provided important information about the distribution of practical theories of action in the field, but without a comparative perspective it is not possible to fully dis-cern whether (and to what extent) patterns of action and discourse are shaped by general characteristics of fields, the mode of cultural production in cuisine, or conditions specific to New York. I thus turn here to San Francisco for a comparative analysis of the two fields.

The two culinary fields differ in significant ways, and this complicates the comparison. First and foremost, the field in New York is much larger than the one in San Francisco. Perhaps more significantly, the most influential restaurant ratings—awarded by local publications in each city—follow different criteria, so they are not quite equivalent. To delineate a more comparable picture of the two fields here, I do not rely on the publications I have used to create the sample, but on the Michelin Guide.[8] For New York, the 2007 guide lists three restaurants with three stars (the highest rating), four with two stars, and thirty-two with one star, with a total of 507 restaurants recommended in the city, a figure that includes rated and unrated restaurants. For San Francisco, the 2007 guide has one restaurant with three stars, four with two stars, and twenty-three with one star, with a total of 356 restaurants recommended, including rated and unrated.[9] These figures alone give a sense of how dissimilar the two culinary fields are.

Relative to New York chefs, chefs in San Francisco are more likely to represent their styles as traditional, and therefore also to claim dedication to morally pure values. What is more, the few who characterize their styles as innovative highlight the importance of flavor, balance of flavors, or ingredients (e.g., "I feel like as a chef . . . you should be able to create, and really push, you know, as long as the ingredients are solid, they are fantastic ingredients, and you are representing them appropriately."), even if some also admit (secondary) attention to morally impure criteria such as the look of dishes or texture. No one among these chefs gives priority to any criteria in cooking other than flavor or ingredients—a significant difference from New York. The principle of flavor becomes an especially important value where there is higher reliance on ingredients (and a de-emphasis of technique), so it makes sense that chefs in San Francisco would claim devotion to flavor regardless of their styles.

Figure 8 adds a mapping of self-representations in San Francisco to the previous figure about New York chefs (Figure 7). The combined information provides a clear picture of the similarities and differences between the two fields. Figure 8 shows that, whereas New York chefs are clustered together by status, those in San Francisco are more dispersed. Because San Francisco chefs are more likely to characterize their styles as traditional and claim they pursue morally pure values regardless of their culinary styles, the association between culinary styles and legitimating claims is weaker in this field, as is that between these claims and status.[10] Only two San Francisco chefs invoke morally impure values (the two left quadrants in Figure 8), but neither is in the upper-left quadrant, where innovation and moral impurity meet, since even those who represent their food as innovative claim dedication to flavor in San Francisco. The two chefs who represent their food as traditional and invoke morally impure values, placed in the lower-left quadrant, are of middle and high status, in contrast to New York, where upper-middle-status chefs are most likely to maintain they pursue morally impure values. However, some caveats are important here, because the middle-status chef is rather close to the boundary between moral impurity and purity, and the high-status chef (the more apparent outlier) works in a restaurant with stunning décor, a feature that constrains her to create dishes that stand up to the setting and therefore makes her deliberatively attentive to the visual appeal of food.

When it comes to chefs who claim to follow morally pure values (the two right quadrants), the associations among representations, culinary styles,

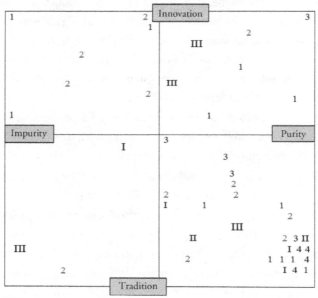

KEY
San Francisco Chefs
I   = Middle-status chef
II = Upper-middle-status chef
III = High-status chef

FIGURE 8. New York and San Francisco Chefs' Self-Representations of Their Styles
NOTE: : I have classified San Francisco chefs into three status categories, rather than the four I used for New York chefs, because there were no restaurants rated with four stars by the *San Francisco Chronicle* at the time I created the sample. For information about how I located chefs in the figure, see the Methodological Appendix and the description of the approach used for Figure 7.

and status also differ across the two fields. Whereas high-status chefs in New York all claim to give priority to morally pure values, and all except for one characterize their food as traditional, a few high-status chefs in San Francisco either characterize their food as innovative or claim to give priority to morally impure values (but never both at the same time). By the same token, in sharp contrast to New York, all upper-middle-status chefs in San Francisco characterize their food as traditional and maintain they pursue morally pure values.

Patterns of Culinary Creation

Strategies of action in creative endeavors are typically explained by status, in that status determines the risks and rewards of different creative styles and therefore the choices individuals make. This notion has been paradigmatically formulated in Bourdieu's theory of fields of cultural production, and furthered by the neo-institutionalist literature in sociology and organizational analysis.[11] The literature shows that innovation is likely to emerge among low-status individuals—often new entrants to the field—as well as high-status persons. As the argument goes, individuals with limited status, hence with limited investment in the field, have little to lose by innovating, and potentially much to gain if their actions prove successful. In addition, being less embedded in the field, they are less likely to take the rules of the game for granted and so are better able to think differently and innovate. For their part, high-status individuals can afford to explore new ideas without jeopardizing their positions, so they are more willing to take risks and innovate.[12] From this perspective, innovation is an instrumental strategy to either increase or maintain one's status (for low- and high-status persons, respectively). If low-status innovators succeed with their novel products, they increase their reputation *and* effect change in the criteria that determine reputation, and thereby transform the social organization of the field itself. If high-status persons succeed, they uphold the criteria and social organization that enabled them to attain—and maintain—their field positions.

Status undoubtedly introduces significant incentives and constraints on creative work, but this does not mean that creative endeavors can be reduced to status-seeking strategic action. In particular, cognitive and social-psychological factors, such as how individuals understand their positions and how secure they feel therein, how invested they are in their work, and how they approach it, significantly inform their choices.[13] Whether chefs identify with the culinary styles of their restaurants and the field positions they have attained influences their inclinations to conform to established ways of doing things or to take risks and innovate. Without question, the risks and rewards they see in innovating will significantly shape their choices, and chefs will strategize about this. However, they are also often driven by other motives (e.g., identification with the occupation, boredom, or a subjectively experienced need to feel creative or stand out), or they act impulsively (with no motive whatsoever) or out of habit. Furthermore, some chefs are so little concerned with status that almost none of their decisions can be explained by it—the chef in the opening example in this chapter is one such case. Chefs with negligible investment in their job, for instance, do the bare minimum to keep the kitchen running and restaurant afloat—this is the goal that drives their choices. If things fail, they know they can obtain another job, even if it comes at the expense of status.

Whereas status concerns point to the degree to which exogenous pressures constrain individual action, cognitive and social-psychological factors point to the ways in which individuals' understandings and approaches to their work inform their responses to constraints.[14] Beyond individuals' motivations, the organizational characteristics of the area of cultural production are also critical for explaining patterns of creation in a field. No single social distribution of risks and rewards to innovating can be generalized to all areas of cultural production, because *what* positions bring risks and *what* positions bring rewards to innovating is associated with modes of cultural production. In cuisine, the for-profit nature of the work, the high costs and competition, and a nonexpert audience introduce a particular distribution of pressures towards conformity to established styles in order to survive in the market and towards originality to differentiate and stand out. Whereas innovating is a reasonable strategy for low-status individuals in areas where the risks of innovating are not too high (where work is not necessarily for profit and costs are low, as in writing poetry), or where audiences are largely able and willing to appreciate innovation (where audiences tend to be experts, as in certain avant-garde arts); this is not the case in cuisine. This is why, contrary to research findings in other areas, innovation is not so common among high-status chefs and middle-status chefs (the lowest-status category in high cuisine), but it *is* common among upper-middle-status chefs.[15]

Just as not all chefs face the same pressures towards conformity and originality in their work, they do not all face the same expectations about the values they stand for, and neither do they all have the same degree of account-ability in justifying their claims. High-status individuals benefit from a slip-page in their legitimating claims that is not there for everyone. This explains why four-star chefs consistently represent themselves as the most traditional and single-mindedly driven by morally pure values, even when their food is not the most traditional and they are not (and cannot possibly be) devoted only to flavor, simplicity, or ingredients. Self-understandings and legitimating claims develop from field positions. Individuals in the highest positions face especially strong pressures to uphold the principles of excellence in their oc-cupation, but they also receive greater benefits, such as being less accountable. Perceptions about the quality of their work, and the moral values behind it, become more rigidified by virtue of their high status, and are therefore more loosely coupled with new external evidence.[16]

I have suggested that culinary styles cannot be dissociated analytically from reflective understandings because chefs make choices about their culinary styles and representations in view of their understandings of the environment. In par-ticular, their strategies to develop styles to differentiate themselves from peers are tightly associated with their attempts to reflectively distance themselves in their self-understandings—a critical task given how important yet hard it is to demonstrate that they have styles of their own. In short, inasmuch as self-understandings inform chefs' responses to the risks and rewards associated with their positions, they mediate the relationship between culinary styles and status.

The Central Chef in the Field

Reflective understandings are inherently associated with how chefs see them-selves vis-à-vis peers, including competitors, chefs they have worked for, those they admire, and chefs they consider like-minded or friends. When they talk about chefs they admire or those with whom they are friends (as I discussed in Chapters Four and Six, respectively), chefs invoke some names much more frequently than others. Even when they talk more generally about peers and restaurants in their field, some names come up much more frequently. Indeed, chefs consistently make comments about one particular person in their field. That chefs do so indicates that this person, and therefore her culinary style, occupies a central position in the field. In turn, this provides information about some fundamental aspects of the logic of creation in that field.

What does it take for a chef to have a central position in a field? First and foremost, a chef attains a central position if she works in a culinary style that has high prestige and visibility in the field, such that she becomes a standard by which others gauge their own styles and, in turn, social positions.[17] But a chef attains a central position only when she is a prototypical representative of the culinary style in question (i.e., her food systematically displays all the attributes that characterize the style).[18] When a person has a central position in a field, she becomes a referent for others to apprehend which culinary attributes are most highly valued, and discern which styles matter, attract attention, and lead to success in the field. Individuals therefore orient their actions towards her in making choices about their culinary styles and careers.

Without any prompting, all the chefs interviewed in New York made comments, at one point in the conversation or another, about Dufresne, the chef at wd-50, at that time the temple of modernist cuisine in the city. Moreover, a good number of interviewees, irrespective of culinary styles, expressed admiration for him, *even* if they generally disapproved of modernist cuisine. By contrast, all the chefs interviewed in San Francisco made comments (and highly laudatory ones) about Alice Waters, the owner of the renowned bastion of seasonal and traditional cooking Chez Panisse. Furthermore, she has earned her unique reputation not so much for the complexity or originality of her food but for having introduced an emphasis on fresh, local, and high-quality ingredients to American eating habits.[19] If she fostered an innovation in cuisine (over thirty years ago), it was about paying respect to ingredients.

In short, whereas the central chef in New York cooked in the culinary style most tightly associated with innovation at the time, and heavily reliant on complex techniques, the central person in San Francisco fostered tradition and simplicity and reverence for ingredients.[20] If chefs talked systematically about them, it is because they are prototypical representatives of the culinary style that is pivotal to each field's dynamics, and therefore ideal referents for others to orient their actions towards. There is another significant characteristic about these two figures, namely that chefs relate to them in consistently amicable terms, either by expressing admiration or signaling friendship ties. This is meaningful because it is not an attribute that should be expected in any and all fields of cultural production. It is sensible to think that at least some individuals might have an adversarial relation to the central person in the field (e.g., those who suffer penalties by being compared to them, whether for being too similar or for lacking any of their highly valued attributes). While other fields may be organized around enmity, culinary fields are structured around cordial ties. Looking closely at the social organization of culinary creation will help explain why this is the case.

Values and Adversarial Cooperation

Chefs look at peers to fully apprehend their own field positions, and from this standpoint shape their culinary styles and representations of their work. Representations are not epiphenomenal to culinary styles. When chefs characterize their work, they effectively identify the attributes of their styles they consider central, distinctive, and enduring, and thus cognitively foreground them; in turn, these attributes will guide the culinary skills and resources chefs choose to cultivate, and thereby shape their styles.[21] Whereas a chef who "sees himself" as innovative will invest himself in learning modernist technical skills, a chef who "sees herself" as traditionalist will direct her efforts towards establishing relations with farmers and purveyors to have access to the best ingredients. I use quotation marks here because self-concepts are neither hard facts nor products of individuals' imagination but a reflective monitoring of their place in the field, and therefore constantly adjusted. Put differently, self-concepts are chefs' theories of their current direction in and through the field. They are usually accurate, though not always, and generally combine descriptive and prescriptive understandings inseparably. They guide chefs in making choices about dishes, career moves, and the skills and resources to be developed, and are in turn shaped by these choices.[22] Chefs thus define their styles and self-concepts concurrently, creating a distinctive identity—manifested materially in culinary styles and subjectively in self-concepts—that is necessary for themselves as well as for their audiences.

Not only do chefs require a distinctive identity, but they are also limited in the extent to which they can stray from it.[23] It stands to reason that their self-representations would highlight their most salient qualities, and that their claims would be shaped by accounts that sound reasonable to them—that is, accounts told repeatedly in their environment and afforded positive values. This implies that representations are part of a cultural repertoire shared by field members—and therefore afforded social facticity—and that there will be a degree of homogeneity in representations in a field.[24] Thus, inasmuch as what defines a chef's job is the creation of dishes, all chefs should be expected to make (at least some) claims about the principle of excellence in their occupation, whether they maintain a single-minded devotion or qualified attention to it. Criteria that do not have to do with flavor, such as the look of dishes or the wow factor, are widely understood to be much less dignifying, even among chefs who admit to attending to them, and thus should be expected to be invoked less often.

The homogeneity of values is reinforced by the tight social network among chefs, because regular face-to-face interaction facilitates the spread of ideas and beliefs (in other words, influence), as well as the monitoring of values and behavior. The form of organizational competition that structures culinary fields also contributes to upholding the homogeneity of values. Elite restaurants compete for customers but rarely have exclusive customers (i.e., diners who patronize only one establishment) and do not require them. Insofar as attracting diners to a restaurant does not necessarily hurt competitors in the long term, chefs do not constitute a system of adversarial competition, as may occur among professionals in occupations where customers are typically exclusive (e.g., law practices or hair salons).[25] Quite the contrary, elite chefs can benefit from each other's success. Arguably, if customers are satisfied with their experiences in elite restaurants, which demand a considerable expense of time and money, they will be inclined to return to these establishments and, given that elite restaurants offer an extraordinary experience (as opposed to the convenience of the neighborhood eatery), (at least some) customers would want to diversify the experience and dine out at a variety of restaurants.[26] In this sense, a field of high cuisine constitutes an organizational space of adversarial cooperation, because chefs compete with one another but collectively benefit from the competition.[27] A structure of adversarial cooperation should be expected to reinforce the homogeneity of values in a field and, in turn, strengthen the collective.

However strong the collective might be, though, the tight social network (the cooperation aspect) is in a delicate coexistence with struggles for differentiation (the adversarial aspect), a coexistence that must be somehow maintained. Chefs actively do so through their culinary styles and career moves, as well as through the reflective management of their identities, social relations, and field positions. Sustaining tight social ties and shared values in a competitive context requires tactful strategies. If chefs try so hard to differentiate from others through multiple strategies, and create accounts that can appear inconsistent with their practices, it is precisely because they are tactfully responding to pressures for differentiation (higher in New York than in San Francisco) while simultaneously upholding a tight social network. They collectively maintain a social order through these practices, an accomplishment made possible by a social order that enables them to manage their actions and relations in the first place.

Cultural Fields and the Mode of Cultural Production

One of the foundational attempts to explain the values and principles that guide action in an organizational field, field theory maintains that individuals internalize a belief in the stakes of the game and (subconsciously) incorporate the logics of the field—this is why the logics are considered a product of the *illusio*.[28] Equipped with the appropriate know-how and a sense of possibilities and limits, individuals delineate lines of action fitting with their social positions, and the social dynamics of the field unfold from the structure of objective relations in which individuals are embedded.[29] In line with these principles, much research in the sociology of culture and organizational analysis makes inferences about the logics of a field, and assumes a certain kind of interested behavior on the part of field members.[30] Field members are often assumed to be driven by instrumental motives and to be embedded in struggles for legitimacy, prestige, and power that collectively shape the field.[31]

When it comes to fields of cultural production, knowledge of the logics that guide action has been limited by the tendency, following Bourdieu's theory, to assume that all cultural fields are organized around two poles—the autonomous pole of artistic consecration and the heteronomous pole of commercial success—and that individuals orient their actions towards one or the other.[32] This reduces explanations of action to either culturalist or materialist motives, in that individuals are assumed to be *either* driven by internalized values (i.e., art for art's sake) *or* instrumentally seeking to improve their status and power.[33] However, any materialist action is inherently cultural, for it is imbued with symbolic meanings, and no cultural act can exist without a material foundation, so posing a dichotomy between cultural and material motives for action is, at the very least, counterproductive and, at worst, untenable.[34] When individuals have to make choices in their work—wherein they must be rational and instrumental—they are faced with the question of what matters to them. They may prioritize economic profit, reputation, social causes, or personal fulfillment. Even when they are at their most calculating, they imbue their actions with meaning, and even when they are driven by their innermost moral values, they are not devoid of reason (at least under normal mental health conditions).[35]

In culinary fields, as I have shown previously in this book, chefs cannot possibly be concerned with *either* artistic worth *or* commercial success, so values and rational calculation cannot be mutually exclusive motives for action. Chefs select paths of action in light of values that matter to them, while also acting strategically so as to keep their restaurants in a secure position or move where they want to be for their careers. They are generally motivated to act by a core value with an ontological specificity that is not quite like the *illusio* because it is neither an abstraction nor misrecognized.[36] Achieving a good balance of flavors is a substantive value inherent to cooking, recognized as such and imbued with very clear meanings. In short, in order to explain how individuals act in cultural fields, attention should be refocused from what fields have in common to how they differ and the dimensions along which they differ. This requires a close examination of the characteristics of the area of activity wherein fields are embedded, because patterns of action are shaped by the mode of cultural production as well as by field dynamics.

Fields of cultural production vary by whether they are localized as well as across areas of activity, but most research examines fields that are not geographically bound, which has reinforced the conceptualization of fields as the product of objective relations rather than actual interactions.[37] This has resulted in a relatively abstract understanding of the dynamics of fields of cultural production, and a lack of knowledge of how localization may shape fields. That culinary fields have some key differences from the most typically studied areas, namely that they are localized and not structured around the opposition between artistic value and commercial success, provided me with instrumental information to analyze some of the dimensions along which fields vary. It also yielded more concrete knowledge of field dynamics, because chefs reported on actual relations with field members rather than theorizing about relations that are more phenomenologically abstract because they lack a regular face-to-face interactive component.[38]

Field dynamics vary across areas of activity because they are structured by the nature of the activity and the substantive logics of action that derive from it, which means simply that they are structured by what individuals produce and how they do it.[39] Five attributes of the mode of cultural production shape patterns of creation: (1) individual versus collective creation; (2) coupling versus separation of creation and execution; (3) managerial versus nonmanagerial roles; (4) commercial versus noncommercial work; and (5) normative versus legal regulation of information exchange. Specifying the dimensions along which cultural creation should be expected to vary better equips us to systematically compare cultural fields, and explain how and why innovation patterns vary across fields and what leads individuals to adopt one creational style or another. The analysis of modes of cultural production allows us to explain how and why patterns of innovation in cuisine are unlike those in areas such as literature or the sciences, as I have suggested, and to speculate about areas that should have patterns similar to those in cuisine, like fashion, architecture, or product design, because they also have individual creation, creators (i.e., those responsible for creation) are also often managers, and work is necessarily commercial.[40] Dynamics of creation may be especially similar in fashion because the regulation of information exchange is also largely normative in that area.[41]

Theorizing Action in a Field

When it comes to explaining individual action in an organizational field, the prevailing tenets are rarely questioned, whether they hold that individuals have an embodied sense of how to act, as in the internalized social structure that constitutes the habitus, or that they follow well-defined, conscious or semiconscious motives.[42] Underpinning these tenets are the assumptions that there is a clear motive that drives action (whether known explicitly or embodied) and that actions are chosen one at a time.[43] Both assumptions stand in contrast to the insights from the literature on subjectivity that show that individuals do not always have a clear sense of what they do in a given situation or why they do it.[44] Pragmatists theorized about this insight early on, offering that individuals do not always understand a situation until it is over, or know how to act until they have already acted, but instead "muddle about," as John Dewey suggests, acting without quite knowing what they are doing.[45] Once a path of action is completed, it may look as though there was a teleology, such that individuals had a clear idea about what to do, but actions accumulate to form a path *as* individuals act, sometimes with more clearly delineated ideas than others but always building on previous actions. Actions are embedded in a sequence of actions, not taken one by one, so that the ends for one action become means for following actions.[46]

Dewey points out that individuals act less driven by particular ends than by the means available to them, because they choose actions based on their capacities, be they in the form of knowledge, skills, or material goods.[47] It follows that individuals' trajectories—that is, the actions they have taken in the past—have a key role informing future actions, not only because they engender dispositions (as Bourdieu would have it), but because they shape capacities. Thus, if chefs vary in their culinary styles and the principles of creation they follow, it is due less to their having different values—as an abstract set of beliefs and moral principles—than to the capacities they have developed throughout their careers. Their careers place them in different field positions, wherein there are different means (material, pragmatic, and cognitive) available for action, as well as different styles and principles of creation fitting with those positions. Chefs' choices about their dishes are so consequential for their careers because they inform the means and ends that will shape future actions.

That chefs make choices about their work implies a degree of purposive behavior, but this is not equal to instrumental rational action as it is traditionally understood, in that purposive behavior results from a choice, but a choice that is profoundly embedded in the conditions of action, so that if chefs follow goals, they are goals that inhere in a particular context.[48] That goals inhere in a context leads Dewey to refer to goals as *ends-in-view*, because they are means for directing action and, in turn, for further ends-in-view.[49] Goals can be constituted by desires, but even these are contingent on context and informed by habits. Individuals may envision what they would like to do, but they adjust their desires as they contemplate options and grapple with information about the consequences of action.[50] Just as ends-in-view are goals within reach, so do desires often involve attainable goals. Bearing in mind that desires are situational facilitates moving beyond the assumption that individuals have a well-defined sense of what they would like to do (whether conscious or embodied) and a ranking of all possible scenarios.[51]

Some desires will prove more enduring than others, however, and those will become solidified into habits. This happens to chefs who are highly motivated to be creative and regularly design original dishes, such that they develop habits of "thinking outside the box" and constantly innovating. Desires, just like inclinations and actions, can thus constitute habits that become central to the self. This implies that desires and habits are not dichotomous forces of action but rather co-constitutive, and therefore that habits cannot be reduced to a mechanical repetition of action.[52] Much of action, as pragmatists argue, is about solving problems and is rarely *either* routine *or* creative. Chefs may begin an action by rote, but facing a problem will lead them to act more imaginatively, and respond to the problem through a combination of habituality and forward thinking, such as when they rely on embodied knowledge and skills to make a dish but, lacking one of the required ingredients, come up with an idea that results in a novel dish. In doing so, they delineate a new kind of action. By the same token, they may conceive a new dish with imaginative thinking but rely on dispositions to design and cook it, as numerous examples throughout this book have shown.

Many of the examples have also shown that actions are shaped by the means chefs have on hand and by the established paths of action that have become embodied and embedded in the physical environment. Chefs generally follow instrumental calculations *and* principles that are meaningful to them, and sometimes act automatically and other times impulsively, with little thought and much less instrumentality. Inasmuch as there is an inherent relationship between value and values, intent and choice, habit and desire, the analysis of action should be sensitive to the many ways in which actions unfold, and to how single actions fit into lines of behavior.[53] How individuals delineate lines of behavior, however, cannot be explained without a close analysis of their self-understandings, themselves constituted by habits, desires, imaginative actions, and values.[54]

Self-Concepts

Psychologists have shown that individuals need a consistent picture of who they are to figure out how to act in different situations.[55] Chefs have such pictures, narratives about who they are that are made up of their dispositions and skills and also their values and desires, informed by ideas available in the environment (in particular how peers talk about themselves), and shaped by their perceptions of how others view them.[56] These narratives guide them, for even when facing all sorts of constraints, chefs make choices that "make sense" to them, which means that the choices are in line with actions they have taken in the past and with the self-image they have developed as a result.[57]

In the early decades of the twentieth century, Charles H. Cooley and George H. Mead developed the foundational theories about how individuals acquire a self-concept through interactions with others, and generations of social psychologists have enriched and specified their insights since then.[58] Many of the existing theories of self-concepts fall squarely in the realm of psychology (focused on issues such as self-esteem or anxiety), but several include characteristics that are instrumental for illuminating the social workings of self-concepts. Here, I review such characteristics, drawing on an overview of the major definitions of *self-concept* compiled by social psychologist Seymour Epstein:[59] (1) the self-concept develops out of experience, especially through interaction with significant others; (2) it is an internally consistent, hierarchically organized schema that fits within a larger framework; (3) it is dynamic, changing with experience; (4) it organizes information from experience into predictable lines of action and helps individuals to avoid overload, inconsistency, or disapproval in paths of action; and (5) it minimizes confusion, disorganization, and stress so that individuals are able to act.

Is the self-concept a stable and solid core, or is it more dynamic, changing with situations? The social-psychological literature is split in this regard; on one side it offers a structural model wherein the self-concept is a stable schema built on personal characteristics and experiences, and on the other side it presents a processual model wherein the self-concept is an active, constantly changing set of self-knowledge.[60] It seems only reasonable to take insights from both models, for self-concepts appear to be relatively stable schemas but changing over time and variable across domains.[61] Individuals develop self-concepts with attributes that resonate with core parts of themselves due to what psychologists refer to as self-consistency, and such a sense of self is required to delineate lines of action that seem reasonable to them.[62] The narratives that constitute self-concepts also need to be consistent for two inherently social reasons. First, because self-concepts are for the self but serve to convey an image to others as well, consistency is important to project an image that appears authentic, and second, self-concepts can have any meaning for the self or others only when they are consistent with familiar narratives.[63]

Though a core part of one's subjectivity, self-concepts are social in nature, not just because they acquire meaning intersubjectively, but because they do so *in relation to* other self-concepts—both similar and different—existing in the social environment. It thus seems sensible to expect that individuals would develop multiple self-concepts, each specific to one of the significant social domains in which they are embedded, in response to the attributes that are socially salient in each domain. This is why I have discussed chefs' professional self-concepts and not the whole sense of identity that goes beyond their occupation.[64] Some of the attributes individuals identify in themselves may be relevant across social domains (e.g., an analytical disposition may inform a chef's work, and perhaps also his music appreciation), but others likely not (e.g., a chef who strives for excellence in the kitchen may be laid-back at the gym). Self-concepts should be expected to vary across social domains, not so much due to the nature of each domain (i.e., an elite chef requires consistent excellence in his work but not in leisure activities) but because they are shaped by the experiences and social interactions individuals have within each domain, and the self-feeling they derive as a consequence (i.e., a chef who achieves excellence may feel good about himself at work but not necessarily at the gym).[65]

It is precisely because self-concepts develop within a specific social domain that they can operate as theories of the field for chefs, as I have suggested in this book, building on the social-psychological insight that the self-concept works as a self-theory, and taking it further to explain how it develops and guides action.[66] Like a scholarly theory, a self-theory is a conceptual tool constructed to fulfill a heuristic purpose, but unlike a scholarly theory, a self-theory is typically built subconsciously.[67] For social psychologists, self-theories help the principle of pleasure, maintain self-esteem, and organize information acquired from experience so that it can be used effectively. The analysis in this book has pointed, in particular, to the importance of self-concepts for a sense of consistency and authenticity, and as a compass for individuals to navigate the environment and focus on the criteria that matter to them so they can delineate lines of action. Like scientists, chefs must solve problems; they make observations, organize them into schemas, and fit these into larger networks of schemas, indeed what we call theories, and use these theories to deal with the problems and dilemmas they face.[68]

The conceptualization of self-concepts I have offered bears a few similarities with one of the recent major sociological elaborations of this notion, developed by Neil Gross, but also has important differences.[69] Like Gross, I consider reflective self-understandings a central component of social action, and key for an organizational analysis of cultural creation, but I depart from him in that he focuses on the *intellectual* self-concept and aims to specify the *causal* role of self-concepts in action.[70] The notion of self-concept I have proposed applies to cultural fields more generally, and constitutes an attempt to formalize the relationship between self-concepts and fields to systematically study how self-concepts develop from field positions and help individuals make choices, and how they collectively contribute to shaping and maintaining a field's structure and dynamics. This entails an always recursive and co-constitutive relationship between self-concepts and field dynamics, and an instrumental heuristic tool to explain both the actions of individuals and the dynamics of a field.

Creativity Within Constraints

Like creators in any cultural field, chefs in elite restaurants in New York and San Francisco vary widely. Some are wildly innovative and value complex intellectual creations, and others favor tradition and simple, sensorial pleasures. Some work in a deliberative and purposeful manner, and others are improvisational, impulsive, or largely automatic. Like creators in any cultural field, chefs also face varying pressures and constraints in their work and self-concepts that are associated with field positions. Yet, no creator in any cultural field is either fully bound by constraints or free from them, which in more general terms means that there is no creativity without constraints and there are no constraints without creativity.[71]

What does it take to do creative work within constraints? First and foremost, it requires knowledge of the constraints, for only then can creators make products that will be accepted by the audience such that they will allow them to maintain their positions and continue to do creative work.[72] Self-understandings guide creators in navigating constraints because they are shaped from within field positions, but this does not mean that self-understandings and field positions are one and the same. Creators' sense of where they are coming from and where they want to go shapes how they understand themselves and their work, and informs the actions they take. That is, reflections on the past and projections into the future come into play in shaping creators' choices as do career paths, skills, and social relations.[73] A young chef at a middle-status restaurant who has trained with the most renowned professionals will make certain choices if he considers his trajectory stellar and his future brimming with potential, and quite different choices if he believes he is not—and will never be—like the chefs for whom he has worked.

Self-concepts serve as a guide for creators to manage their way through the field and negotiate a balance between constraints and their own inclinations. Not all creators have the same ability to negotiate this balance, as some face more pressures, others are better equipped to resist pressures and find a compromise, and still others are more inclined to take risks. The ability to negotiate the balance between creativity and constraints will also vary across areas with different modes of cultural production. While being "too creative" is a bad career strategy in cuisine and, likely, in areas with similar characteristics, such as fashion, architecture, or product design, it would be less risky in areas where work is not necessarily commercial, and the creation and the execution of products are separated into two roles, as in contemporary academic music or avant-garde theater, so that creators can get prestige from their creations even if these are not profitable, or hardly performable.

Areas with varying modes of cultural production introduce different pressures and constraints for creators to both remain within the bounds of tradition *and* demonstrate creativity. There is plenty of information about the pressures to keep to tradition, as well as about the potential of constraints to foster creativity given that they can encourage creators to innovate even when doing so was not the original intention. But there are also pressures to be creative, and these can be constraining in that they may lead creators to prioritize easy ways of conveying originality at the expense of creations that require more time and work or, even worse, at the expense of quality. This is a not uncommon occurrence in cuisine, evidenced when chefs, too keen on making innovative food to attract attention, disregard flavor and make dishes that lack the right balance.

It may not be possible to ever fully understand how creativity works.[74] As an actual process that goes from an initial idea to the production of an object, and from a lone thinker to the social organization of work, it is too complex and elusive and too multifaceted to reduce to a straightforward socio-logical explanation. A good beginning, however, is to liberate creativity from the bounds of constraints within which it has been placed in sociological and organizational research so as to gain a more thorough understanding of the forces that inform creativity, ranging from the more constraining to the imagi-native, contingent, and even accidental. I have suggested that understanding creativity in cultural creation requires an analysis of the organizational dynam-ics of a field to explain its social structure and internal logics; attention to the mode of cultural production to understand the distribution of constraints on and incentives for creativity in a particular area; and an examination of self-concepts to explain how and why individuals vary in their values, motivations, and responses to external pressures. This multilevel approach allows for an ex-planation of individuals' choices in their creative endeavors and of the patterns of cultural creation that develop across fields and areas of activity. Compara-tive research across areas of activity is key to moving the extant understanding of creativity forward. It would not reveal the elusive nature of creativity alto-gether, but this may be welcome because it means, among other things, that the study of creativity has no end in sight.

Methodological Appendix

The Research

This study is largely based on in-depth interviews I conducted with forty-four elite chefs and non-participant observation of how each of them works in the kitchen of an elite restaurant in New York City or San Francisco. I concentrated my research on chefs because their creative processes were of central interest, and I relied on semi-structured, in-depth interviews to get the descriptions and accounts I needed to explain how and why chefs make choices about their dishes. Observing chefs and their staff in the kitchen gave me a good background to better understand their work, and the tensions among the creative, the administrative, and what chefs call the "robotic" parts of their jobs. But to explain how chefs plot a trajectory through a culinary field, I also talked, both formally and informally, with about sixty individuals in other ranks and occupations in the restaurant world, both during my kitchen observations and outside them.

To answer my main questions, I wanted to know about chefs' careers, how they got started in cooking and why they chose the occupation, and about all the jobs they had along the way. We spent a good deal of time talking about their food; chefs described how they come up with new ideas, and how they go from the initial idea to the point where they consider the dish ready to be added to the menu. I used their menus and reviews of their restaurants to prod them with questions. I often picked dishes from the menu or dishes described in reviews and asked chefs how they decided to put given ingredients together or cook them in a particular way, a technique that was especially helpful with interviewees who struggled to explain their work processes. If they paired halibut with thyme, for example, I wanted to know why they did not use tarragon or marjoram instead. I also used menus and reviews as a means of checking further into chefs' descriptions and eliciting fuller explanations. When chefs claimed their food was faithful to culinary traditions and not inventive at all, I could point to an original combination of ingredients on the menu and ask about it, or bring up comments made by restaurant critics. I asked how they got ideas for dishes and whether they read cookbooks or ate out at restaurants for inspiration. I wanted to know how they designed a menu and how often they changed their menus. I asked about their kitchen staff and the criteria they used for hiring. Chefs told me about the restaurants they visit, where they travel, the food they like, and also the chefs they consider interesting, those they admire, and those they wish they had worked for earlier in their careers. They also told me about their future plans.

Fieldwork took place in 2004 and 2005 in New York, and in 2004 in San Francisco. For most of the interviews, I met with chefs at their restaurants, typically in the late morning or early afternoon before they became busy with preparations for dinner. In a few cases, I interviewed chefs in a nearby café because they feared having too many interruptions at the restaurant. Interviews lasted between one and three hours and were around one hour and a half on average; they were all tape-recorded and transcribed. I do not use the names of chefs or their restaurants because the interviews were anonymous and confidential.

During interviews, I sought to set up a relaxed environment that allowed chefs to elaborate on the choices they made in their work. Quite in contrast to the quiet and reflective ambiance of the interviews, the kitchens were fast-paced, intense, and stressful environments during service. Numerous dishes must be flawlessly prepared within minutes, and chefs are there to make sure everything is made to perfection. So I got to see another side of chefs in kitchens during service, one with little room for reflectivity. I was also able to see the dishes they described in interviews, and gain a more rounded understanding of how chefs approach their work. The observation of the kitchen was usually on the same day as the interview. I generally went to the kitchen during the early part of dinner service on a weekday, because the kitchen at that time was sufficiently busy that I could see chefs and cooks work, but not so hectic that I became a disturbance in what were often cramped quarters. How long I could stay in a kitchen varied between one and several hours, and depended on the size of the kitchen and how busy it was. In very small and busy kitchens, a non-participant observer is an evident obstacle (i.e., no matter where you stand, you are never out of the way), so I was not able to stay long in those restaurants. However, a couple of hours were generally all the time required to obtain the information I needed.[1] In larger kitchens, with more staff, more dishes, and a more complex organization, there were more things to observe, staff I could potentially talk with, and room to stand somewhat unobtrusively, so I stayed longer.

I spent most of my time in kitchens during dinner service because it was the best time to observe the dishes chefs described during their interviews and to get a sense of how the kitchen worked when most of the staff were there, so I got to see each person's job, the work pace, and the attention chefs and cooks gave to the cooking and presentation of dishes. I took note of the kitchen layout and the number, demographics, and skill levels of the staff. I also observed the social dynamics in the kitchen, whether the environment was collaborative or friendly, tense, calm, or hectic. I was interested in the presentation of dishes, including the style (whether dishes were intricately decorated, minimalist, carefully plated, or rustic) and how much attention was paid to that presentation. I also looked closely into the roles of the various ingredients in each dish, whether they were there for decoration (e.g., texture, color, volume), balance of flavors (e.g., sweetness, acidity, bitterness), or dietary purposes (e.g., protein, vegetables, carbohydrates). Watching the dishes was an effective way to better understand—and identify contrasts with—chefs' comments about their food, especially the aspects they claimed to focus on for making a good dish. When a chef highlighted contrast of colors as an important element in cooking, I could see how he approached this, and when another chef claimed he was unconcerned with the presentation of dish, I could check how much attention was actually paid to presentation vis-à-vis other tasks in the kitchen.

I observed chefs in particular, noting what they did in the kitchen (whether they cooked, executed, or oversaw the staff), how they did it, and how they interacted with staff. I took note of how the staff worked, and the responsibility, autonomy, and trust they were afforded. The number and skill levels of staff, along with the physical amenities of a kitchen, constrain the kinds of dishes chefs can serve, so it was important to observe all that. If the kitchen was not too busy while I was there, I talked with chefs and asked more specific questions about the dishes they were preparing. Whenever possible, I talked with chefs de cuisine, sous-chefs, cooks, and service staff, and asked about their backgrounds and training, the restaurant's style, and the food they were preparing. If they collaborated with the chef on the creation of dishes, I asked more questions about the food. I generally took note of conversations among the staff, whether they were focused on the work in front of them, talked about the dishes they were preparing or restaurants they visited recently, or joked around.

I spent a lot of time around chefs, both in and outside their kitchens, so I heard them talk about many topics that went beyond those I addressed in interviews. I learned about their opinions of peers, restaurants, the cookbook business, the role of media ratings and reviews, TV food shows, and websites and blogs, and also about the strains of life as a chef. I sometimes revisited chefs after the interview and observation, and had more conversations about their work and the world of cuisine. Some invited me to spend time in the kitchen during the day while they worked on specials, so that I could observe the process of creation in action. Others invited me to go to farmers' markets with them, because they develop ideas for dishes while seeing what is available and what looks good at the market. Still others let me participate in meetings with all the kitchen staff, where they explained the dishes for the day and organized each person's work or discussed problems that needed to be solved.

Doing ethnographic work involves developing relationships with one's research subjects and spending time with them beyond the more formalized instances of data gathering. Conversations in unstructured contexts provided important information for gaining a full understanding of chefs' jobs and culinary fields. I had a chance to talk with chefs I did not formally interview, and to have conversations with pastry chefs, chefs de cuisine, sous-chefs, and cooks working at restaurants included in my sample (between thirty-five and forty informants in total). These individuals talked about their jobs and careers and the restaurant world, offering additional perspectives that helped me better understand the culinary profession and field dynamics. I also talked to other professionals working in the world of high cuisine. I talked formally and informally with restaurateurs, restaurant managers, food writers, service staff, and professionals such as lawyers, architects, and food purveyors associated with the restaurant industry in New York (about eleven informants in total). As insiders, these professionals provided valuable complementary information. I asked them about their view of the field, trends and changes in the restaurant world, the nature of the restaurant business, customers' preferences, and what they thought of particular restaurants. I also conducted ten formal interviews and observation periods with chefs, cooks, managers, and service staff at another location in the New York area, outside Manhattan but with a high concentration of good restaurants, as part of a pilot study prior to the fieldwork in New York and San Francisco.[2] Several chefs working in that location had previously worked in Manhattan and trained at the best culinary schools and restaurants; due to their direct knowledge and proximity to the New York culinary field, they provided useful information and a supplementary perspective on the field. Though I do not draw on these interviews in this book, they informed my knowledge of the restaurant world.

In addition to the ethnographic research, I collected menus from all the restaurants included in the sample to examine their content and form and, when available, other documents that chefs provided (e.g., PR materials, curricula vitae, and formal models chefs devised as blueprints to develop new recipes). I also collected reviews of all the restaurants included in the sample (and evaluated them through content analysis, as I describe below), and numerous articles on food and chefs in New York and San Francisco published during the time of my research. All this information provided necessary background for understanding the two culinary fields.

The Sample of Restaurants

In culinary fields, where the fate of chefs and restaurants is heavily dependent on external appraisals, ratings from the media are a logical guide to selecting restaurants for the research sample. Yet, as dependent as a field may be on external forces, the dynamics of the field ultimately lie in its internal logics, so the opinion of insiders is also critical for ensuring that the sample includes key players in the field. I therefore selected the forty-four restaurants with a two-part sampling strategy. First, I used criteria from influential media, namely the number of stars and price of a meal, to create a sample with three status categories—middle, upper-middle, and high—from which I selected cases randomly.[3] I augmented the stratified sample with field sampling once the research was under way, using the references that my informants made to other chefs and restaurants to chart where the relevant players were and include cases of pivotal importance in each field. I sampled purposively and as systematically as possible from these references, adding cases that were not in the initial sample only when I heard repeated references to any one single chef. One would be unlikely to understand world politics in the 1960s from a random sample of the United Nations that omitted both the USSR and the US; so too one cannot explain the workings of a culinary field without including key chefs.

New York and San Francisco made the two best case studies because they are considered the first and second best culinary destinations, respectively, in the United States, so they share a certain degree of competition and pressures for excellence, and also have significant differences, including the cuisines and trends that are most influential in each city. This made San Francisco a good control case to discern whether the patterns of culinary creation I found in New York have to do with characteristics particular to this city or are more general.

To create the initial restaurant sample, I relied on the most influential publication in each city—that is, the *New York Times* or the *San Francisco Chronicle*—and supplemented the latter with the magazine *San Francisco* to increase comparability, because the way restaurants were rated varied significantly between the two newspapers. For New York, I selected and classified restaurants following the *New York Times*'s ratings, including both stars and prices:[4]

Middle status: one or two stars and "expensive."[5]

Upper-middle status: one or two stars and "very expensive."

High status: three or four stars.

In San Francisco, I selected cases by cross-referencing lists of "best restaurants" from several sources: the *San Francisco Chronicle*, the *San Francisco* magazine, *The Rough Guide to San Francisco Restaurants*, the *Zagat Survey*, and the website *Open Table*.[6] I chose restaurants that were mentioned in at least two of these source and, with research under way, used field sampling following the same logic as in New York. Because the stars scale of the *San Francisco Chronicle* was not comparable to that of the *New York Times* (*all* San Francisco restaurants I sampled in 2004 were awarded three or three and a half stars by the *San Francisco Chronicle*), I used both the *Chronicle*'s ratings and the ratings of the *San Francisco* magazine, and relied on the newspaper for the price category:[7]

Middle status: three stars in the newspaper but two in the magazine and "expensive."[8]

Upper-middle status: three stars in the newspaper and magazine and "expensive."

High status: three stars in the newspaper and magazine and "very expensive."

Tables 1 and 2 present the composition of the samples of restaurants in New York and San Francisco.

TABLE 1. New York City Restaurant Sample

	N	Stars	Price
Middle status	15	1 star: 8 2 stars: 7	Moderate: 3 Expensive: 12
Upper-middle status	11	1 star: 2 2 stars: 9	Very expensive: 11
High status	8	3 stars: 4 4 stars: 4	Expensive: 2 Very expensive: 6

TABLE 2. San Francisco Restaurant Sample

	N	Stars	Price
Middle status	3	3 stars *SFC*: 3 2 stars *SF*: 3	Moderate: 1 Expensive: 2
Upper-middle status	2	3 stars *SFC*: 2 3 stars *SF*: 2	Expensive: 2
High status	5	3 stars *SFC*: 5 3 stars *SF*: 5	Very expensive: 5

NOTE: *SFC* = *San Francisco Chronicle*; *SF* = *San Francisco* magazine.

The Basic Interview Questionnaire for Chefs

CAREERS

How did you become a chef?

Did you go to culinary school?

If so, where did you study?

What did you learn?

Please tell me where you have worked, the positions you had, and how long you stayed in each restaurant.

How long have you been the chef in this restaurant for?

What kind of food does the restaurant make? How would you describe it?

Please tell me about your kitchen staff. How many people work in each position in the kitchen?

What kind of training do they have?

What criteria do you use for hiring kitchen staff?

CREATING DISHES

What do you think makes a dish good/bad?

What does it take for a dish to be successful for you?

What makes a dish successful for your customers?

How does your view differ from that of customers? Why?

How do you decide which ingredients will go well together?

How do you go about creating a new dish?

Please give me an example of a dish you created and describe what you did, from the initial idea until you added the dish to the menu.

Do you do trial and error?

What things do you consider when creating a dish?

What factors influence the choices you make when designing a dish to be added to the menu?

What sources do you use for inspiration to make new dishes?

How do you design the menu? What factors do you consider?

Do you have specials on the menu?

If so, how do you create them and decide to add them to the menu?

INFLUENCE, DIFFERENTIATION, AND INNOVATION

If you were to start your career again, who would you have liked to work with? Why?

What chefs do you admire? Why?

What restaurants do you like to eat at?

Who do you consider innovative? Why?

What would make a dish "different" or innovative?

What would you consider to be an innovation in cuisine?

Categories and Classifications in Cuisine:
Content Analysis of Restaurant Reviews

In Chapter Three, to code and analyze how critics understand and assess innovation, I selected the reviews from the *New York Times* and the *San Francisco Chronicle* for each restaurant included in the sample. Relying on the same sources I used for the sample ensured consistency with the rest of the analysis. Also, because these publications are the most influential in each city, respectively, their assessments of innovation in cuisine carry especially high weight.

I coded the content of reviews to analyze how critics view innovation. I wanted to know whether critics assessed innovation positively or negatively, and what factors contributed to their assessment. Critics may use the words *innovation* or *innovative* or other words that denote the same phenomenon, including *creative, original, inventive, experimental, surprising, different, unusual,* and *playful.* They may also use adjectives such as *whimsical, wild,* or *wacky,* and may qualify dishes as *re-creations* or *reinterpretations* of classical recipes. Of course, there is wide variance in the degree of innovativeness that these words capture—a dish described as *experimental* will be assumed to be much more innovative than a dish that is said to be a *re-creation* of a traditional recipe. Critics may also write about "the genius of a chef" in combining flavors; if the context indicated that the combination of flavors in question was innovative in the critic's eyes, I counted it as a mention of innovation. Because I wanted to capture all the different ways in which critics write about innovation, I took an inductive and interpretive approach to coding reviews (instead of identifying keywords and using software to count mentions).

It was through this inductive approach that I found that critics distinguish innovation by degree and type. The degree of innovation has to do not only with excess (failing to have a balance between originality and familiarity), but also with whether the innovation comes at the expense of flavor. Critics make comments about four types of innovation: in ingredients, ingredient combinations, technique, and presentation. And they write differently about the four types. Although their assessment of a type of innovation is combined with degree (i.e., innovative technique may be appreciated, but not if there is too much of it), some types of innovations are treated as more inherently positive than others. Innovative ingredient combinations have the most positive valuations, because they are perceived as strong indicators of creativity, and have to do with flavor. Innovative presentations are at the other end of the spectrum as the most likely to be met with disapproval, especially if they appear gratuitous.

In addition to counting the mentions of each type of innovation (see Tables 3 and 4), I noted how critics valued each type. I also coded and analyzed comments that highlighted the simplicity of the food to examine how this interacted with assessments of innovation (or lack thereof). In effect, a very high value is placed on the combination of innovation with simplicity, restraint, or subtlety, something that is especially apparent in reviews of high-status restaurants (innovation is expected in these establishments, but simplicity is not). Because innovation is so often seen to be accompanied by excess (too many ingredients, textures, or technical flourishes added to "wow" diners), it is praised especially highly when it is achieved with restraint.

TABLE 3. Indicators of Innovation in Restaurant Reviews in New York

	Innovative Ingredient	Innovative Ingredient Combination	Innovative Technique	Innovative Presentation	Total	Average Innovations per Restaurant
Middle status	4	31	1	9	45	3
Upper-middle status	1	29	5	9	44	4
High status	1	15	2	5	23	3.3

NOTE: N = 33 reviews total: 15 middle status, 11 upper-middle status, and 7 high status.

TABLE 4. Indicators of Innovation in Restaurant Reviews in San Francisco

	Innovative Ingredient	Innovative Ingredient Combination	Innovative Technique	Innovative Presentation	Total	Average Innovations per Restaurant
Middle status	0	3	0	0	3	1
Upper-middle status	0	2	0	0	2	1
High status	0	15	0	0	15	3

NOTE: N = 10 reviews total: 3 middle status, 2 upper-middle status, and 5 high status.

Once each statement about innovation and simplicity was coded, I analyzed the general tone of each review. I wanted to know whether the critic ultimately conveyed a positive image of the chef or the restaurant, what elements contributed to positive and negative valuations, and which attributes of the chef or restaurant were highlighted the most. In particular, I found that not only was innovation in ingredient combinations the most frequently mentioned by far, and the most enthusiastically reviewed, but also that critics devoted more space to discussing this type of innovation than any other. A contextual interpretation suggests that innovation in ingredient combinations provides the most pleasure in the dining experience for critics.

Mapping Out Creative Patterns:
Chefs' Self-Representations of Their Styles

In Figure 7 in Chapter Seven, I located chefs in the New York culinary field based on (1) how they understood their culinary styles, in particular in terms of their innovativeness, and (2) the claims they made to represent and legitimate their choices of culinary styles. In Figure 8, I located chefs in the San Francisco culinary field along with the New York chefs shown in Figure 7 based on the same criteria. To organize their remarks on a scale, I scored the arguments they used to justify their character-izations, the number of arguments they raised, and the order in which they raised them. If they said that their styles were "innovative," emphasizing that their food was boundary breaking, I gave them the highest score for innovation, and placed them next to the innovation end on the vertical axis. If they said that their styles were "dif-ferent" or "original" because of some minor twists (i.e., not boundary breaking), I gave them a lower score and placed them just below the self-represented innovators on the vertical axis. If they said they took classical dishes and tweaked them to re-create the classics and make them "interesting," I gave them a midpoint score, higher if they emphasized the originality of their dishes and lower if they highlighted the traditional sources, and placed them accordingly towards the center on the vertical axis. If they characterized their styles as traditional but interesting because their dishes were a "re-creation of classics" by means of minor tweaks, I gave them a low score for innovativeness and placed them close to the traditional end on the vertical axis. If they characterized their styles as "traditional," "classic," or "regional," and maintained that they relied on old recipes, I gave them the lowest score for innovativeness and placed them next to the traditional end on the vertical axis.

Regarding claims about principles of culinary creation, I scored chefs on the basis of the characteristics they mentioned, the total number of elements they brought up, and the order in which they did it. If they said that flavor is *the* most important ele-ment in a dish, and that all they cared about was making food that tastes good, or that good ingredients are the only requisite for making a good dish, I gave them the highest score for the moral purity of the values they uphold, and placed them on the purity end on the horizontal axis.[9] If they said that flavor is a key concern but contrast of textures is important too, I gave them a lower score in moral purity, and placed them next to the purity end of the axis. If they singled out contrast of textures as the most important aspect of a dish, noting that balance of flavor is also important, I gave them a lower score and placed them near the center on the horizontal axis. If color was the first aspect of a dish they invoked, followed by texture or contrast of tastes, I gave them yet a lower score and placed them midway between the center and the impurity end. If they talked first about the look of dishes, or the wow factor, and then mentioned other criteria, I gave them a lower score in moral purity and placed them close to the impurity end. Lastly, if they talked only about the wow factor or the elegant look of dishes, I gave them the lowest score and placed them next to the impurity end.

Notes

Chapter One: Exploring the World of Elite Chefs

1. This figure (U.S. Census Bureau 2014a, 2014b) includes the restaurants in all five boroughs of New York City. Manhattan, the area of the city where my research was focused (Brooklyn, a magnet for new and trendy restaurants in the early 2010s, had not yet developed as a dining destination when I conducted the research) has about 4,200 restaurants. The figures from the U.S. Census Bureau include only full-service restaurants, which are establishments that offer food for customers who order and are served while seated, and pay after eating.

2. About 400 of these restaurants are in Oakland, and the remaining 200 are in Berkeley (U.S. Census Bureau 2014a, 2014b). The available figures do not provide an accurate picture of the fields of high cuisine in New York and San Francisco because they comprise a wider range of restaurants (including non-elite restaurants and establishments serving strictly defined ethnic fare) than the elite establishments that constitute these two culinary fields.

3. For literature on the nature of French and Italian cuisines, see Capatti and Montanari 1999; Cheminski 2005; Ferguson 1998, 2004; Steinberger 2009; and Trubek 2000.

4. For good descriptive accounts of kitchen work, see Boulud 2003; Buford 2006; Chang, Meehan, and Ying 2012, 2013; Cheminski 2005; Fine 1990, 1995, 1996; Hamilton and Kuh 2008; Ruhlman 2001; and Steinberger 2009.

5. It must be noted that one dimension along which chefs do not vary extensively is gender, especially in New York (but see the *New York Times* article [Moskin 2014] about a recent controversy sparked by "The 13 Gods of Food," a *Time* magazine cover story in November 2013 that barely mentioned women in a long list of personalities around the globe who are changing the food world). If throughout this book I use mostly male pronouns, it is because a large majority of chefs are men, and most of my interviewees were men (more so in New York than in San Francisco). The latter reason also explains why I do not discuss how gender may shape creativity in cuisine (for literature on the role of gender in high cuisine, see Hollows 2003 and Swenson 2009).

6. I will use the terms *cuisines*, or *regional cuisines*, to distinguish them from what I will call *culinary styles*, which comprise regional origin and innovativeness.

7. The lowest category is middle status because these are all elite restaurants, so no restaurant in the sample is low in status. I created the status classifications using the categories of stars and price points awarded by restaurant reviews in the *New York Times* and in the *San Francisco Chronicle* and *San Francisco* magazine for each city, respectively (see the Methodological Appendix for detailed information about the classification process). Insofar as chefs acquire status through the restaurants where they work, they cannot be dissociated from restaurants in any effort to understand their social positions; this is why I have used restaurant reviews to classify chefs. Along the same lines, Rao, Monin, and Durand (2005) consider the chef-restaurant dyad as the basic unit of analysis in their study of French cuisine, and also use originality to classify chefs.

8. Galenson (2007) notes a similar distinction in his study of artistic creativity. He argues that there are two types of artists in the modern world, differing not by their styles but by their methods: aesthetically motivated experimentation or conceptual execution. This distinction, Galenson suggests, is associated with artists' goals.

9. But see Molotch's ([2003] 2005) book on product designers for a very good example of research on how individuals create cultural products in the context of day jobs.

10. For literature on the occupation of chef, see Ferguson and Zukin 1998; Fine 1996; Trubek 2000; and Whyte 1948.

11. The kinds of occupational ranks found in restaurant kitchens vary widely, depending on the size and status of the restaurant, as I describe later in the chapter.

12. A wide range of research has contributed to our knowledge of patterns of innovation. Bourdieu (1976, [1992] 1996, 1993) has theorized about the social distribution of strategies of creation given the risks and rewards attendant on different social positions in a field (for literature that relies on field theory to analyze patterns of creation in a variety of areas of activity, see DiMaggio 1991; Karpik 2010; Thompson 2010; and van Rees and Dorleijn 2001). Much organizational analysis (implicitly sharing many of the assumptions of field theory) examines how risks and rewards shape patterns of innovation (Clemens 1997; Frickel and Gross 2005; Lounsbury 2002; Morrill 2001; Phillips and Owens 2004; Phillips, Turco, and Zuckerman 2013; Phillips and Zuckerman 2001; Rao, Monin, and Durand 2003, 2005; Zuckerman 1999). From a different standpoint, the production of culture perspective looks at a host of social factors, including organizational, legal, and technological factors, that facilitate or hinder innovation (Anand and Peterson 2000; Baumann 2007b; Dowd 2004; Peterson 1997). Network analysis, for its part, sheds light on the role of social networks on innovation (Burt 1992, 2004; Faulkner [1983] 1987; Owen-Smith and Powell 2004). The literature on valuation and evaluation, especially the line of research developed by Lamont (Lamont 2009, 2012; Lamont, Guetzkow, and Mallard 2004), provides knowledge of how shared meanings and values inform patterns of innovation.

13. The individualization of creation and significance of status are common attributes in many areas of cultural creation, including the fine arts, music, film, and academic research.

14. When a dish does not taste good, it is not always easy to discern whether the original idea or the execution is at fault.

15. In chefs' eyes, food critics are more like customers than like chefs because these critics typically have no training in cooking, whether at culinary school or through work experience.

16. Chefs could seek legal protection of intellectual property, but they almost never do. Among the legal tools available to them, patents or trademarks could protect technically complex recipes, and treating recipe ingredients as trade secrets could protect information that might afford a potential economic advantage. The only form of legal protection of intellectual property that is common in cuisine is copyrights, but these protect cookbooks as combinations of recipes along with descriptions and explanations, not the listing of the ingredients that go into an individual recipe.

17. For example, Becker 1982; Becker, Faulkner, and Kirshenblatt-Gimblett 2006; Bourdieu [1992] 1996, 1993; Faulkner [1983] 1987; Gross 2008; Lena 2012; Molotch [2003] 2005; Peterson 1997.

18. The classical argument that all complex social configurations introduce inherent contradictions was developed by Marx ([1867] 1889), drawing on Hegel ([1837] 1997), and was elaborated on in the context of modern institutions by Benson (1977). For literature on how individuals deal with the complexity of organizational fields, see Fligstein 1996; Fligstein and McAdam 2012; and Porac et al. 1995. Several major perspectives in sociology and organizational analysis have contributed to the understanding of how these competing pressures shape organizational dynamics in occupations, most prominently the production of culture perspective (Anand and Peterson 2000; Peterson and Anand 2004) and the neo-institutionalism in organizational analysis (Phillips and Zuckerman 2001; Zuckerman 1999).

19. Without question, restaurants in New York and San Francisco also have tourists in their dining rooms, but tourists do not make up their customer base. Furthermore, chefs bear local customers in mind when they design their food and restaurants. As for chefs' immediate competitors, these are peers at elite restaurants and not chefs at lower-end establishments (e.g., fast food establishments or the corner joint) or at establishments serving strictly *ethnic* fare (a term I use phenomenologically, following chefs' own understandings). Elite chefs are not affected by the actions of those working at these other places, and therefore do not need to know what these chefs are doing. This means that neither lower-end nor ethnic establishments are part of a field of high cuisine. For literature on ethnic restaurants in New York, see Ray 2010, 2011.

20. Bourdieu [1992] 1996, 1993. This conceptualization of a culinary field draws the boundaries of the field more narrowly than other extant definitions. In her foundational work on the field of cuisine, Ferguson (1998, 2004) extends this social space to the national level, and includes individuals beyond those who make food. But Ferguson writes about the *gastronomic field*, a social space constituted by all those interested in food (not just those involved in the world of restaurants), including food writers, producers, and consumers. Rao, Monin, and Durand (2003, 2005), for their part, follow Ferguson's conceptualization. To the extent that the concept of a field is a heuristic device, the object of study will largely determine how the boundaries of a field are drawn, hence the culinary field as I conceptualize it has more narrow boundaries than the gastronomic field.

21. Attuned to the texture and form of interactions between individuals and groups, Simmel (1950, p. 10) noted that supra-individual organizations "are nothing but immediate interactions that occur among men constantly, every minute, but that have become crystallized as permanent fields, as autonomous phenomena."

22. Bourdieu 1976; DiMaggio 1991; Savage and Gayo 2011; van Rees and Dorleijn 2001.

23. Bourdieu 1993. In several other areas of cultural production, artists may create products for the sake of commercial success, prioritizing audiences' preferences and economic incentives. Some high-end contemporary art is a good example of this. However, a key difference between cuisine and the fine arts is that for painters it is possible to acquire artistic reputation without commercial success and to remain as players in the field. That is, painters have the option of acting towards one impulse or the other because the two poles of artistic reputation and commercial success are not inherently fused.

24. There is much literature on the constraints on creativity and innovation from the perspectives of field theory and organizational and network analyses (Burt 1992, 2004; Ferguson 1998, 2004; Owen-Smith and Powell 2004; Phillips and Zuckerman 2001; Rao, Monin, and Durand 2005; Zuckerman 1999).

25. The approach suggested here is in line with the sensemaking perspective developed by Weick (1995), the inhabited institutions perspective (Hallett and Ventresca 2006), and Porac's approach (Porac et al. 1995).

26. I suggest here that traditional styles and originality—along with status—are basic coordinates at both the individual level (as principles of action) and the field level (structuring the field). In some sense, whether one sees the individual or the social level, as Simmel (1950, p. 8) insightfully noted long ago, has to do with the distance from which one looks at the phenomenon; see also Martin 2009, p. 17.

27. See Mead [1934] 1967 for the foundation of the notion of self-concept developed in this book, and Gross 2008 for a formulation of the role of self-concepts in cultural creation along the lines proposed here. Like Gross, I take self-concepts in a relatively narrow sense as having to do with the beliefs and self-understandings that pertain to individuals' occupations.

28. Not surprisingly, the use of French terms co-varies with restaurant status as well. Higher-status restaurants are more likely to have kitchen structures closer to the French model and to use French terms.

29. Chefs are rarely the sole owners of their restaurants in New York and San Francisco. Given the high costs of the restaurant business in these cities, they generally have financial partners, whether particularly trusted persons or willing investors.

30. Such a structure, as Abbott (1988, p. 128) points out, brings about hierarchical social dynamics.

31. The expertise required for pastry is different than that required for savory cooking, so much so that career lines rarely cross between savory cooking and pastry. If a cook does make this leap, he will most commonly move from pastry to savory cooking, as technical skills for pastry are considered to be more difficult to acquire than those for savory cooking (see Ferguson and Zukin 1998). Moreover, pastry chefs

orient their actions to what pastry chefs in other restaurants are doing, and their work and careers are affected by pastry chefs' actions, and not so much by savory chefs' actions (Bourdieu 1993).

32. This three-person kitchen is not uncommon in small, one star restaurants (with about sixty seats).

33. Young cooks go through a process of stripping away of any positive feeling about the self that is quite similar to what patients with mental illnesses experience in the initial phases of their careers in total institutions, as described by Goffman (1961).

34. Abbott 1988, p. 126.

35. This is what Bourdieu calls *symbolic capital*; see, for example, Bourdieu 1977.

36. Staff turnover varies with changes in the economy: higher in better times, lower during recessions. In the first quarter of 2013 (the latest period for which a report was available at the time of this writing), the annual employee turnover in fine dining was estimated at 48.8%, down from 60.7% in the last quarter of 2012 (People Report 2013, p. 13). A report on the restaurant industry published in early 2014 provides a significantly lower figure (28%) for turnover in kitchens in upscale, fine-dining establishments (Batt, Lee, and Lakhani 2014). The difference between the two figures is most likely explained by the operationalization of the "fine dining" category and sampling (more narrow in the latter case). To compare this with other industries, consider that the U.S. Bureau of Labor Statistics (2014) reported a total annual turnover in the United States in 2013 of 38%, with a median of 31%. The annual turnover rate in accommodation and food services was the second highest, at 62.6% (after arts, entertainment, and recreation, at 72.4%), and the lowest annual turnover in the private sector was in the manufacturing of durable goods, at 21.9%.

37. About 30% of new restaurants in the United States are said to fail within their first year, and about 60% within the first three years (Parsa et al. 2005). Few data on restaurant failure rates are available (due at least to some extent to the fact that reports are not required when a business closes), and what information is available is often either not sufficiently broken down into categories (e.g., types of food establishments or geographic location) or too narrow (e.g., only for restaurants in Boulder, Colorado). There is also a lot of information with little validity (much of it consisting of myths), and the more serious reports also suffer from a lack of a consistent definition of restaurant failure (Parsa et al. 2005, p. 305).

38. Ferguson 1998; Rao, Monin, and Durand 2003, 2005.

39. Similarly, White and White (1965) show the shift in organization in painting in nineteenth-century France, and demonstrate how that shift led to an increased structuring of actions, social connections, and organizations.

40. Hirsch 1972.

41. This pressure towards mobility is characteristic of episodic careers such as professionals in cuisine or musicians in orchestras (Faulkner [1983] 1987; Westby 1960).

42. White and White 1965. Where career decisions are of great consequence, jobs are means whereby individuals enact social ties (see Faulkner [1983] 1987) and, in turn, means whereby they enact status.

Chapter Two: Career Paths in High Cuisine

1. Working at a restaurant during high school or college is indeed quite common in the United States. That should not be surprising, given that the restaurant industry is the second largest employer in the private sector in the country, employing around 13 million individuals, or 10% of the workforce (National Restaurant Association 2014).

2. Culinary schools are more common in Europe now than when current chefs began their careers, so some culinary professionals working in Europe now start in ways that are more similar to career approaches in the United States, rather than through formal apprenticeships.

3. These stories have a high degree of typicality (Cerulo 2006; Rosch 1978).

4. Though the two stories are not mutually exclusive, chefs tend to resort to either one or the other. The story of "falling into" cooking after working in restaurants in high school or college more clearly points to an unintended beginning than the narrative of growing up in a food-loving family does, but even when telling the latter story, chefs give an impression of not having made a career choice purposefully but of somehow naturally ending up in cuisine due to their early experiences.

5. Oliver and Johnston 2000; Swidler 1986, 2003.

6. Cf. Granovetter 1974. Episodic careers are typical of freelancers in the arts but are also common among some regularly employed artists, such as musicians employed full-time in a symphony orchestra (see Faulkner [1983] 1987 and Westby 1960).

7. I am following Bourdieu's (1977, [1984] 1993) understanding of capital here.

8. With the growth of attention devoted to food in the media (TV programs and channels, magazines, websites, blogs, radio shows), a professional career in cooking has gained status in the past few years. But it was seen as a blue-collar job when many of the chefs I interviewed chose this career. Younger culinary professionals moving into high positions now may have chosen this occupation in a social environment in which cuisine was being afforded more status.

9. These few cases are all in San Francisco. I explain below why this is the case.

10. Much more public information about professional cooking is now available due to the growth in media devoted to chefs and food. The change in restaurant design, which now often features open kitchens, also increased the availability of information about chefs' jobs, as well as the chance of having a personal connection with chefs (for those who can afford to go to the better restaurants), because chefs are now more out in the open in their restaurants. Personal connections with individuals in an occupation explain career choices of other occupations, such as book editor (Coser, Kadushin, and Powell 1982). When it comes to occupations whose subject matter is not regularly taught at school, like design, individuals also choose them as careers after work experience in the area (Molotch [2003] 2005).

11. Dewey [1922] 2002, [1939] 1967; Whitford 2002; Winship 2006.

12. Intense collective activity and socializing are of course not sufficient for a strong professional identity; norms and values that guide and regulate activity in a field are also key (see Larson 2005). Celebrity chefs who own several restaurants or have television shows are more likely to socialize with individuals outside their occupation.

They do not do much cooking and are not as tied to restaurant hours as other chefs. Also, being celebrities, they are much more likely to be in social settings where they meet elites in other occupations.

13. That individuals may move to the culinary profession after successful careers in other occupations, particularly in lucrative ones, ought not to be surprising. Having sufficient personal economic capital facilitates a career in cuisine because income is very low in the first few years, when individuals are in kitchens' lower ranks.

14. Many undertake these entrepreneurial pursuits while being chefs, often after they have attained a celebrity status and are running a fleet of restaurants—they require a high reputation for these other pursuits to work. These related businesses are means for ensuring a good retirement, given that it is difficult to work as a chef in one's later years because the job is taxing and hard on individuals' bodies.

15. For research on the effect of labor markets on mobility patterns, see Carroll and Mayer 1984, 1986; Hachen 1990; Rosenfeld 1992; and Tuma 1985.

16. This is what Bourdieu (1976, 1977, [1992] 1996, 1993) refers to when he writes about the nontransferability of certain forms of capital that are specific to a field.

17. The same phenomenon exists in other areas where practitioners have a strong professional identity, such as symphonic music (Westby 1960). The distinction between organizational and cognitive constraints is analytical, of course, as the two are intrinsically connected. For classical references concerning access to information about other jobs, see Blau et al. 1956; Granovetter 1974; Marsden and Campbell 1990; and Sørensen 1975. For references addressing cognitive constraints in organizations, see Clemens 1997; Clemens and Cook 1999; and DiMaggio and Powell 1983, 1991. Findings from the neo-institutional literature and social network analysis show that social connections with individuals in other areas open access to different cognitive frameworks, thereby increasing the likelihood that individuals will conceive of new ideas (Burt 1992, 2004; Clemens 1997; Clemens and Cook 1999; Giuffre 1999; McLaughlin 2001; Mische 2008; Morrill 2001; Owen-Smith and Powell 2004).

18. That is, their moves function as what Podolny (2005) refers to as *status signals* and thus are used to judge their achievement.

19. Althauser and Kalleberg 1990; Spilerman 1977. This makes Spilerman (1977) suggest that employees are insulated from nonemployees in competing for promotions.

20. For examples of other areas where social ties are essential for opportunities for mobility, see Bearman 2005; Powell 1985; and Westby 1960.

21. Whereas culinary professionals in New York almost never skip these positions in their upward path, those in San Francisco may do so. I explain this difference later in this chapter. There is only one case among the chefs I interviewed of becoming a chef-owner without being an executive chef before, an unusual trajectory all in all.

22. Internal promotion and social ties are common in labor markets where similar social attributes are salient (e.g., Bearman 2005; Faulkner [1983] 1987; Zuckerman et al. 2003).

23. The social connections individuals enact through work (see Faulkner [1983] 1987) convey skill as well as status.

24. In his work on status in markets, Podolny (1993, p. 835) suggests that using

status as a proxy for skill (as chefs do) decouples a person's prestige—the outcome of past accomplishments—from her current work, because the latter is less significant to her current status. Taking this insight further, just as past work is relevant for a person's present status, present work is of consequence for future status (Podolny [1993, 2005] uses *reputation* to describe what I mean by *status*—i.e., field position). Whereas status (or reputation) is an outcome of field position, prestige is an outcome of an actor's past production—so they are two related but analytically different phenomena. Higher-status chefs face a greater decoupling between their status and current work than lower-status counterparts do because their high status leads to critics' and customers' preconceived ideas about the quality of the food. When the quality of high-status chefs' food declines, it can take a long time for these chefs to fall in status. Restaurants are not reviewed frequently, so restaurant ratings remain in effect for many years, even if a restaurant's quality is no longer present.

25. This is not humorous; violence is known to happen in restaurant kitchens. Besides the narratives published in the media or books (see Bourdain 2000 and Buford 2006), I have heard numerous stories about chefs who throw hot pans at cooks, hurl plates, wield knives, or burn cooks with various hot utensils, among other forms of physical aggression.

26. Some chefs claim they even prefer hiring cooks with no skills because lack of training means that cooks have no preconceived ideas about how things should be done, so they are more likely to follow orders about how to do things. Psychological criteria are also given preference in other occupations where specific skills are not easily detectable and relevant skills are generally disdained, such as among editors in the publishing industry (Coser, Kadushin, and Powell 1982).

27. Abbott 1988, p. 131.

28. Cf. Granovetter 1974. In his study of doormen, Bearman (2005) underscores the role of chance in doormen's explanations of how they find (otherwise difficult) jobs easily. Unlike doormen, chefs are aware that their social ties often helped them gain entry to places that would be blocked for outsiders.

29. Zuckerman et al. (2003) suggest that using a simple identity (i.e., typecasting) filters the unskilled from the multitalented in many cases, including the film industry, the area of their study. Typecasting is instrumental in occupations where careers are stochastic, built from salient jobs and not gradual progressions through positions. Paradigmatic examples of these occupations are acting and performing music (Faulkner [1983] 1987; Zuckerman et al. 2003). Classifying individuals into categories facilitates sorting potential candidates into those who may fit the job and those who do not. Typecasting is thus advantageous for employers but even more so for intermediaries (i.e., agencies) in a labor market because classifying individuals into categories is their job. However, in the labor market in cuisine there are no intermediaries, and given the occupational structure of kitchens, skills that are useful for one position are also often valuable for higher positions, so typecasting (based on distinctions among skills) is not so helpful for selecting personnel.

30. This means, in other words, that there is no easy system of social closure (cf. Parkin 1974; Weber [1922] 1978).

31. The long training in the arts protects insiders from outsiders as well, as Becker (1982) shows.

32. Some contributions in the literature do point out that occupational classifications have a role that varies by status (Faulkner [1983] 1987; Hsu, Hannan, and Pólos 2011; Zuckerman et al. 2003).

33. Lena (2012, p. 162) suggests the same is the case in popular music. The structural difference in the perception of occupational classifications across status categories is consistent with the finding from the sociology of culture that higher status actors are more likely to be omnivorous in their cultural practices because, having multiple and heterogeneous social networks, they have more varied access to a diversity of cultural practices and therefore better chances to communicate with multiple social groups (Clemens et al. 1995; DiMaggio 1987; DiMaggio and Mukhtar 2004; Erickson 1996, 2007; Fischler 1990; Peterson 2005; Peterson and Kern 1996; Peterson and Rossman 2007; Warde, Martens, and Olsen 1999).

34. The chefs I interviewed sought a culinary degree only once they were fully committed to the occupation. However, enrollment in culinary school prior to work experience has become more common, in particular for individuals who want to make a career change to cuisine later in life, because they are less willing than younger individuals to put up with years of apprenticeship, starting at the very bottom of the kitchen hierarchy to learn the trade and move up the ladder. Attendance in culinary schools has also increased in the last few years, likely due to the growth in media attention to food, the faddish status of food and cuisine, and the phenomenon of the celebrity chef. The Career Index compiled by Education News (see Capuzzi Simon 2014) estimates a 25% growth in culinary school graduates between 2010 and 2014, while others had earlier estimated 20% growth per year (see Webley 2011). The situation has changed in Europe as well; formal apprenticeship was once the only entryway to a culinary career there, but multiple entryways are now opening. The establishment of the European and American models of professionalization in cuisine is consistent with the history of professions in the two regions (Abbott 1988; Larson 1977). Due to a large extent to state control, professions developed in a rigid framework in continental Europe, and careers were perceived as lifelong projects (Stovel, Savage, and Bearman 1996), but careers developed in a more flexible and dispersed structure in the United States and were thus more individually managed, which led to a high rate of mobility within as well as across occupations (Abbott 1988).

35. Cf. Merton 1961.

36. The CIA and Johnson & Wales have other campuses in the United States, but these are the most prestigious. All chefs and cooks I interviewed or talked to who attended either of these schools did so on these campuses. The organizations that rank institutions of higher education, such as U.S. News, do not rank culinary schools, so there are only unofficial rankings based on each school's reputation. The ranking of culinary schools to which I refer here is based on chefs' views, and represents widely agreed-upon perceptions.

37. I report figures only for chefs here because I do not have exact data for all kitchen staff. However, the data I collected during ethnographic observation, talking

to chefs de cuisine, sous-chefs, and cooks, are consistent with the tendencies described here for chefs. Dishwashers and prep cooks are largely Latin American immigrants, mostly from Mexico, in New York and San Francisco restaurants.

38. When reporting the percentage of CIA graduates, I have used the total of American chefs in my study (instead of all chefs) because that conveys a better sense of the position that the CIA occupies in the world of high cuisine in New York and San Francisco. There are several foreign chefs in elite restaurants in these two cities, and they tend to come to the United States with training from their countries of origin.

39. The findings are representative of the population of chefs in elite restaurants in New York and San Francisco in general; an assessment I make based on my conversations with other chefs and cooks conducted doing fieldwork, as well as on analysis of material from the media.

40. Some might wonder if there is a reproductive effect, as chefs have social connections with culinary schools that could operate as conduits for new recruits, but it is unlikely. Few chefs have strong connections (be they institutional, social, or symbolic) with their alma maters. Culinary schools are unlike universities; programs are generally shorter and do not lead to strong bonds among classmates or faculty or to a strong emotional bond with the school. In other words, culinary schools do not attain the symbolic position of colleges or universities.

41. Just as the subdisciplines within which scholars work make their professional identities (Clemens et al. 1995), so do culinary styles make chefs' occupational identities (Rao, Monin, and Durand 2003, 2005). Research shows that the first faculty position, and not the institution that grants scholars their PhD degree, is the most consequential for scholars' careers, as measured by the ranking of the universities where they obtain jobs throughout their careers (Long 1978; Long, Allison, and McGinnis 1979). This is similar to chefs' experiences in cuisine.

42. It is relatively common for young chefs who have worked for renowned chefs at French restaurants to move away from French food when they open their own restaurants. If several young chefs have gone on to open Italian restaurants in the late 2000s and early 2010s, it is in part because Italian food experienced a surge in popularity, but also because elite chefs, especially in New York, who are likely to have trained at renowned French (or New American) restaurants, are also likely to move away from the recognized styles of those restaurants.

43. Faulkner [1983] 1987.

44. Podolny (1993, 2005) maintains that when high-status individuals open businesses in lower-status categories, they always do it under a different identity, so as not to harm their reputation.

45. This is the case in the publishing industry. There are a few positions above that of editor, but they involve tasks that are more managerial and administrative than editorial, and many editors are not interested in them (Coser, Kadushin, and Powell 1982; Powell 1985).

46. In orchestras, for instance, promotion is institutionally discouraged for fear of causing tension by turning equal relationships into hierarchical ones (Westby 1960).

47. This is the case for editors, again, who establish close relationships with their

authors—helping them get published and in return receiving valuable information on new talent—and are likely to change jobs frequently (Coser, Kadushin, and Powell 1982; Powell 1985).

48. Doormen are a paradigmatic example; they typically establish strong relations with their supers and tenants (Bearman 2005, pp. 141–142).

49. Given the work and effort it takes to arrive at the top positions in the culinary fields of New York and San Francisco, chefs who have arrived should be expected to be invested in their careers.

50. See Anderson 2013. For literature on creative work, see Taylor and Littleton 2012. Unlike editors, who prefer to remain editors rather than move up to higher positions that would entail spending less time on their craft, as Coser, Kadushin, and Powell (1982; see also Powell 1985) note, chefs do pursue the positions of executive chef and chef-owner, even though these jobs will entail spending less time in the kitchen. Yet chefs are like editors in seeing themselves as creative and looking for new jobs to fight the tedium of their daily routines.

51. Lahire (2003, p. 349) expresses this notion elegantly in claiming that to the extent that the social world is composed of individuals, the singular is not necessarily the unique.

52. Stovel, Savage, and Bearman 1996, p. 361. In a similar vein, Rosenfeld (1992, p. 40) notes that the notion of career implies coherence or progress, which conceals the randomness that can apply to careers; see also Wilensky 1960.

53. Vacancy chains unfold when persons take up the positions left by others (White 1970). When career paths are interdependent, career patterns show the entirety of individuals' trajectories in terms of vacancy chains (Smith and Abbott 1983, p. 1163).

54. It must be noted that reliable data on each occupational rank, restaurant, and length of tenure were not always available. Sometimes I had access to chefs' full curricula vitae; at other times chefs told me about their careers but understandably, given the number of jobs they accumulate over their careers, mixed the order of jobs they had long ago or provided partial information. Most typically, chefs mentioned the restaurants where they worked but not necessarily the occupational rank. In some cases rank can be reliably inferred, but in others it is not so easy. Some chefs were reluctant to give much information about their careers. Whenever possible, I obtained data from other sources—because the interviewees were elite chefs, many of the needed data were available in the media. The reliability of these data cannot be taken for granted either, but I have taken measures to look across media outlets, look for reliability, and cross-reference data.

55. Prestigious middle-status restaurants are in a particularly ambivalent position, because a review that was just slightly more positive could have put them in the upper-middle category.

56. This does not necessarily follow from the fact that all these chefs ended up at prestigious middle-status restaurants. In principle, they could obtain their first executive chef position without sacrificing status, or be internally promoted to executive chef, just as the rest of the middle- and high-status chefs were. By the same token, they could in theory obtain their first executive chef job at less prestigious middle-status restaurants.

57. This model of professionalization is in evidence in the long, formal apprenticeship typical in European restaurant kitchens. In that context, individuals follow standardized paths, which they tend to experience as somewhat beyond their control (see Abbott 1988). This pattern has surely changed in Europe (and the rest of the world) in recent times, because it is increasingly rare for someone to remain in the same job throughout her career. For analyses of sociocultural models of careers, see Larson 1977 and Stovel, Savage, and Bearman 1996.

58. Stovel, Savage, and Bearman 1996.

59. Mobility, both within and across occupations, is higher in the United States than in other countries (Abbott 1988, p. 132). Moving across occupations, Abbott points out, is more difficult where there is a more formal structure of professions, such as in Europe.

60. *Stages* only partially explain the variance in number of steps in professional trajectories, given that more chefs have only one *stage* and fewer have multiple *stages*.

61. Many chefs at lower-status restaurants also have social connections with higher-status chefs, either in their own field or abroad, but higher-status chefs are more likely to have more and better connections and to be more effective at securing *stages* for their staff.

62. Here, I do not consider the first restaurant jobs individuals have in their youth. Most elite chefs begin their careers in lower-status domestic fields. What is consequential for their careers is a move to those fields after they have held the first cook position in a restaurant in New York or San Francisco.

63. Only two individuals moved from cook to executive chef within the same restaurant, so the possibility of an association between a nonstandardized, nongradual occupational ladder (i.e., skipping the position of sous-chef or chef de cuisine) and internal promotion as a means of mobility can be rejected.

64. Only one chef I interviewed temporarily moved to a nearby town—still within the Bay Area—to be an executive chef at a higher-status restaurant. This is also one of the few San Francisco chefs with international experience. He became a chef-owner in San Francisco subsequent to this move.

65. The difference also stems from the standing of regional cuisines in each field. With an especially high standing in New York, French cuisine puts French professionals at a clear advantage there, but French cuisine is not indisputably at the top of the hierarchy in San Francisco, where the local California cuisine, originated in the Bay Area and with roots in Italy, has been greatly influential and prestigious for decades. Even the (still plentiful) high-end French restaurants in San Francisco are generally run by chefs born and trained in the United States.

66. One chef even took a break in the middle of his culinary career to pursue a college degree (a theoretical program related to food), a case for which there is no evidence in New York.

67. Kadushin 1969.

68. For example, this is the case for medical students. As Becker et al. (1961) show, being constantly denied responsibility, which reminds them that they are not doctors, prevents medical students from developing a professional self-concept early.

69. This is consistent with a pattern that has been identified as typical of occupations in the United States, namely that individuals tend to feel that they control their own careers (Abbott 1988). Faulkner ([1983] 1987) suggests that the fact that success or status is somewhat random (not an outcome of productivity or networks), and therefore unpredictable, may give individuals pleasure or hope in a hierarchical organization that might otherwise make them feel hopeless.

70. Both chefs and the media represent careers in this way. In being episodic, culinary careers are akin to the careers of freelancers such as filmmakers or musicians (Faulkner [1983] 1987).

71. For literature on the role of the future in the understanding of action, see Beckert 2013; Emirbayer and Mische 1998; and Mische 2008, 2009.

72. Dewey [1922] 2002, [1939] 1967. See Swidler 1986 for a claim about action much along the same lines.

73. Faulkner [1983] 1987, p. 236.

Chapter Three: Categories and Classifications in Cuisine

1. Ferguson 1998, 2004; Pearlman 2013; Steinberger 2009; Trubek 2000.

2. For this count, I considered to be French any restaurant that was classified solely as French or French along with some other category, including Californian, Mediterranean, or Seafood. To put these figures in perspective, among the many categories used to classify restaurants are French, Italian, Mediterranean, Bistro, Spanish, Portuguese, German, Russian, American, New American, Asian, Chinese, Korean, Japanese, Sushi, Noodles, Mexican, Latin American, Steakhouse, Eclectic, Fusion, Vegetarian. Proportionally fewer highly rated (with three or four stars) restaurants were classified as French in the *San Francisco Chronicle*, only ten of the total of eighty-six (11.6%) in the spring of 2014. This is not surprising, however, given that the culinary field in New York leans more towards France and that of San Francisco more towards Italy.

3. Cf. Zuckerman 1999.

4. Boundaries also weaken where more cuisines are available. For a good explanation of boundaries, see Lamont and Molnár 2002 and Pachuki, Pendergrass, and Lamont 2007. For a conceptualization of boundaries that departs from the more common understanding in the sociology of culture, see Abbott 2001.

5. Hosking 2006.

6. France is considered to be the birthplace of modern Western cuisine (Ferguson 1998, 2004; Ferguson and Zukin 1998), hence its role as the foundation of cuisines in the West. *Modern* here refers not to contemporary times but the historical period following the Renaissance and continuing up to current times (Leschziner 2006; Leschziner and Dakin 2011).

7. Ferguson 2004; Rao, Monin, and Durand 2005.

8. Farrer 2010; Ray and Srinivas 2012; Trubek 2000.

9. *Modernist* is the most common label used nowadays to refer to this culinary style, but other terms also in use are *molecular gastronomy, hypermodern, avant-garde,* and more generally, *innovative*. Chefs who cook in this style have been called "mad scientists," though that term is heard less often as time goes by.

10. Many of these changes in traditional techniques started in the 1960s and 1970s with the development of the nouvelle cuisine in France (Rao, Monin, and Durand 2003; Steinberger 2009).

11. Just as the foundational personalities and bibliographic materials of traditional French cuisine are renowned chefs with classical styles and their books (e.g., Escoffier 1979; *Larousse Gastronomique* 2001), the key figures of modernist techniques are scientists. Hervé This (2006), a French physico-chemist, developed many of the principles that led to modernist cuisine. Harold McGee (2004), an American expert on the chemistry of food, is considered a sort of guru among science-inclined chefs; his book *On Food and Cooking* has a unique status among these chefs (Ankeny 2006). Nathan Myhrvold is the latest entry in this group. He is a former chief technology officer at Microsoft who spent years studying science and cuisine and published a book titled *Modernist Cuisine: The Art and Science of Cooking* (Myhrvold, Young, and Bilet 2011), in which he applies scientific and technological principles to innovative culinary techniques. He coined the term *modernist cuisine*, which has replaced the formerly used *molecular gastronomy*.

12. At the time of my fieldwork, foams were at the height of their popularity and that is why there are more references to foams than to gelées or powders in interview excerpts. Having become too common, foams have lost their appeal and are now showcased much less frequently.

13. Lamont and Molnár 2002; Pachuki, Pendergrass, and Lamont 2007. DiMaggio (1987) suggests that categories differ according to their hierarchy and potency; some boundaries separating categories are stronger than others, and some categories are more important than others. Rao, Monin, and Durand (2003, see also 2005) also point out that techniques are more clearly defined cultural markers than ingredients are, and therefore they take techniques (and not ingredients) as indicators of borrowing practices in their study of French chefs.

14. Bourdieu 1976, 1977, [1984] 1993, [1992] 1996; DiMaggio 1987. Theories of categorization show that phenomena that do not fit neatly into existing categories are especially subject to contestation (Rosch 1978; Zerubavel 1997).

15. Another factor that has increased the popularity of cooking sous-vide is that it allows for precooking, easing the pressure of work during service and potentially lowering costs because fewer staff may be required in the kitchen during service (e.g., even a steak can be cooked early in the day and then briefly seared when ordered). At the same time, cooking sous-vide requires expensive equipment and advanced knowledge of the chemical properties of ingredients and of cooking temperatures and times specific to the technique, so it is not accessible to any and all chefs.

16. Of course, much of the porosity of boundaries between regions has to do with geopolitics, areas that were once not so differentiated but were then divided into different nations.

17. French chefs began to incorporate ingredients from other lands, and make lighter and simpler food, with the rise of nouvelle cuisine, a tendency that has only increased since then.

18. The New American cuisine is, as the name suggests, of relatively recent origin.

There are some traditional regional cuisines in the United States but, as such, they are geographically bounded.

19. Lamont and Molnár 2002; Pachuki, Pendergrass, and Lamont 2007.

20. Rao, Monin, and Durand (2005) point out that when categories are seen as complementary, the boundaries separating them are particularly weak.

21. The reconfiguration of the relationship between French and Japanese food applies only to the realm of high cuisine, not to lower-status and/or traditional French or Japanese restaurants, which are still expected to remain within the older bounds of each cuisine.

22. When high-status chefs open restaurants aside from their high-end flagship, serving comfort food such as pizza, pasta, or sausages, they also increase the symbolic value of these foods, and other chefs with relatively high status begin to incorporate these foodstuffs into their menus. Examples of this pattern abound. Mac and cheese, hamburgers, pork belly, sausages, and tacos are just a few examples of the foodstuffs that were symbolically banned from elite restaurants only a few years ago but are commonly served in these establishments now.

23. See DiMaggio 1987. Boundaries, as White (1992, p. 127) puts it, are the complex outcome of actions of individuals; see also White and White 1965. Though in a very different realm (poverty relief practices at the turn of the nineteenth century in New York), Mohr and Duquenne (1997) point to a duality between categories and actions similar to that discussed here.

24. Rao, Monin, and Durand (2005) note a similar pattern in France.

25. The Michelin Guide, originally published in and for France but now published in countries across the world, launched its first restaurant guide to New York City in November 2005 (2006 edition) and to San Francisco in 2006 (2007 edition). While this publication is the most influential restaurant reviewer in France, where it is even said to have led chefs to commit suicide upon losing one of the coveted stars, it does not have (at least for now) nearly as much power in New York and San Francisco as the publications that have a long-standing reputation in each of these cities. Awards bestowed by global organizations are also becoming increasingly influential for restaurants. In particular, the *Restaurant Magazine*'s "World's 50 Best Restaurants" list can change a restaurant's position on the local and global stage, including its reputation and financial success. Websites and blogs have also become increasingly influential, especially for the commercial success of a restaurant.

26. By classifying restaurants into culinary categories, the media turn qualitative attributes into commensurable objects (Espeland and Sauder 2007; Espeland and Stevens 1998). The publications I mention in the text also classify restaurants into price categories and neighborhoods. The process of classification itself makes certain characteristics of culinary categories salient and others insignificant; see Lena 2012, p. 147.

27. That being said, *eclectic cuisine* and *modernist cuisine* are formal categories and certainly connote innovation.

28. Sifton 2010. To protect the confidentiality and anonymity of interviewees, I do not cite reviews of restaurants whose chefs I have interviewed. This is why the reviews that I cite as examples were published after the completion of fieldwork.

29. Bruni 2008.

30. With the statement "Lupa meets wd-50," Bruni denotes the blend of flavorful traditional Italian cooking (as found at the very successful rustic restaurant Lupa) with wild flights of inventiveness (as found at the temple to modernist cuisine that was the restaurant wd-50).

31. Bruni 2007.

32. I analyzed reviews of the *New York Times* and the *San Francisco Chronicle* for each city, respectively—the same publications used to sample and classify the restaurants included in this study (see the Methodological Appendix for detailed information about the content analysis). Though a relatively small sample, the reviews included in the content analysis are representative of how restaurants are typically reviewed in these and other publications.

33. Sometimes, before the review comes out, critics will call the restaurant to obtain such information after they have dined there for the purpose of writing a review.

34. Information about the source of ingredients has become increasingly available to the diner, as it is much more common for restaurants now to list their purveyors on the menu when these are local farmers or prestigious stores (e.g., Murray's Cheese, a renowned cheese store in New York). Restaurants may list local farms but not wholesale purveyors that bring food from afar (whether nationally or internationally). Generally, farms are named on menus when they have already acquired a reputation, so that they add symbolic capital. Obviously, if these farms are already highly reputed, they cannot be taken to be an original source and therefore an indicator of creativity.

35. I coded each mention of innovation separately (i.e., if there are four mentions of a type of innovation in a review, I coded that as "four").

36. Whereas status, culinary styles, and innovativeness are important criteria for chefs, they tend to disregard age, gender, or ethnicity when they talk about the restaurant world. This certainly does not mean that age does not matter, or that there is no gender or ethnic inequality in restaurant kitchens, but that these are not attributes formally used in the classification of restaurants, and therefore not deliberatively considered by chefs to make sense of their environment.

37. There is a clear understanding among chefs about which publications matter, so much so that there is no need to mention the names of the key publications (the *New York Times* and *San Francisco Chronicle* in each city, respectively) when commenting on restaurant ratings or reviews. Simply saying that someone is a three-star chef suffices.

38. Bothner and White 2001; see also Hsu and Hannan 2005. That chefs rely on reviews for information does not mean that they respect reviews or the critics who write them. They generally find critics unknowledgeable and more like customers than culinary professionals because they lack training in cuisine. Chefs also often consider critics too driven by fads, partial in their judgments, and blinded by the allure of celebrity. Not all chefs I interviewed expressed views about critics, and those who did varied in their comments. Some chefs were openly negative, others voiced moderately critical opinions, and still others were visibly political in talking about critics, conveying a subjectively experienced need to show gratitude towards critics who wrote positive reviews about their restaurants. If chefs tend to have such strong opinions—or

cautiousness—about critics, it is due to the power of critics over chefs' professional fate. External assessments are especially influential in highly heteronomous fields, like cuisine, because the work is targeted at audiences that are outside the field. In a similar vein, Hsu and Hannan (2005) suggest that, whereas the identity of an organization has been traditionally thought to be shaped by the organization's members themselves, audiences' perceptions are just as important.

39. Glynn and Abzug 2002; Lounsbury and Glynn 2001.

40. More senior chefs often remark that they experienced a much stronger need to develop unique styles, so as to establish their authorship and place in the field, when they were younger.

41. Seeing their styles in all their complexity, individuals will likely note more qualities than those captured by any existing category. Furthermore, as Simmel (1950, p. 31) notes, individuals tend to be more aware of difference than similarity, even when the two are equally salient. According to Simmel, because awareness of differences is so important in social life, similarity fades to the background.

42. "The creation of the mass, that is, the leveling of heterogeneous persons, can be brought about only by the lowering of the higher elements, which is always possible, rather than by the raising of the lower elements, which is rarely if ever possible" (Simmel 1950, p. 38; see also Simmel 1910, p. 378).

43. Though New York also has a stock of low-quality Italian American restaurants in a tourist area (Little Italy), I have not heard chefs in this city express fear of a negative connotation if they characterize their restaurants as Italian. This indicates that the association between the term *Italian restaurant* and low-quality, inauthentic food was weaker by the early 2000s in New York than it was in San Francisco.

44. Furthermore, once a chef's restaurant is classified, undertaking creative projects that violate the understood boundaries of the given category is to risk a penalty (Hahl and Richardson Gosline 2011; Kovács, Carroll, and Lehman 2013; Zuckerman 1999).

45. In a similar vein, Lena (2012, p. 159) notes that systems of classifications and ratings tend to be reactive, so that individuals modify their behavior in view of how they will be evaluated.

46. Lounsbury and Glynn (2001) coined the term *cultural entrepreneurship* to refer to the creation of stories to depict one's style and shape how it will be perceived; see also Wry, Lounsbury, and Glynn 2011. Along similar lines, Glynn and Abzug (2002) rely on organizations' names to show that organizations need to select an existing identity to be afforded legitimacy by outsiders. They note that there are homogenizing tendencies, or a "symbolic isomorphism," in corporations' names. That individuals use familiar frames or stories, however, does not necessarily imply that they do so instrumentally—it is the likely outcome of relying on cultural tools that are already widely shared. Rao (1994) points out that in selecting a story and objectifying a style, individuals also reduce uncertainty and generate order.

47. Using stories that resonate with their own experiences (hence with what "feels right") as well as with the stories other chefs tell is more likely to be effective for individuals in anchoring their self-projects and delineating courses of action; see Weber, Heinze, and De Soucey 2008. To the extent that schemas help individuals create solu-

tions for the situations and problems they face (what Hutchins [1995] calls "mediating structures"), they persist in time only if at least some individuals find them useful and adopt them; see also Strauss and Quinn 1997, p. 125.

48. Goffman 1959.

49. This tendency is in line with what has been identified as a cognitive pattern to code phenomena into binary sets (Douglas 1986; Lévi-Strauss [1962] 1968, 1973; Lloyd 1966; Sahlins 1976, 1981, 1985, 2000; Sewell 1992).

50. Joas 1996; see also Dalton 2004. See Dewey [1922] 2002 for the pragmatist development of these ideas.

51. Dalton 2004; Joas 1996; March 1991; Peterson 1997. For information on the positive attributes afforded to creativity or innovation in various areas of cultural production, see Farrell 2001; Galenson 2007; and Molotch [2003] 2005. For an especially clear account of the positive values afforded to originality, see Lamont's study of academia (Lamont 2009; Lamont, Guetzkow, and Mallard 2004). For an insightful take on the ever-present dialectical relationship between conformity and originality, see Simmel 1904, pp. 131–132. As Simmel saw it, innovation happens through the conflicts and compromises between conformity and individuality.

52. Bourdieu's theory (e.g., [1979] 1984) can be interpreted as an example of this tendency to the extent that action is not instrumental-rational but objectively strategic, in that there is a lawful connection between some means and ends of which individuals are not aware.

53. Bourdieu 1976, [1984] 1993, [1992] 1996; Burt 2004; Collins 1998; Farrell 2001; McLaughlin 2001; Mulkay 1972; Phillips, Turco, and Zuckerman 2013; Phillips and Zuckerman 2001; Sawyer 2003.

54. Clemens 1997; Clemens and Cook 1999; James Evans 2010; Hollingsworth 2000; Morrill 2001; White and White 1965.

55. Burt 2004, Clemens 1997, Clemens and Cook 1999, Giuffre 1999, McLaughlin 2001, Morrill 2001; Owen-Smith and Powell 2004.

56. Elsbach and Flynn 2013; Gross 2002; Lamont, Guetzkow, and Mallard 2004; Rao, Monin, and Durand 2003.

57. For perspectives in organizational analysis that consider cognition and emotions central to the explanation, two schools of note are the sensemaking perspective of Daft and Weick (1984) and the "inhabited institutions" approach developed by Hallett and Ventresca (2006).

58. The examples I use here are imaginary because the confidentiality of interviews prevents me from using real dishes. However, these dishes are entirely plausible, as they are along the lines of the dishes that the chefs I interviewed serve in their restaurants.

59. Whereas all chefs use this logic, an average diner rarely thinks of function when enjoying a meal, which leads to a decoupling between how chefs understand their styles and how others view them (cf. Meyer and Rowan 1977).

60. The restaurant reviewer for the *New York Times*, for instance, wrote that this chef had a good idea about his restaurant, where he serves food with good, bold flavors, and fresh and seasonal ingredients, and the critic noted the thrill that comes

with the balance, precision, and clarity of flavors in some of the dishes. In writing about the previous chef, another critic for the *New York Times* had offered that she followed her own muse, and that she began a trend that, while not new in and of itself, was made novel by her take on it. This puts in high relief the fact that chefs' different representations of their styles have to do largely with how they see their role as chefs. I do not quote the texts or cite the reviews here (or in following cases) to maintain the anonymity of the chefs and restaurants.

61. This is in line with Bourdieu's (1976, [1992] 1996, 1993) understanding of fields of cultural production.

62. Of course, chefs may well see themselves in ways that are inconsistent with how others view them. In the context of romantic relations, Swidler (2003) shows that individuals seek resonance between their actions and beliefs, even if their discourses can seem inconsistent to outsiders.

63. How individuals see themselves has been shown to guide the type of information they seek out (Verplanken and Holland 2002). For the importance of consistency for one's sense of self, see Epstein 1973. For literature on how individuals make decisions in an organizational field where there is too much information and too many factors that bound their work, see Fligstein 1996; Fligstein and McAdam 2012; Porac et al. 1995; and Porac, Thomas, and Baden-Fuller 2011.

64. Identity theorists point out that individuals strive to maintain consistency between their actions and self-understandings, and when there is some inconsistency, they make adjustments to reduce it (Burke 2006; Burke and Stets 2009).

65. Though a meal at a high-end restaurant is costly, these restaurants generally have few seats and exceptionally high ingredient and labor costs, so there is little margin for profit.

66. Chefs often make efforts to highlight the aspects of the job that are in line with their views in order to find consistency between the type of cooking they are doing and their self-concepts; see Burke 2006 and Burke and Stets 2009. Some of these efforts are, of course, easier than others; chefs can find themselves in jobs that are so out of line with their styles and views that it is hard to find a significant point of agreement between their standpoints and their jobs.

Chapter Four: Managing a Culinary Style

An early version of this chapter was published in "Kitchen Stories: Patterns of Recognition in Contemporary High Cuisine," *Sociological Forum* 2006, 22, pp. 77–101.

1. More general than the other types of intellectual property, trade secrets protect any kind of information that may afford an organization a potential economic advantage.

2. In line with this, Fauchart and von Hippel (2006) suggest that cuisine is a norm-based knowledge-exchange regime; see also Di Stefano, King, and Verona 2014.

3. Leschziner 2007. Lena (2012, p. 161) makes the same point for the case of music, comparing the fuzzy articulation of musical conventions to the more clearly and rigidly organized world of science.

4. Peterson (1997) suggests that demonstrating authenticity requires a combina-

tion of conformity to a style and originality; see also Rao, Monin, and Durand 2005. Simmel (1950, p. 30) went so far as to note that similarity and difference are the great principles of individual and social development and, what is more, that the cultural history of mankind can be seen as the history of the struggles and attempts at reconciliation between the two. Because similarity and difference can never be equally satisfied, there are always conflicts and compromises that, in and of themselves, create the possibility of advancement in social life, according to Simmel (1904, p. 131).

5. This is a pattern also found among French elite chefs (Rao, Monin, and Durand 2003, 2005).

6. Burt 2004; Clemens and Cook 1999.

7. Signaling that ingredients are from a local farm, fisherman, or butcher shows concern with buying foodstuffs that are fresh, local, and humanely raised.

8. Hirsch 1972; Simmel 1904.

9. "Man is a differentiating creature" (Simmel 1950, p. 410). Simmel, in several works, points out a few reasons for this nature. First, it is only through difference that an individual acquires perspective and objectivity (Simmel 1910, p. 378). Second, individuals only feel their own significance when they contrast themselves to others, so they may end up seeing differences where there is no real basis for them (Simmel 1950, p. 31). Research in other economic markets has also showed that cognitive interpretations (rather than purely economic criteria) guide the decisions individuals make in the market (Porac et al. 1995; see also Porac, Thomas, and Baden-Fuller, 2011). This is especially the case in markets with high heterogeneity and where market cues are not clear.

10. Again, I understand the category of ethnic cuisines phenomenologically. It obtains its meaning and validity as is used by chefs intersubjectively.

11. Leschziner 2006; see also Leschziner and Dakin 2011.

12. It might be argued that chefs claim a preference for low-key restaurants serving ethnic or simple food to avoid mentioning names of other chefs or restaurants in a context that could indicate preferences, connections, or allegiances—in other words, they might be making conduits of influence explicit. Their attitudes about naming colleagues vary, from a refusal to name them to a complete openness in talking about them. In few instances, chefs' preferences for not citing names are evidently political, and in these cases, choosing ethnic or downscale foods saves them from manifesting any social connections to peers.

13. For literature on cultural omnivorousness, see DiMaggio 1987; DiMaggio and Mukhtar 2004; Erickson 1996, 2007; Fischler 1990; Fishman and Lizardo 2013; Johnston and Baumann 2007, 2010; Lizardo 2014; Lizardo and Skiles 2009, 2012; Peterson 2005; Peterson and Kern 1996; Peterson and Rossman 2007; and Warde, Martens, and Olsen 1999.

14. These claims are not a mere instrumental strategy to distance themselves from competitors. The desire for novelty and rarity, as Simmel (1950, p. 30) has noted, is an intrinsic part of the discriminatory power of individuals.

15. It is important for restaurants that their managers and wine program directors also dine out in the city and sometimes that they travel as well. At some restaurants

these front-of-the-house employees benefit from a financial arrangement similar to that for the kitchen staff.

16. This is akin to what Cerulo (2006) calls *cognitive asymmetry*, a cultural pattern whereby individuals in a group (such as an organization, an occupation, or a society) focus on certain phenomena and disregard others. Cerulo writes about what she calls *positive asymmetry*, a tendency to focus on and exaggerate the best sides of scenarios, outlooks, experiences, or memories, and disregard the negative sides.

17. See Lamont 1992, 2009 for research on the role of moral values.

18. Emotions constitute a phenomenologically and socially interactive process, as much a reaction as an action meant to elicit a response from the other person in turn; see Goffman 1956, 1967 and Katz 1999.

19. Even for a wine program, which may be the least adaptable part of the restaurant business from one country to another (given that the economics of the wine business vary across countries), there are plenty of ideas that could be borrowed, including the organization of wine lists or wine pairings, and new wines that could be made available in the United States.

20. If a chef serves a blatant copy of a foreign chef's dish and is found out, an accusation of plagiarism may spread through informal means (gossip, especially through blogs), and this has happened. But such copying is an extreme and rare case, the most common practice is for chefs to borrow ideas—not entire dishes—from chefs in foreign countries and adapt these ideas to their own styles. Drawing on research on social norms, Fauchart and von Hippel (2006) note that norm-based knowledge-exchange regimes, such as cuisine, create a particularly high level of communalism within the group. Di Stefano, King, and Verona (2014) go further than most research on social norms in knowledge-exchange to explain individuals' willingness to share information with others. They note that this willingness has to do not so much with the characteristics of the individuals willing to share information or the role of norms (the common arguments of research on social norms) but with these individuals' knowledge of the persons with whom they would share information and these persons' visibility.

21. In their study of Italian chefs, Di Stefano, King, and Verona (2014) also show that self-interested motives and normative behavior are intrinsically related, such that a "thick rationality" explains action. See also Spillman 2012 for recent research into the connection between economic calculation and moral and emotional motives for explaining action in economic markets.

22. See Di Stefano, King, and Verona 2014 and Fauchart and von Hippel 2006. Fashion and academia are similar cases in this regard. See also Raustiala and Sprigman 2009.

23. Coleman 1990; Granovetter 2005. The informal control of misbehavior is all the more effective with the availability of virtual channels. Accusations of plagiarism are sometimes launched on websites or blogs that thrive on gossip. One of the most renowned accusations of plagiarism of the past few years began on eGullet, often referred to as an influential website for culinary insiders (Wells 2006).

24. I paraphrase Marx to suggest that, just as one's opinion of someone is not based on what he (or she) thinks of himself (or herself), the logic of creation in a field

cannot be understood by looking only at individuals' discourses on their practices. In the preface to *A Contribution to the Critique of Political Economy*, Marx ([1859] 1970, p. 15) writes, "Just as our opinion of an individual is not based on what he thinks of himself, so can we not judge of such a period of transformation by its own consciousness; on the contrary, this consciousness must be explained rather from the contradictions of material life, from the existing conflict between the social productive forces and the relations of production." Along the same lines, chefs' discourses about their practices can be understood only in light of the mode of cultural production in cuisine.

25. Zerubavel (2002, pp. 24–25) notes that there is a normative organization of attending and ignoring, sustained by an *optical socialization*. As he points out, ignoring is as active and deliberate as noticing. Sociologists have recently begun to appreciate that what is not seen, not done, not spoken of, is at least as sociologically informative as overt actions, calling attention to these areas of social life that have traditionally been overlooked. See Brekhus 2003; Eliasoph 1998; Eliasoph and Lichterman 2003; Lamont 1992; Lichterman 2005; Mullaney 2005; and Zerubavel 2002.

26. Goffman's (1956) work on embarrassment is a good example of how the practices of attending and ignoring are sustained. He describes and explains the social management of uncomfortable situations, as individuals cooperate to downplay the significance of an uncomfortable scene (by looking the other way or making jokes about it) to make the situation less socially disruptive.

27. In the past few years, some sociologists of culture have shed light on the fact that cognitive schemas are properties of both particular groups and settings (DiMaggio 2002; Eliasoph and Lichterman 2003).

28. For cogent explanations of the effects of connectedness through indirect ties, see the literature on structural equivalence in network analysis: Burt 1987, 1988, 1992; White 1992.

29. Sometimes professional cookbook writers who have a large stake on the writing of the book are listed as coauthors, but always second to chefs and generally in smaller print.

30. Since chefs do not seek to protect their ideas through intellectual property laws, this strategy effectively works to treat certain things like trade secrets. It may be argued that chefs emphasized their low opinions of the usefulness of cookbooks in the interviews because they assumed that, as an outsider, I did not understand that a cookbook is of less value to a culinary professional than a home cook, but the extent to which they went to undermine the value of these books clearly goes beyond this point.

31. Fauchart and von Hippel 2006, p. 4.

32. Wells 2006.

33. See also Di Stefano, King, and Verona 2014.

34. Professional lineage is not unlike a genealogy in that both serve to transfer social and symbolic capital; see Zerubavel 2012, p. 24. For a good explanation of how social connections bestow status on individuals, see Podolny 1993, 2005.

35. Zerubavel 2012, p. 10.

36. In this sense, shaping one's professional lineage is not unlike delineating one's genealogical tree. The latter involves blood ties, of course, but also socially shared

ideas about principles of relatedness that indicate who is connected to whom, and norms about which ties are the most significant and which can be forgotten. Drawing on a wide range of examples, Zerubavel (2012) shows how even the most seemingly genetics-based genealogies are built on what he calls norms of selective remembrance, which involve norms about remembering, denial, and forgetting.

37. DiMaggio 2002, p. 277. The understanding that individuals respond to their perception of what the context calls on them to do originates in pragmatists' ideas (see Dewey [1922] 2002, [1939] 1967; see also Martin 2011, pp. 181–190).

38. In total, the chefs I interviewed in New York selected 116 admired chefs (this is not to say 116 different names, but the total number of names invoked) and 66 chefs (again, the total number of names invoked, not 66 different names) with whom they would have wanted to work. On average, they selected four chefs they admire, and two they would have wanted to work with.

39. The restaurant world is fast-changing, so chefs' portfolios (i.e., the restaurants they own and whether they own other businesses or host TV shows) have, in many cases, changed since I obtained these responses.

40. Ferguson 1998, 2004; Ferguson and Zukin 1998. New York interviewees tended to select Europeans as chefs they would have wanted to work with, whether or not they had spent time working in Europe.

41. E.g., Bourdieu [1992] 1996, 1993; DiMaggio and Powell 1983, 1991; Phillips, Turco, and Zuckerman 2013; Phillips and Zuckerman 2001; Porac et al. 1995, Rao; Monin, and Durand 2005; Zuckerman 1999.

42. The figures for New York would be lower if I included only the chefs selected who are currently in the field. Some of the chefs selected were dead, and others work at traditional Asian restaurants. If nonfield members are eliminated, the proportion of admired chefs in New York goes down a few percentage points. Of the chefs selected in other fields, whether as admired or as chefs with whom respondents would have wanted to work, 90% are in Europe.

43. The figures are significantly lower in San Francisco because the sample of chefs in this city is significantly smaller, as is the culinary field.

44. Bourdieu (1993, p. 137) argues that "intellectual or artistic position-takings are also always semi-conscious *strategies* in a game in which the conquest of cultural legitimacy and of the concomitant power of legitimate symbolic violence is at stake."

45. Simmel (1950, p. 30) noted that differentiation is the force that challenges and determines individuals' activities. Only through the observation of differences can individuals figure out how to act, especially how to act vis-à-vis others (see also Simmel 1910, p. 378, 1950, pp. 31, 410).

46. The general formulation of how individuals respond to their environment by means of their reflective self-understandings should be traced back to pragmatism (Dewey [1922] 2002; Mead [1934] 1967). The connection between the objective and subjective realms I suggest here is key to field theory; see Bourdieu 1977, 1990.

47. The association between access to good-quality ingredients and de-emphasis of technique is widespread beyond the American context. It is the classic explanation for the difference between Italian and French cuisines.

48. E.g., Geertz 1973; Parsons [1937] 1968. The contemporary sociology of culture has moved away from the earlier notion of *culture* as a set of beliefs and ideas, and instead emphasizes the inherent connection between culture and structure (e.g., DiMaggio 1997, 2002; McDonnell 2014; Mohr and Duquenne 1997; Swidler 1986, 2003).

49. More analytically, discourses, attitudes, and behavior develop from the patterning of the social relations that constitute a field—with more pressures for differentiation in one field than the other—because individuals orient their actions in response to such patterning and their place in it. This argument is, of course, in line with the principles of field theory; see Bourdieu 1977, 1990.

50. It could be argued that chefs in San Francisco have a lesser interest in having information about culinary trends due to their higher reliance on ingredients. This may have something to do with their lack of interest in modernist cuisine, but their lower tendency to seek out information goes beyond this. For one thing, even very traditional chefs in New York, opposed to recent fads, have information about the latest culinary trends. In addition, San Francisco chefs manifest little interest not only in the latest technical developments but also in monitoring peers, regardless of the peers' styles.

51. Chefs in New York also experience a potential for cooperation, and indeed do cooperate, but to a somewhat lesser degree. Di Stefano, King, and Verona (2014) similarly argue that being in the same market niche both frames others as rivals and triggers a potential for identification and cooperation given similarities in style and market position. Here, I specify that there is variance in the potential for identification and cooperation across fields, given that some environments facilitate the sense of identification and cooperation more than others.

Chapter Five: Cognitive Patterns and Work Processes in Cooking
A brief section of this chapter was previously published in "Thinking About Food and Sex: Deliberate Cognition in the Routine Practices of a Field," *Sociological Theory* 2013: 31, pp. 116–144 (with Adam Isaiah Green).

1. When chefs comment on tastes, they almost always mention salty, sweet, acid (i.e., sour), and bitter. In recent years, umami—generally defined as "savoriness"—has begun to be considered a fifth taste, one that is commonly found in foodstuffs with high protein levels and "meaty" flavors, such as meat, mushrooms, broths, and cheese. Receptor cells on the tongue have been identified for all five tastes. Foodstuffs are classified into different sets of tastes in other world cuisines, notably in South Asia, where they often amount to five categories, sometimes including umami (originally discovered in Japan) and at other times categories such as pungent.

2. Whereas the four tastes constitute a rigid set of categories (backed up by scientific studies of taste receptors in the tongue), textures are a more flexible group. For instance, some chefs point out that there should always be something soft and something crunchy in a dish, without mentioning any other textures, whereas others mention smooth and crispy, and still others mention a wider range.

3. I derive these three culinary principles phenomenologically, from how chefs talk about cooking, not from criteria that *could* guide thoughts on cooking. This is

why smell—a critical sense for the appreciation of food—is not included among the culinary principles. Chefs rarely mention it; a few of them talk about using the sense of smell for gauging whether something has been cooked properly, but it is almost never mentioned as an important component of a dish. That chefs rarely talk about smell is not surprising. Retronasal smell (the smell that we get when we breathe out) is what allows human beings to apprehend flavor, but we rarely recognize it as a distinct sense, and as the sense that actually gives us the capacity to taste flavor, because it is always associated with the senses of taste and touch. The three of them together form the sense of flavor, which appears to us as something that comes from the mouth, and not the nose (Shepherd 2012, p. 31).

4. There is a similar intuitive understanding in other occupations. When asked about what makes a "cool" product, industrial designers respond that "you know it when you see it," as Molotch ([2003] 2005) shows in his study of product design.

5. See Haidt 2001 for a clear explanation of how deep intuitions work.

6. The notion of practical logic is central to Bourdieu's (1977, [1979] 1984) conception of the habitus, which operates precisely through the internalization of practical knowledge into dispositions.

7. For the variance (ranging from detailed schema to loose guidelines) in how individuals use categories in improvisation in the arts, see Sawyer 2003.

8. Field theory and the neo-institutional literature theorize the process whereby individuals incorporate codified rules and principles through formal and informal channels, which go on to constrain their work (Bourdieu 1976; DiMaggio and Powell 1983; Larson 2005; Mohr 1994; Mohr and Duquenne 1997; Zucker 1977, 1987; Zuckerman 1999; Zuckerman et al. 2003). Contrary to this assumption, Bergesen (2005) maintains that if individuals are not aware of the ideas that bound their work, it is because they have never learned them. Indeed, Bergesen argues against the assumption that there is socialization into classificatory schemas in the arts. It seems sensible to maintain (if challenging to demonstrate) that it is precisely the lack of awareness of rules that is evidence of the extent to which such rules may have been internalized.

9. Nonetheless, well-established chefs at high-end restaurants, who are the most experienced, are particularly likely to taste foods constantly. They are especially sensitive to the subtle daily changes of ingredients and, facing strong pressures for excellence, tend to control quality closely.

10. For literature on organizational analysis that elaborates on the multiplicity of frames that exist in an organizational field, see Clemens and Cook's 1999 review; see also Mische 2008.

11. In opposition to the homogenizing view that pervaded the understanding of culture until the late 1970s (expounded with particular force by Parsons [1937] 1968, 1964), contemporary scholarship in the sociology of culture has been increasingly pointing to the need to investigate variations across individuals' repertoires of action, an approach most prominently developed by Swidler (1986, 2003) and widely followed by others; see Cerulo 2010; Lizardo and Strand 2010; Ortner 1984; and Vaisey 2008b, 2009.

12. See March 1991. For an application of March's concepts to the arts, see Faulkner 2006.

13. For literature on dispositions, see Bourdieu 1998 and Lahire 2003. The neo-institutionalism in sociology and organizational analysis classically theorized the tendency for actions to become habitual in a field (cf. DiMaggio and Powell 1983, 1991).

14. The organizational literature shows that the age and size of an organization affects the likelihood that individuals will take an active role in creating opportunities; see Daft and Weick 1984.

15. The organizational literature also suggests that individuals' inclination to innovate is also related to their perceptions of their ability to figure out the state of the market. For organizational literature on the perception of markets, see Child 1974; Daft and Weick 1984; and Hedberg 1981. Daft and Weick, in particular, offer a good explanation of how perceptions influence individuals' choices in an organization. For an example of empirical research that applies this perspective, see Weber, Heinze, and De Soucey 2008.

16. See DiMaggio 2002, p. 278, and Swidler 2003, pp. 175–180, for a similar point. Recent scholarship in the sociology of culture, echoing this insight, calls attention to the interrelation of dispositions and contexts; see Eliasoph and Lichterman 2003; Lizardo and Strand 2010; and Mische 2008. Eliasoph and Lichterman (2003) developed the concept of *group style* to address this very phenomenon. Group styles are not preestablished schemas that individuals (or groups) bring to situations (as Bourdieu [1977, (1979) 1984] might have it) but are instead developed in a social context, where stable cultural patterns and forms of social interaction intersect. This notion is akin to the principle of co-constitution of meaning and practice (see, for instance, Mohr and Duquenne 1997), even if the two arguments come from different theoretical perspectives and methodologies.

17. This is the embodied nature of habitual action, a phenomenon captured by Bourdieu's notion of habitus (see, for example, Bourdieu 1977).

18. Such processing of information is often a retrieval of memory that happens automatically in the brain, which remains obscure to individuals.

19. The two examples from the same chef put in high relief individuals' tendency to adjust their practices—cognitive approaches and actions—to particular contexts (see DiMaggio 2002; Eliasoph and Lichterman 2003; Lizardo and Strand 2010; Mische 2008; and Vaisey 2008b, 2009).

20. Alter (2003) argues that innovation begins intuitively, driven by a belief in a positive outcome, because it is a more uncertain endeavor than creating products by means of established ideas. Once started, he suggests, innovation becomes a process, first "normed" and then normative, in time generating a new established way of doing things.

21. See Joas 1996, p. 156. Joas (1996, p. 158) writes: "According to this view, our perception of the world appears to be structured by our capacities for, and experiences of, action. Even when we are not pursuing any immediate intention of action, the world exists not simply as an external counterpart to our internal self, but in the form of possible actions." For an insightful elaboration of this point, see Martin 2011, pp. 181–190.

22. For literature on the process of bricolage, see de Certeau 1984 and Lévi-Strauss [1962] 1968.

23. Moreover, this chef regularly reads art books to develop his aestheticized style, a practice chefs, even the most innovative ones, rarely mention.

24. For a sociological explanation of how dispositions work, see Bourdieu 1977, [1979] 1984, and for a philosophical explanation, see Bourdieu 1998. See Dewey [1922] 2002, pp. 40–42, for a theorization of imaginative, forward-looking action. See Evans 2012, p. 128, for a cognitive psychological explanation of the emotional, cognitive, and metacognitive factors that lead individuals to rely on established ways of thinking and acting (Type 1 processing) or analytical thinking and forward-looking action (Type 2 processing).

25. Chefs do not necessarily like to keep these dishes on the menu, but they are best-sellers and, even more importantly, are demanded by customers.

26. Swidler 1986. For a good application of the notion of toolkits in organizations, see Weber 2005.

27. For research on the "aha" moment, see Thompson and Morsanyi 2012 and Topolinski and Reber 2010.

28. Cognitive scientists and cognitive psychologists use various terms to refer to the deliberative process, including *cold* or *controlled cognition, System 2* or *Type 2 processes*, or the *new mind* (see Jonathan Evans 2010, 2012; Haidt 2001; and Lieberman 2007).

29. See Dalton 2004; see also Joas 1996. In line with the position I put forth here, Dalton argues for a coupling of habit and creativity in the conception of action.

30. These two approaches to cuisine should be viewed as ideal types (cf. Weber [1922] 1978), presented here for heuristic purposes. In practice, they are the two extremes on a continuum, and chefs' views of the process of creation generally fall at varying points along that continuum.

31. These varying views of cuisine extend to the writing of restaurant menus. Whereas some chefs see menus as finished products, others view them as works in progress. For the former, it is not acceptable to have dishes that are works in progress on the menu because it means treating customers as guinea pigs, but for the latter, menus are more flexible, so dishes can go on or off a menu as they see fit.

32. For research that shows the limitations of a dual view of cognition, see Elqayam and Over 2012; Evans 2012; Frank, Cohen, and Sanfey 2009; Oaksford and Chater 2012; Roser and Gazzaniga 2004; and Thompson and Morsanyi 2012.

33. For cognitive explanations of how mental schemas work, see D'Andrade 1995, p. 142; Norman 1986, p. 536; and Strauss and Quinn 1997, p. 49. For cognitive research on mental structures, see Neisser 1967 and Rumelhart 1980. For especially clear explanations of the automatic model of cognition, see D'Andrade 1995; Haidt 2001; Quinlan 1991; and Strauss and Quinn 1997.

34. See D'Andrade 1992, p. 29, 1995, pp. 136, 142, and Norman 1986, p. 536. Cognitive psychologists have found that there are four properties that make connectionist networks very good representations for the schematization processes that happen in the brain: an ability to use default information to fill in for what is missing; a capacity to learn abstract and nuanced characteristics and find the structure that underlies information; a sensitivity to context; and an ability to combine interpretations

formed out of disconnected bits of information into a synthesis that makes sense; see D'Andrade 1995, pp. 139–140.

35. For explanations of serial symbolic processing, see D'Andrade 1995, p. 137; Fodor and Pylyshyn 1988, 1995; Newell and Simon 1972; and Strauss and Quinn 1997.

36. For cognitive research on dual-process models of cognition, see Bargh 1994; Bargh and Chartrand 1999; Chaiken and Trope 1999; Greenwald and Banaji 1995; Haidt 2001, 2005; Lieberman 2007; Wegner and Bargh 1998; and Zajonc 1980. See Lizardo and Strand 2010 and Vaisey 2008a, 2008b, 2009 for a sociological discussion of the relationship between the connectionist model in cognitive psychology and the sociological notion of cultural toolkits.

37. For clear explanations of the factors that may lead to deliberative thinking, see D'Andrade 1995; DiMaggio 1997; Haidt 2001; and Strauss and Quinn 1997.

38. This tripartite understanding of cognition and action is inspired by phenomenology and heterophenomenology (see Dennett 2003; Dreyfus and Kelly 2007; Husserl 1960; and Merleau-Ponty 1962). I delineate three paths of action for heuristic purposes here, but other options are feasible. In particular, individuals could strategically choose to continue doing what they have been doing, or they could make a change by accident, through automatic action.

39. For the sociological literature on culture and cognition that follows dual-process models for the explanation of cognition and action, see Cerulo 2010; Lizardo and Strand 2010; Martin 2010; and Vaisey 2009. For a critique, see Leschziner and Green 2013. In contrast to much of the literature on dual-process models, I follow Evans (2012, p. 123) in arguing that the two modes of thinking are not opposite in that only deliberative thinking can achieve logical reasoning. For one thing, automatic thinking can achieve instrumental rationality (by associative processes rather than rule following), and deliberative thinking can be quick or can follow routine heuristics with little conscious thought.

40. On this point, see Joas 1996, pp. 126–144. This notion is in line with the pragmatists' view of creative action, what Joas (1996, p. 133) calls "a theory of situated creativity." In particular, it recalls Dewey's ([1934] 2005, p. 35) understanding of those experiences that are "rounded out" because they have a special meaningfulness that makes them more whole, such that they stand above the flow of actions.

41. This is another example of the insight that is experienced as an "aha" moment. The new idea appears suddenly and with unexpected ease because it is not created through a slow, conscious process but originates in knowledge that is engaged with routinely. Because the new idea appears unexpectedly and effortlessly, it triggers a positive affect that endows the person with confidence in it. These cognitive and emotional mechanisms together turn the experience into an "aha" moment (Thompson and Morsanyi 2012; Topolinski and Reber 2010; Topolinski and Strack 2009).

42. See Evans 2012, p. 128. There is experimental evidence that self-identities guide individuals not only in their actions but also in their cognitive processes. For instance, a multidisciplinary group of scientists led by Jennifer Murphy, a psychologist at the Army Research Institute, conducted experimental research on bomb detection among army troops, and found a significant difference between those who see

themselves as prey and those who see themselves as predators (Shingledecker et al. 2010) in that the latter were much better at noticing bombs. Researchers suggest that a self-image as a predator itself may contribute to reduced stress. A brain that is over-whelmed by stress or anxiety, however perceptive and observing, will miss subtle clues. Research in neuroscience has also shown that a cognitively overloaded brain will suffer an impairment in logical reasoning; see DeWall, Baumeister, and Masicampo 2008.

43. For especially compelling explanations of what leads individuals to switch from automatic to deliberative thinking, see Evans 2012 and Thompson and Morsanyi 2012.

44. For cognitive research on neuronal connections, see Kandel, Schwartz, and Jessell 1995, p. 479; Merzenich and Sameshima 1993, p. 190; and Strauss and Quinn 1997, p. 90.

45. This suggests that the kind of food chefs make constrains future opportuni-ties, not only through the skills and culinary styles chefs learn but also through the cognitive patterns they develop in making food, for these will shape the ideas they will come up with in the future, as well as the opportunities they will pursue. This argument has similarities with Swidler's (1986, 2003) toolkit theory of action, which posits that individuals are unlikely to undertake an action if they have not mastered the necessary skills for that action, or if they could not justify the action a posteriori. Such a view is in line with the pragmatists' understanding that individuals perceive and respond to their environments in ways that are shaped by their capacities to act, and delineate paths of action from there; see Dewey [1922] 2002 and Joas 1996.

46. The tendency to combine routine work with more exploratory and imagi-native practices is common in cuisine, as well as in other realms. Faulkner (2006) shows how jazz musicians oscillate between and combine exploitation of standards and exploration of new ideas, particularly through improvisation; see also Faulkner and Becker 2009.

47. Being at one of the most prestigious restaurants in the country gives him a flexibility that is not available to all chefs. For one thing, he is assured of having cus-tomers (at least for some time) based on his reputation alone, and being at the very top of the field, he faces less competition and therefore fewer pressures to constantly change the menu. Chefs at the most elite restaurants are also less pressured to change menus often because their establishments are "destination restaurants," no.t typically visited frequently by any one patron.

48. See Dalton 2004 and Joas 1996. For exemplary work on individuals' imagina-tive and forward-looking action, see Emirbayer and Mische 1998 and Mische 2008, 2009; see also Lahire 2003. The conceptualization of creation I propose here is along the lines of contemporary understandings of culture (DiMaggio 1997, 2002; Eliasoph and Lichterman 2003) in the effort to specify the variation of behavior across situa-tions. DiMaggio (2002, p. 279) insightfully defined *culture* as the product of disposi-tions and situations. Though his definition does not make reference to individuals' desires and inclinations, his discussion of the role of hot and cool affects is evocative of these phenomena.

49. The molten chocolate cake resulted from a mistake in baking such that a chocolate cake came out of the oven not fully baked but with a liquid center. This

shows that relying on well-established ideas and incorporated knowledge can still lead to innovation, not mere reproduction or even the "improvisatory reaction" theorized by Bourdieu (e.g., 1977).

50. See, for example, Bourdieu 1977. Research on cognition shows that routine and habitual action is made possible by the implicit and procedural knowledge that is gained through repeated action and stored in what is referred to as the *old mind*, or the intuitive part of thinking; see Evans 2012, p. 125.

51. For this definition of dispositions, see Dewey [1922] 2002, pp. 41–42. Dewey ([1922] 2002, p. 41) writes that "the word disposition means predisposition, readiness to act overtly in a specific fashion whenever opportunity is presented . . . and that attitude means some special case of a predisposition, the disposition waiting as it were to spring through an opened door."

52. For a philosophical explanation of this characteristic of dispositions, see Bourdieu 1998, pp. 39–53, and Goodman 1955. On this point, Dewey ([1922] 2002, p. 42) writes: "The essence of habit is an acquired predisposition to *ways* or modes of response, not to particular acts except as, under special conditions, these express a way of behaving. Habit means special sensitiveness or accessibility to certain classes of stimuli, standing predilections and aversions, rather than bare recurrence of specific acts. It means will."

53. See Evans 2012, p. 124.

54. This conceptualization is akin to Hennion's (2003) notion of innovation as performative action. Hennion suggests that in making innovative products or services, individuals produce and prescribe the innovative style.

Chapter Six: Culinary Styles and Principles of Creation

1. Some argue that it was the French chef Michel Bras who invented the cake, not Vongerichten, and his possible authorship is acknowledged even more rarely, even among culinary professionals (Khong 2011).

2. Bourdieu 1993.

3. Latour 2005. But see Knorr Cetina 1997 for a conceptualization that is more akin to what I propose here. The notion I suggest is along the lines of Marx's ([1867] 1889) theory; Marx not only notes that objects are imbued with social relations but that this is obscured by established social processes, what he has famously labeled the *fetishism of commodities.*

4. Breiger 1974. Breiger followed Simmel's (1955) insight on the duality of individuals and groups (as elaborated in his formal sociology, nicely exemplified in his analysis of dyads and triads) to develop the "membership network analysis" in this seminal article.

5. Bourdieu 1977, [1992] 1996, 1993.

6. This is one of the basic premises of Mead's ([1934] 1967) pragmatist theory and the symbolic interactionism developed by Blumer ([1969] 1986).

7. Bourdieu 1993.

8. Bourdieu 1976; Collins 1998; Frickel and Gross 2005; Gross 2008; Whitley [1984] 2000. This is a broad generalization, as there is much variance in the degree of

autonomy found across disciplines (e.g., a department of philosophy is typically more autonomous than a business school) and across areas within disciplines (e.g., work in social theory is more autonomous than empirical research on contemporary social issues). In addition, exogenous factors, such as an economic recession that reduces universities' budgets and access to grants, can affect any area of knowledge.

9. Baumann 2007b; Hsu 2006; Zuckerman et al. 2003. Much research on cultural fields, inspired by Bourdieu's theory, has focused on academia and the movie industry, along with a few other areas such as literature, music, and the fine arts (Bourdieu 1976, [1984] 1993, [1992] 1996, 1993; Karpik 2010; Lamont and Fournier 1992; Savage and Gayo 2011; van Rees and Dorleijn 2001; Velthuis 2005).

10. A large area of research in sociology examines the distinction between pure and mass production in cultural fields that derives from the antagonism between artistic reputation and commercial success, in particular focusing on the consumption of cultural products. Much of this research argues that the once sharp boundary between highbrow and lowbrow products has been blurred in the past few years, because individuals are more likely to have diverse cultural tastes and to attain social distinction not by rejecting lowbrow products but through omnivorous cultural behavior (DiMaggio 1987; DiMaggio and Mukhtar 2004; Erickson 1996, 2007; Fischler 1990; Peterson 1997; Peterson and Kern 1996; Peterson and Rossman 2007; Warde, Martens, and Olsen 1999). Some research, however, shows that patterns of cultural consumption have not changed in the past few years, and that omnivorous behavior is less widespread than has been shown; see Lizardo and Skiles 2008, 2009.

11. One line of research on cultural fields examines knowledge production in academic fields, where action is driven largely by reputation concerns (Camic, Gross, and Lamont 2011; Collins 1998; Frickel and Gross 2005; McLaughlin 2001; Owen-Smith 2001). Another line of research investigates knowledge exchange in the financial or corporate worlds or the biotechnical industry (Burt 2004; Haveman and Rao 1997; Owen-Smith and Powell 2004; Zuckerman 1999), where, in contrast to academic fields, action is driven by the impulse of economic success, and where knowledge production is therefore a more heteronomous process.

12. In fact, the word *chef* refers to an occupational position (*chef* is French for "boss"), not an activity.

13. Food trucks may be an exception, but for one thing, not all foods can be prepared in a food truck. Indeed, food trucks are not equivalent to restaurants; what is more, they often serve as stepping-stones towards opening a restaurant.

14. Leschziner 2010. In symphony orchestras, for instance, musicians resort to artistic values and administrators to economic values to legitimate themselves (Glynn 2000).

15. In any market, products must be familiar to audiences in order to be recognizable and perceived as legitimate offers (Zuckerman 1999). Their failure to be recognizable to audiences in a market leads to what Zuckerman (1999) calls the "illegitimacy discount." If products do not fit any existing category, they generally fail to attract attention and/or to be perceived as legitimate offers.

16. Many times, chefs cannot make any choice at all. If they are hired to work at

an existing restaurant or a restaurant to be opened by another restaurateur, they have little freedom to choose the style, for it is already determined; at most, they can try to adapt that style towards their preferences over time. But they face constraints even when they open their own restaurants, including the interests of financial backers, the culinary trends of the moment, and the economic climate (e.g., an economic recession can easily change a chef's plan to open a high-end restaurant and lead him to veer towards a more downscale style).

17. Chefs are also motivated to change their culinary styles for a number of other reasons, including that they may be coming out of a situation where they were constrained to cook in a style they never liked or may be experiencing the boredom that comes with cooking the same foodstuffs over a long period. At the same time, there are strong incentives to continue to work with the same styles, especially the mastery that is gained over time. As a result, chefs rarely have significant shifts in culinary styles subsequent to opening their first restaurants.

18. In organizational terms, this is referred to as membership in a category (Zuckerman 1999).

19. See Gould 1993.

20. There is a growing body of literature on the exchange of ideas in cuisine (e.g., Di Stefano, King, and Verona 2014; Fauchart and von Hippel 2006; Rao, Monin, and Durand 2005), but it rarely examines how chefs reflectively deal with the exchange of ideas.

21. Although not all chefs who work in corporate groups said that they obtained ideas for dishes from other chefs with whom they met on occasion, all those who acknowledged obtaining ideas from other chefs were in corporate groups.

22. For a sociological analysis of the role of friendship in collaborative circles in other areas of cultural creation, see Farrell 2001.

23. This allows him to maintain the definition of the situation in a kitchen where he is in command; see Goffman 1959.

24. The MAD annual symposium (run by a not-for-profit organization founded by culinary professionals) is the most renowned example of such gatherings. It has become an influential, two-day conference with about six hundred attendees from all over the world, including culinary professionals, purveyors, farmers, butchers, food writers, and activists.

25. The network literature distinguishes two mechanisms for diffusion of ideas: structural equivalence (Burt 1987, 1988, 1992; White 1992) and structural cohesion (Coleman, Katz, and Menzel 1957; Laumann, Marsden, and Galaskiewicz 1977; Laumann and Pappi 1973). The first model posits that knowledge diffuses through individuals in similar structural positions because ideas are adopted by looking at competitors. The second model posits that ideas diffuse through proximity in a network, so information is likely to travel between individuals who have connections devoid of many intermediaries. Along these lines, Owen-Smith and Powell (2004, p. 8) distinguish between two types of connections: open channels, which are diffuse, reaching centrally located as well as loosely connected persons, and closed conduits, which are legally controlled, limiting the exchange of information to membership in a group.

The two cases I am describing here involve social proximity and (likely) similar structural positions.

26. Research in network analysis and neo-institutionalism shows evidence of how social connections with members of other groups lead to innovative ways of thinking in areas as varied as social movements, biotechnology, or corporations (Burt 1992, 2004; Clemens 1997; Clemens and Cook 1999; Giuffre 1999; Mische 2008; Morrill 2001).

27. Network research also shows that innovative thinking tends to arise among elites because they are likely to be connected to elites in other fields, who are also often innovators; in more technical terms, innovation is likely to diffuse through elites across fields because there is a transfer of ideas through actors in similar structural positions across organizational fields (Laumann, Marsden, and Galaskiewicz 1977; Laumann and Pappi 1973).

28. With similarly nontraditional work schedules, professional dance musicians, for instance, have also been shown to be unlikely to meet individuals in other occupations (Becker 1951). Celebrity chefs who own several restaurants and run large businesses are not tied to restaurant schedules, and they move in wide social circles (due to a large extent to their celebrity), so they do have friends and acquaintances in other areas, many of whom are elites themselves. However, these chefs do not make any comment about getting ideas or inspiration from such friends or acquaintances either. What is more, these chefs are rarely among the most innovative, at least not at this stage in their careers.

29. Only one person, an innovative chef at a high-status restaurant in New York, suggested that he looks at art books for inspiration. The media sometimes report that chefs take inspiration in the arts, but typically in reference to presentation, not the substance of a dish. In any event, this is not something I have personally heard chefs comment on.

30. The structural equivalence model contends that individuals identify competitors through shared audiences (Burt 1987, 1988, 1992; White 1992). Hsu and Hannan (2005) suggest that ties to audiences are also key for the classification of organizations. They thus argue that the notion of *structural equivalence* is restrictive, and propose instead the concept of *automorphic equivalence* to capture the tendency of organizations that are similarly classified by their audiences (on the basis of organizational identity) to relate to audiences in a similar way.

31. To the extent that chefs rely on established criteria to identify competitors and orient their decisions to them, they collectively maintain the criteria and, in turn, they maintain an institutional stability in the field (see White 1981). By the same token, precisely such institutional stability makes it possible for individuals to rely on established criteria in order to develop practical theories of action and strategize effectively.

32. Rao, Monin, and Durand (2003, 2005) identify similar patterns whereby new ideas diffuse in the French culinary field.

33. See Podolny 1993, 2005. Podolny elaborates on the important role of social ties for conveying information about one's social standing; this is why he calls them *status signals*. See McLean 2007 for a sophisticated analysis, in the context of Renaissance

Florence, that shows how and why individuals pursue social ties, not just to obtain resources but also as a means to define themselves in relation to others.

34. Chefs with similar styles are more likely to be connected to this chef in the first place, given that they come together at specialized industry events, and social gatherings.

35. Vonnegut 2011, p 110.

36. See Podolny 1993, 2005. Chefs in New York would likely not talk about Wylie Dufresne as much now as they did a few years ago, when I conducted my fieldwork, and this is precisely because their references to him had little to do with Dufresne's personal charisma and much to do with the position of modernist cuisine in New York, which was at its highest then. That wd-50 closed in November 2014 (even though prompted by real estate issues) shows how much the scenario has changed.

37. The notion that individuals tend to prioritize some aspects over others in their representations is along the lines of what Cerulo (2006) identifies as the *relevance structures* that constitute the cognitive asymmetry in a group. D'Andrade (1989), for his part, represents this common aspect of cognition somewhat more cynically, characterizing all individuals as opportunistic information processors; see also Hutchins 1995, p. 157.

38. Lounsbury and Glynn 2001, p. 560.

39. Many chefs made comments about the change they experienced in their palates over time. Like this chef, they generally pointed out that their palates get tired after tasting and eating rich foods regularly, so they long for stronger flavors and more acidity.

40. In more analytical terms, chefs create and re-create themselves in an ongoing process of cognition and action (Weick 1979, 1995).

41. *Enjeu* translates (less succinctly) as "that which is at stake" (Bourdieu 1976, 1977, [1984] 1993, [1992] 1996). The concept of field can be further traced to Weber's ([1920] 1963, pp. 323–324) notion of value spheres, which were conceptualized as follows: "The individual spheres of value are prepared with a rational consistency which is rarely found in reality. But they *can* appear thus in reality and in historically important ways, and they have." Weber's conception of value spheres is one example that shows that, much before Bourdieu, there was already an interest, particularly among the German neo-Kantians associated with the philosophy of history, in finding the set of principles that organize the logic of action in a sphere and lead to consistent forms of behavior (see Rickert 1913; see also Martin, 2003, p. 20, 2011, pp. 249–250).

42. The traditional understanding that main dishes ought to have meat, carbohydrates, and vegetables has its foundation in classical French cuisine. The normative proportion of each component varies by location; the size of the meat and the carbohydrates in a dish is estimated to be smaller in New York and San Francisco than in the rest of the country. These components were traditionally arranged—following classical French cuisine—with the meat placed closest to the diner. In more recent times, this tradition was replaced by an arrangement that typically places the carbohydrates and/or vegetables in the center of the plate, and the meat on top of them. More modern styles now have presentations that depart from this, with small pieces of ingredients arranged throughout the plate in a highly aestheticized style, playing with textures, shapes, and colors.

43. Elite restaurants that have been around for a long time are re-reviewed every few years.

44. Insofar as chefs rely on technique to understand cooking, a style that uses some of the modernist techniques may be seen as modernist. This is especially the case with modernist cuisine because, more than other styles, it is essentially defined by technique.

45. This kind of cognitive process is not unlike the tendency of persons to rank themselves as middle class when asked to place themselves on a social class scale in a survey. Just as there is always someone with a higher level of socioeconomic status, there is always a chef who is more highly reliant on modernist cuisine.

46. For a classic elaboration of the principle of cognitive economy, see Rosch 1978.

47. Douglas 1986; Lévi-Strauss [1962] 1968, 1973; Lloyd 1966; Needham 1973, 1979; Sahlins 1976, 1981, 1985, 2000; Sewell 1992. For a sociological analysis of the tendency to think with binary constructs, see Fine 1992.

48. Gieryn 1983.

49. Claiming a single-minded pursuit of flavor entails a loose coupling (Meyer and Rowan 1977) between practices and discourse, given that most chefs strive to make flavorful food *and* distinguish themselves from others to stay in the game, even if to varying degrees. Moreover, chefs interpret culinary styles—their own as well as those of peers—in light of their perceptions of orientations of action, whether they have firsthand information about motives or are making inferences about them. Understandings about logics of action are, of course, subject to contestation (such understandings are what Bourdieu ([1992] 1996) calls *nomos*). This leads Bourdieu ([1992] 1996, p. 132) to view the formation of a field as the "institutionalization of anomie," because no one has a monopoly over the principles that structure the logic of creation or configuration of the field.

50. DiMaggio 1997. In his classic piece on boundary work, Gieryn (1983) describes a similar shift between logics in discourses that depends on the context of conversation.

51. This understanding was theorized by Simmel (1910, p. 380): "Within a sphere which has any sort of community of calling or of interests, every member looks upon every other, not in a purely empirical way, but on the basis of an a priori which this sphere imposes upon each consciousness which has part in it."

52. Bourdieu 1990.

53. Baumann 2007a; Ferree and Merrill 2000; Johnston and Baumann 2007; Lounsbury and Glynn 2001; Oliver and Johnston 2000. Building on Oliver and Johnston's (2000) distinction between frames and ideologies, Ferree and Merrill (2000) view discourses, ideologies, and frames on a continuum ranging from vague and incoherent to cognitively tight. Johnston and Baumann 2007 applied this understanding to the study of gourmet food. Here, I do not make a distinction among the three notions along these lines. What I show, instead, is how individuals draw on well-defined cognitive schemas that are available in their environment, and improvise on them as they respond to present conditions in a local context.

54. E.g., Bourdieu [1992] 1996, 1993; Burt 2004; Collins 1998; DiMaggio and Powell 1983; Farrell 2001; Lena 2012; Rao, Monin, and Durand 2005.

55. Cf. Bourdieu 1993; DiMaggio and Powell 1983, 1991.

56. Porac et al. 1995, p. 224; Porac, Thomas, and Baden-Fuller 2011.

57. A field is constituted by schemas for perception and actions that have reached a stable—though dynamic—patterning, what White (1992, p. 6) calls a "dynamic equilibrium." There is a history to the patterning of relations that is an intrinsic part of the field, and to the extent that there are multiple schemas and paths of action, there is always potential for dissensus and therefore for instability. Bourdieu (e.g., 1977, [1984] 1993, [1992] 1996) noted that a field is constituted by the history of its struggles, an idea in line with these principles.

58. Cf. Bourdieu 1976, 1977, [1992] 1996. For a comprehensive overview of Bourdieu's conceptualization of the dynamics of fields, and its relevance for organizational analysis, see Emirbayer and Johnson 2008.

59. Baumann 2007a, p. 51; van Rees and Dorleijn 2001, p. 332.

Chapter Seven: Mapping Out Creative Patterns

1. With the exception of this case, the chefs I interviewed cooked during service only when they had small kitchens and few staff, and nobody was hired solely to expedite.

2. Research on other organizations also shows that individuals with lower status levels, lacking the legitimacy and prestige that come with high status, are more constrained to conform to widely recognized and well-established styles to survive in a market (e.g., Hsu and Hannan 2005; Phillips and Zuckerman 2001).

3. Bourdieu [1992] 1996, p. 149. A public self-presentation that conveys devotion to the principle of excellence undoubtedly yields a positive image, which elicits a more favorable coverage in the press and, in turn, higher reputation.

4. Hsu and Hannan (2005) also show, with the case of the Hollywood film industry, that high-status individuals have fewer pressures to conform to established styles—what Hsu and Hannan call *form-level identities*—but more pressures to conform to their own styles—what these authors call *organization-specific identities*. They suggest that this happens because perceptions of status tend to be associated with perceptions of an organization's distinctiveness, and high-status individuals—being more distinctive—face higher expectations.

5. As with any generalization, there are a few exceptions here, in particular upper-middle-status chefs who could have been placed in the high-status category if they had received even a marginally better review in the *New York Times*. These chefs have profiles as high as those of high-status chefs, and culinary styles just as distinctive, so they also face strong pressures to be loyal to their styles.

6. Laumann, Marsden, and Galaskiewicz 1977; Laumann and Pappi 1973.

7. Actions can be strategic without necessarily being instrumental-rational, since they can be objectively strategic, shaped by a connection between means and ends of which individuals are not conscious (see Bourdieu [1979] 1984, 1993, p. 137).

8. The first Michelin Guide for New York was the 2006 edition, published in late 2005, and for San Francisco the 2007 edition, published in late 2006. I use the Michelin Guide for 2007 because it is the first year for which guides were published for both New York and San Francisco (the latter guide includes the Bay Area and wine

country). I do not use later editions of the Michelin guide because the 2007 edition is a closer representation of the culinary fields I studied. That Michelin focused its first U.S. guide on New York and the following year added a guide to San Francisco is further evidence of the perception that New York and San Francisco are, respectively, the first and second best dining destinations in the country. After initiating guides for these two cities, Michelin released guides for Los Angeles, Chicago, and Las Vegas, though it has already ceased to publish the Los Angeles and Las Vegas editions.

9. Note that this guide covers the whole Bay Area, and that the only three-star restaurant is in Napa Valley and two of the four two-star restaurants are in Los Gatos (Santa Clara County) and Sonoma.

10. That San Francisco chefs are more dispersed may also be partly explained by the fact that the sample is much smaller.

11. Bourdieu 1976, [1984] 1993, [1992] 1996, 1993; Frickel and Gross 2005; Lounsbury 2002; Monin and Durand 2003; Owen-Smith 2001; Phillips and Owens 2004; Phillips, Turco, and Zuckerman 2013; Phillips and Zuckerman 2001; Rao 1994; Rao, Monin, and Durand 2003, 2005.

12. E.g., Phillips and Zuckerman 2001.

13. In line with this argument, Phillips and Zuckerman (2001) suggest that identification with a role and a sense of security in the role influences the likelihood that individuals will innovate.

14. This proposition combines the insights of two models of markets, one that sees markets as role structures (White's [1981] work is foundational here; see also Zuckerman 1999), and another that views them as status structures (Podolny [1993, 2005] is a leading figure here). Whereas the former model emphasizes individuals' identification with their role in a market, and the importance of their conforming to expectations of their roles for maintaining market stability, the latter highlights the importance of perceptions of quality, tightly associated with status positions, for the organization and stability of markets; see Phillips and Zuckerman 2001, p. 421.

15. Cf. Phillips and Zuckerman 2001.

16. Meyer and Rowan 1977; Podolny 1993, 2005.

17. Rosch (1975, 1978) argues that individuals use core categories as referents in judgments of similarity. I extend her idea to suggest that individuals use core categories as referents to judge both how similar or different they are from these categories. In a related vein, Lena (2012, p. 163) points out that reputations develop from a social process whereby some characteristics are afforded salience and significance while others are disregarded, and notes that reputations begin from direct social interaction and concatenate from there. Her insights apply well to the case of cuisine.

18. As Rosch (1978) notes, a concept (a culinary style, in this case) is an effective cognitive tool if it has the critical attributes that define the category (i.e., cases in a category can be considered equivalent without sharing all attributes, just the critical ones), a notion best conceptualized by Wittgenstein ([1953] 2003) as "family resemblance" (see Cerulo 2006).

19. Indeed, she is credited with having taught Americans to appreciate organic and local ingredients and with spearheading the development of farmers' markets.

20. Modernist cuisine was still a recent phenomenon at the time of my fieldwork, and other styles that occupy significant positions now, such as the New Nordic cuisine and the nose-to-tail and farm-to-table movements, did not have much of a presence in New York or San Francisco then. Chefs' comments about chefs and restaurants in their field, particularly in New York, would likely differ now.

21. See Albert and Whetten 1985; see also Glynn 2000.

22. Self-concepts constitute reflective theories of action regardless of the type of action individuals follow, whether individuals act dispositionally or in imaginative and forward-looking ways.

23. Straying from the identity they claim to embody threatens the impression that they are authentic (Carroll and Wheaton 2009; Hsu and Hannan 2005), and risks alienating customers who go to their restaurants expecting to find the styles they associate with these restaurants.

24. That a repertoire of representations is shared by field members does not mean that all field members share all ideas (at all times). The repertoire is likely familiar to all field members, but individuals will prioritize different claims and might very well do so relative to circumstances, an idea consistent with recent approaches to culture and cognition; see DiMaggio 1997; Eliasoph and Lichterman 2003; and Swidler 1986, 2003.

25. Individuals may have different lawyers for different areas of the legal system (e.g., family and commercial law) but are less likely to alternate law firms for legal support in a single area in the way one alternates restaurants, fashion stores, or travel destinations.

26. Evidence from fieldwork suggests that exclusive patrons are indeed rare at elite restaurants in New York and San Francisco.

27. I am indebted to Edward Laumann for suggesting this point.

28. Bourdieu 1977, [1992] 1996, 1993. For the earliest sociological formulation of the notion that any sphere of action has a value that is internal to it, see Weber's ([1920] 1963) theorization of *spheres of value*.

29. Friedland 2009, p. 911.

30. Santoro 2011, p. 14. A fundamental assumption in the neo-institutionalism in sociology and organizational analysis (cf. DiMaggio and Powell 1983, 1991), much like field theory, is that individuals unreflectively incorporate the cognitive schemas and norms central in their field (for a critique, see Fligstein and McAdam 2011, 2012; Friedland 2009; and Stark 2009).

31. The emphasis on subconscious habitual thinking and on the constraints on thinking and action associated with social positions is central to field theory and the organizational and network literatures (Bourdieu 1977; Burt 2004; DiMaggio 1991; DiMaggio and Powell 1983, 1991; Frickel and Gross 2005; Gross 2008; Owen-Smith and Powell 2004; Powell et al. 2005).

32. Bourdieu [1992] 1996, 1993.

33. Friedland 2009; Stark 2009. In a related vein, Friedland (2009, pp. 894, 905) argues that Bourdieu theorized fields in too general and abstract terms, organized around universal principles and devoid of any substantive logics.

34. Boltanski and Thévenot [1991] 2006; Friedland 2009; Sahlins 1976; Stark 2009; Zelizer 1997, 2011. Boltanski and Thévenot ([1991] 2006) indeed reject the notion that there is a dichotomy between material and cultural realms.

35. Swidler (2003) made this same point in her book *Talk of Love*, where she states that hers is an "identity" theory of culture, with identity being not a core, consistent part of the self but the answer to the question of what matters to oneself that one asks before acting.

36. Bourdieu [1997] 2000, p. 11.

37. This is the case in research that explicitly follows Bourdieu's general principles of fields, as well as in the organizational and network literatures (Bourdieu 1976, 1993; Burt 2004; DiMaggio 1991; Owen-Smith and Powell 2004; Savage and Gayo 2011; van Rees and Dorleijn 2001). For a similar critique, see Bottero and Crossley 2011, p. 100, and Santoro 2011. But see Green's (2008, 2011) work on sexual fields for research that takes into account the role of space in shaping sexual fields. Green argues that these fields are necessarily local and small-scale, as individuals orient their actions to others who share certain common attributes and are in the same geographic area; see also Leschziner and Green 2013.

38. Along similar lines, Santoro (2011, p. 14) argues that the concept of field does not suffice to account for the structural positions of individuals and practices and that a mediating term is required to account for the variance in practices in a field. He suggests the term *situations* as one that stands between *habitus* and *field*. Because situations are concrete instances of social action, they are better suited for sociological analysis (for a similar argument, see Bottero and Crossley 2011). That is, individuals do not act in fields—these are just an abstraction—but in field-specific situations.

39. In a similar vein, Friedland (2009, p. 905) criticizes Bourdieu's field theory for focusing on the structural question of the distribution of goods as opposed to the systemic question of the legitimacy and practical logic of goods. In other words, he argues that Bourdieu focuses on who gets what as opposed to what and how goods are produced.

40. Baumann 2007b; Becker, Faulkner, and Kirshenblatt-Gimblett 2006; Bourdieu 1976, [1992] 1996; Farrell 2001; Faulkner and Becker 2009; Galenson 2007; Molotch [2003] 2005; Powell et al. 2005; van Rees and Dorleijn 2001.

41. Raustiala and Sprigman 2009.

42. Bourdieu 1977, 1990; Coleman 1990; DiMaggio and Powell 1983, 1991; Parsons [1937] 1968.

43. That individuals do not choose one action at a time is a point made by Swidler (1986) almost thirty years ago in her article on the toolkit theory of action. There, she forcefully argued against the idea that individuals choose their actions based on the values they hold, because actions are embedded in more encompassing trajectories, such that they are selected because they fit with individuals' ways of doing things rather than with specific motives.

44. Among the major theories explaining various aspects of this phenomenon are those developed by Blumer [1969] 1986; Dewey [1922] 2002; Goffman 1967; and Swidler 2003.

45. Dewey [1939] 1967. See also Goffman 1959 and Winship 2006. Dewey ([1922] 2002, p. 36) writes that "we do not know what we are really after until a course of action is mentally worked out." Individuals hypothesize about paths of action based on knowledge they have gained through past experience. Winship (2006) proposes the notion of "puzzling" to characterize a type of action wherein individuals do not know the end they are following but instead look for and determine possible options.

46. Dewey [1922] 2002, [1939] 1967. The connection to Swidler's (1986) toolkit theory of action is obvious here. It is surprising that Dewey is not referenced in her seminal article, given that she makes the same argument, namely that action should not be understood as isolated acts but rather as instances that fit within a broader set of practices.

47. For Dewey ([1939] 1967), means and ends are constantly shaping one another. No end can be only an end and never a means for action (see also Whitford 2002, p. 360, n. 53), because what was an end can promptly become a means for a following action). Understanding that social action is continuous, Dewey ([1939] 1967, p. 43) maintains that "nothing happens which is final in the sense that it is not part of any ongoing stream of events." Means and ends are two names for the same thing, differing only temporally and relationally (Dewey [1922] 2002, [1939] 1967, p. 43).

48. The traditional view of instrumental rational action to which I refer here is that proposed by rational actor models (e.g., Becker 1976; Coleman 1990; Hechter and Kanazawa 1997). March (1982) argues that the choice of action is based on four elements: knowledge of alternatives, knowledge of (or beliefs about) the consequences of the alternatives, an ordering of preferences (i.e., desires), and a procedure for making choices among the alternatives. This is another example of an understanding of action as purposive but not necessarily instrumental rational. The local conditions of action (especially access to information), as well as desires, have an important role in guiding action.

49. Dewey [1922] 2002, p. 225; see also Winship 2006, p. 338.

50. Dewey [1922] 2002, p. 202.

51. Whitford 2002, p, 344; see Swidler 2003 for a similar point.

52. Dewey 1931, pp. 181–182. Dewey notes that even impulsive action entails a commitment to a whole line of behavior, not just an isolated action.

53. For a good explanation of how, as White puts it, individuals "get action," see White 2008, pp. 279–333.

54. This proposition is in line with contemporary perspectives in organizational analysis that point to the inherent relationship between organizational dynamics and meaning-making processes, and which emphasize the co-constitutive role of practice, beliefs, and values in shaping the dynamics of fields, such as Friedland and Alford's (1991) *institutional logics* and Boltanski and Thévenot's ([1991] 2006) *orders of worth* (see also Hallett and Ventresca 2006; Friedland 2009; and Stark 2009).

55. Demo 1992, p. 307.

56. Narratives are built from an existing set of types, which means that they are typological (Gross 2008, pp. 263–264). That narratives are informed by the factors I point out here follows from the insight offered by Cooley's ([1902] 2006) "looking-

glass self," and elaborated upon by Mead ([1934] 1967), that individuals require social interactions to develop a sense of self, and that this sense is built in response to the meanings derived from those interactions.

57. Much research, ranging from social psychology to some of the recent perspectives in organizational analysis, has noted the emotional and affective dimensions of action (e.g., Demo 1992; Hallett and Ventresca 2006; Porac and Thomas 1994; Weick 1979), showing how cognition and emotion, developed from past experiences, together inform action (see also Gross 2008, pp. 260–261).

58. Cooley [1902] 2006; Mead [1934] 1967.

59. Epstein 1973, p. 407. Because I ignore the most purely psychological characteristics, I depart somewhat from the general picture drawn by Epstein.

60. For the structural model, see Demo 1992, p. 305, and also Markus and Sentis 1982. For the processual model, see Markus and Wurf 1987, p. 306.

61. Demo 1992, p. 306.

62. For social psychological literature on self-consistency, see Higgins 1987; Morse and Gergen 1970; and Swann et al. 1987. For a similar point made in sociology, see Gross 2008, p. 272. That individuals tend to undertake actions that they can justify to themselves and others is a point made by other scholars in sociology as well (e.g., Boltanski and Thévenot [1991] 2006; Swidler 2003).

63. It must be noted that here I am using the notion of consistency in two different ways—the first one refers to a self-concept's internal consistency, and the second to consistency among self-concepts within one's social environment. For a sociological elaboration of the notion of authenticity, see Peterson 1997.

64. See Gross 2008, p. 267, for a similar point.

65. In addition to Cooley [1902] 2006 and Mead [1934] 1967, see Schütz 1945 and Blumer [1969] 1986 for the development of these ideas.

66. For the understanding of the self-concept as a self-theory, see Epstein 1973.

67. Epstein 1973, pp. 407–408.

68. Epstein 1973, pp. 415–416.

69. Gross 2008.

70. Gross argues that the self-concept's causal role in action is stronger when status pressures subside (in his study, through tenure in the American academic system). It could be argued that if self-concepts have causal power only in the absence of status concerns, status remains the main explanatory factor. Gross's analysis hinges on conditions that are specific not just to academic life but to a particular academic life organized by a tenure system. Nonetheless, Gross has provided helpful correctives to the overly structural approaches to the study of intellectual creation offered by Bourdieu (1976, 1988, [1992] 1996, 1993) and Collins (1998), whose organizational and network analyses, respectively, lack a social psychology, or more precisely, a theory of the self (Gross 2008, p. 261).

71. The complex reality of creative work notwithstanding, it is typically discussed as an either-or endeavor (e.g., Burt 2004; Clemens 1997; Clemens and Cook 1999; Dalton 2004; Gardner 1993; Joas 1996; Peterson 1997).

72. Zuckerman 1999.

73. For sociological literature on the role of the future in shaping social action, see Beckert 2013; Emirbayer and Mische 1998; and Mische 2009.

74. Even the degree to which creativity relies on conscious or subconscious cognitive processes is, to this day, largely unknown in the sciences of the mind (Macchi, Over, and Viale 2012, p. 1).

Methodological Appendix

1. In effect, in small and busy kitchens, staying longer did not yield additional useful information.

2. I keep the name of the location confidential to protect the individuals I interviewed. These pilot interviews and observation were conducted in 2001. Half of the interviewees were kitchen staff (three chefs, a chef de cuisine, and a cook), and the others were front of the house staff (three managers and two servers).

3. I eliminated ethnic restaurants from the sample, following chefs' own phenomenological views, because these do not constitute part of the fields of high cuisine in New York City and San Francisco—chefs in ethnic restaurants have different training, careers, and social networks, and use different categories for thinking about food. In short, elite chefs do not need to know what these chefs in ethnic restaurants are doing to maintain their own positions in the field. Additionally, in the New York sample, I included only restaurants in Manhattan (a choice that would make less sense in 2014, with the explosion of the Brooklyn dining scene, than it did ten years prior), and in the San Francisco sample, I included restaurants in Berkeley and Oakland in Alameda County as well as in San Francisco.

4. Stars were an insufficient measure for distinguishing the middle-status restaurants from the upper-middle-status ones. The boundaries between a decent neighborhood place, a relatively good restaurant, and a special-occasions destination are somewhat fuzzy among restaurants of middling status, so I combined stars with price to distinguish between the middle and upper-middle categories. The adjudication of prestige is much less contentious for high-status restaurants, so the number of stars is sufficient to distinguish these from the rest. To corroborate that the distinction made by the *New York Times* between "very expensive" and "expensive" was meaningful and reliable, I randomly selected ten menus from restaurants with one or two stars and falling in one or the other of these two price categories and calculated the mean prices for entrées. I used two measures: first, I calculated the average price for entrées in each group, and second, I chose the two most common and comparable entrées (chicken and salmon, and in the few cases where salmon was not offered, striped bass) and compared prices across groups. Both measures showed consistency in the distinction between the categories "very expensive" and "expensive."

5. In the final sample, there were three restaurants that were classified as "moderate" in price by the *New York Times*. These exceptions were made either because the restaurants were part of field sampling, or because they had been rated by the newspaper long before I selected them and their pricing had effectively changed since then.

6. I cross-referenced "best of" lists from several sources because it was critical to

include the prestigious and influential restaurants in San Francisco, given the small sample size.

7. Only two restaurants in the sample had three and a half stars (and both were "expensive"), so I collapsed them into the three-stars category and do not distinguish them here. Note then, that in Table 2, each of the two upper-middle-status restaurants actually had three and a half stars from the *San Francisco Chronicle*.

8. There is one exception in this middle-status group, a restaurant classified as "moderate" in price by the *San Francisco Chronicle*. I included it as part of field sampling, using the same strategy as was used in New York.

9. The idea of purity applied here follows Bourdieu's (1993) understanding that in every field of cultural production, there are two poles, one leading towards what Bourdieu calls restricted production—that is, *art for art's sake*—and the other leading towards the mass market. Insofar as the former is concerned with artistic criteria, it involves a certain moral purity of values, whereas the latter entails more morally impure concerns with commercial success.

Bibliography

Abbott, Andrew. 1988. *The System of Professions: An Essay on the Division of Expert Labor*. Chicago: University of Chicago Press.

———. 2001. *Time Matters: On Theory and Methods*. Chicago: University of Chicago Press.

Albert, Stuart, and David A. Whetten. 1985. "Organizational Identity." *Research in Organizational Behavior* 7:263–295.

Alter, Norbert. 2003. "Innovation organisationnelle entre croyance et raison." In *Encyclopédie de l'innovation*, edited by Philippe Mustar and Hervé Penan. Paris: Editions Économica.

Althauser, Robert, and Arne Kalleberg. 1990. "Identifying Career Lines and Internal Labor Markets Within Firms: A Study in the Interrelationship of Theory and Methods." In *Social Mobility and Social Structure*, edited by Ronald Breiger. Cambridge, UK: Cambridge University Press.

Anand, N., and Richard Peterson. 2000. "When Market Information Constitutes Fields: Sensemaking of Markets in the Commercial Music Industry." *Organization Science* 11:270–284.

Anderson, Brett. 2013. "When One Kitchen Isn't Enough." *New York Times*, November 11.

Ankeny, Rachel. 2006. "The Rise of Molecular Gastronomy and Its Problematic Use of Science as an Authenticating Authority." In *Authenticity in the Kitchen: Proceedings of the Oxford Symposium on Food and Cookery 2005*, edited by R. Hosking. Totnes, UK: Prospect Books.

Bargh, John A. 1994. "The Four Horsemen of Automaticity: Awareness, Intention, Efficiency, and Control in Social Cognition." In *Handbook of Social Cognition*. Vol. 1, *Basic Processes*, edited by Robert S. Wyer and Thomas K. Srull. Hillsdale, NJ: Lawrence Erlbaum.

Bargh, John A., and Tanya L. Chartrand. 1999. "The Unbearable Automaticity of Being." *American Psychologist* 54:462–479.

Batt, Rosemary, Jae Eun Lee, and Tashlin Lakhani. 2014. *A National Study of Human Resource Practices, Turnover, and Customer Service in the Restaurant Industry*. New York: Restaurant Opportunities Centers United.

Baumann, Shyon. 2007a. "A General Theory of Artistic Legitimation: How Art Worlds Are Like Social Movements." *Poetics* 35:47–65.

———. 2007b. *Hollywood Highbrow: From Entertainment to Art*. Princeton, NJ: Princeton University Press.

Bearman, Peter. 2005. *Doormen*. Chicago: University of Chicago Press.

Becker, Gary. 1976. "Altruism, Egoism, and Genetic Fitness: Economics and Sociobiology." *Journal of Economic Literature* 4:817–826.

Becker, Howard. 1951. "The Professional Dance Musician and His Audience." *American Journal of Sociology* 57:136–144.

———. 1982. *Art Worlds*. Berkeley: University of California Press.

Becker, Howard, Robert Faulkner, and Barbara Kirshenblatt-Gimblett, eds. 2006. *Art from Start to Finish: Jazz, Painting, Writing, and Other Improvisations*. Chicago: University of Chicago Press.

Becker, Howard, Blanche Geer, Everett Hughes, and Anselm Strauss. 1961. *Boys in White: Student Culture in Medical School*. Chicago: University of Chicago Press.

Beckert, Jens. 2013. "Imagined Futures: Fictional Expectations in the Economy." *Theory and Society* 42:219–240.

Benson, J. Kenneth. 1977. "Organizations: A Dialectic View." *Administrative Science Quarterly* 22:1–21.

Bergesen, Albert. 2005. "Culture and Cognition." In *The Blackwell Companion to the Sociology of Culture*, edited by Mark Jacobs and Nancy W. Hanrahan. Oxford, UK: Blackwell.

Blau, Peter, John Gustard, Richard Jessor, Herbert Parnes, and Richard Wilcock. 1956. "Occupational Choice: A Conceptual Framework." *Industrial and Labor Relations Review* 9:531–543.

Blumer, Herbert. [1969] 1986. *Symbolic Interactionism: Perspective and Method*. Berkeley: University of California Press.

Boltanski, Luc, and Laurent Thévenot. [1991] 2006. *On Justification: Economies of Worth*. Princeton, NJ: Princeton University Press.

Bothner, Matthew, and Harrison White. 2001. "Market Orientation and Monopoly Power." In *Simulating Organizational Societies: Theories, Models and Applications*, edited by Alessandro Lomi and Erik Larsen. Cambridge, MA: MIT Press.

Bottero, Wendy, and Nick Crossley. 2011. "Worlds, Fields and Networks: Becker, Bourdieu, and the Structures of Social Relations." *Cultural Sociology* 5:99–119.

Boulud, Daniel. 2003. *Letters to a Young Chef*. Cambridge, MA: Basic Books.

Bourdain, Anthony. 2000. *Kitchen Confidential: Adventures in the Culinary Underbelly*. New York: Bloomsbury.

Bourdieu, Emmanuel. 1998. *Savoir faire: contribution à une théorie dispositionnelle de l'action*. Paris: Seuil.

Bourdieu, Pierre. 1976. "Le champ scientifique." *Actes de la Recherche en Sciences Sociales* 2:88–104.

———. 1977. *Outline of a Theory of Practice*. Cambridge, UK: Cambridge University Press.

———. [1979] 1984. *Distinction: A Social Critique of the Judgment of Taste*. Cambridge, MA: Harvard University Press.

———. [1984] 1993. *Sociology in Question*. Thousand Oaks, CA: Sage.

———. 1988. *Homo Academicus*. Cambridge, UK: Polity Press.

———. 1990. *The Logic of Practice*. Stanford, CA: Stanford University Press.

———. [1992] 1996. *The Rules of Art: Genesis and Structure of the Literary Field*. Stanford, CA: Stanford University Press.

———. 1993. *The Field of Cultural Production: Essays on Art and Literature*. New York: Columbia University Press.

———. [1997] 2000. *Pascalian Meditations*. Stanford, CA: Stanford University Press.

Brekhus, Wayne. 2003. *Peacocks, Chameleons, Centaurs: Gay Suburbia and the Grammar of Social Identity*. Chicago: University of Chicago Press.

Breiger, Ronald. 1974. "The Duality of Persons and Groups." *Social Forces* 53:181–190.

Bruni, Frank. 2007. "An Italian Spot, Larded with Drive." *New York Times*, January 17.

———. 2008. "When a Trattoria Goes Avant-Garde." *New York Times*, August 20.

Buford, Bill. 2006. *Heat: An Amateur's Adventures as Kitchen Slave, Line Cook, Pasta-Maker, and Apprentice to a Dante-Quoting Butcher in Tuscany*. New York: Alfred A. Knopf.

Bureau of Labor Statistics. 2014. *Job Openings and Labor Turnover—January 2014*. News Release, March 11.

Burke, Peter J. 2006. "Identity Change." *Social Psychology Quarterly* 69:81–96.

Burke, Peter J., and Jan E. Stets. 2009. *Identity Theory*. New York: Oxford University Press.

Burt, Ronald. 1987. "Social Contagion and Innovation: Cohesion Versus Structural Equivalence." *American Journal of Sociology* 92:1287–1335.

———. 1988. "The Stability of American Markets." *American Journal of Sociology* 94:356–395.

———. 1992. *Structural Holes: The Social Structure of Competition*. Cambridge, MA: Harvard University Press.

———. 2004. "Structural Holes and Good Ideas." *American Journal of Sociology* 110:349–399.

Camic, Charles, Neil Gross, and Michèle Lamont, eds. 2011. *Social Knowledge in the Making*. Chicago: University of Chicago Press.

Capatti, Alberto, and Massimo Montanari. 1999. *Italian Cuisine: A Cultural History*. New York: Columbia University Press.

Capuzzi Simon, Cecilia. 2014. "Culinary Schools Speed the Rise of Hopeful Chefs." *New York Times*, March 18.

Carroll, Glenn R., and Karl Mayer. 1984. "Organizational Effects in the Wage Attainment Process." *Social Science Journal* 21:5–22.

Carroll, Glenn R., and Karl Mayer. 1986. "Job-Shift Patterns in the Federal Republic of Germany: The Effects of Social Class, Industrial Sector, and Organizational Size." *American Sociological Review* 51:323–341.

Carroll, Glenn R., and Dennis Ray Wheaton. 2009. "The Organizational Construction of Authenticity: An Examination of Contemporary Food and Dining in the U.S." *Research in Organizational Behavior* 29:255–282.

Cerulo, Karen. 2006. *Never Saw It Coming: Cultural Challenges to Envisioning the Worst*. Chicago: University of Chicago Press.

———. 2010. "Mining the Intersections of Cognitive Sociology and Neuroscience." *Poetics* 38:115–132.

Chaiken, Shelly, and Yaacov Trope. 1999. *Dual-Process Theories in Social Psychology*. New York: Guilford Press.

Chang, David, Peter Meehan, and Chris Ying, eds. 2012. "Cooks and Chefs." *Lucky Peach*, no. 3.

———, eds. 2013. "Cooks and Chefs 2.0." *Lucky Peach*, no. 9.

Cheminski, Rudolph. 2005. *The Perfectionist: Life and Death in Haute Cuisine*. New York: Gotham Books.

Child, John. 1974. "Organization, Management and Adaptiveness." Working paper, University of Aston.

Clemens, Elisabeth. 1997. *The People's Lobby: Organizational Innovation and the Rise of Interest Group Politics in the United States, 1890–1925*. Chicago: University of Chicago Press.

Clemens, Elisabeth, and James Cook. 1999. "Politics and Institutionalism: Explaining Durability and Change." *Annual Review of Sociology* 25:441–466.

Clemens, Elisabeth, Walter Powell, Kris McIlwaine, and Dina Okamoto. 1995. "Careers in Print: Books, Journals, and Scholarly Reputations." *American Journal of Sociology* 101:433–494.

Coleman, James. 1990. *Foundations of Social Theory*. Cambridge, MA: Harvard University Press.

Coleman, James, Elihu Katz, and Herbert Menzel. 1957. "The Diffusion of an Innovation Among Physicians." *Sociometry* 20:253–270.

Collins, Randall. 1998. *The Sociology of Philosophies: A Global Theory of Intellectual Change*. Cambridge, MA: Harvard University Press.

Cooley, Charles H. [1902] 2006. *Human Nature and the Social Order*. New Brunswick, NJ: Transaction.

Coser, Lewis, Charles Kadushin, and Walter Powell. 1982. *Books: The Culture and Commerce of Publishing*. New York: Basic Books.

D'Andrade, Roy. 1989. "Cultural Cognition." In *Foundations of Cognitive Science*, edited by Michael I. Posner. Cambridge, MA: MIT Press.

———. 1992. "Schemas and Motivation." In *Human Motives and Cultural Models*, edited by Roy D'Andrade and Claudia Strauss. Cambridge, UK: Cambridge University Press.

———. 1995. *The Development of Cognitive Anthropology*. Cambridge, UK: Cambridge University Press.

Daft, Richard L., and Karl E. Weick. 1984. "Toward a Model of Organizations as Interpretation Systems." *Academy of Management Review* 9:284–295.

Dalton, Benjamin. 2004. "Creativity, Habit, and the Social Products of Creative Action: Revising Joas, Incorporating Bourdieu." *Sociological Theory* 22:603–622.

de Certeau, Michel. 1984. *The Practice of Everyday Life*. Berkeley: University of California Press.

Demo, David. 1992. "The Self-Concept over Time: Research Issues and Directions." *Annual Review of Sociology* 18:303–326.

Dennett, Daniel. 2003. "Who's on First?: Heterophenomenology Explained." *Journal of Consciousness Studies* 10:19–30.

DeWall, C. Nathan, Roy F. Baumeister, and E. J. Masicampo. 2008. "Evidence That Logical Reasoning Depends on Conscious Processing." *Consciousness and Cognition* 17:628–645.

Dewey, John. [1922] 2002. *Human Nature and Conduct*. New York: Modern Library.

———. 1931. *Ethics*. New York: Henry Holt.

———. [1934] 2005. *Art as Experience*. New York: Perigee.

———. [1939] 1967. *Theory of Valuation*. Chicago: University of Chicago Press.

Di Stefano, Giada, Andrew A. King, and Gianmario Verona. 2014. "Kitchen Confidential? Norms for the Use of Transferred Knowledge in Gourmet Cuisine." *Strategic Management Journal* 35:1645–1670.

DiMaggio, Paul. 1987. "Classification in Art." *American Sociological Review* 52:440–455.

———. 1991. "Constructing an Organizational Field as a Professional Project: The Case of U.S. Art Museums." In *The New Institutionalism in Organizational Analysis*, edited by Walter J. Powell and Paul DiMaggio. Chicago: University of Chicago Press.

———. 1997. "Culture and Cognition." *Annual Review of Sociology* 23:263–287.

———. 2002. "Why Cognitive (and Cultural) Sociology Needs Cognitive Psychology." In *Culture in Mind: Toward a Sociology of Culture and Cognition*, edited by Karen Cerulo. New York: Routledge.

DiMaggio, Paul, and Toqir Mukhtar. 2004. "Arts Participation as Cultural Capital in the United States, 1982–2002: Signs of Decline?" *Poetics* 32:169–194.

DiMaggio, Paul, and Walter Powell. 1983. "The Iron Cage Revisited: Institutional Isomorphism and Collective Rationality in Organizational Fields." *American Sociological Review* 48:147–160.

———. 1991. "Introduction." In *The New Institutionalism in Organizational Analysis*, edited by Paul DiMaggio and Walter Powell. Chicago: University of Chicago Press.

Douglas, Mary. 1986. *How Institutions Think*. Syracuse, NY: Syracuse University Press.

Dowd, Timothy. 2004. "Concentration and Diversity Revisited: Production Logics and the U.S. Mainstream Recording Market, 1940–1990." *Social Forces* 82:1411–1455.

Dreyfus, Hubert, and Sean D. Kelly. 2007. "Heterophenomenology: Heavy-Handed Sleight-of-Hand." *Phenomenology and the Cognitive Sciences* 6:45–55.

Eliasoph, Nina. 1998. *Avoiding Politics: How Americans Produce Apathy in Everyday Life*. Cambridge, UK: Cambridge University Press.

Eliasoph, Nina, and Paul Lichterman. 2003. "Culture in Interaction." *American Journal of Sociology* 108:735–794.

Elqayam, Shira, and David Over. 2012. "Probabilities, Beliefs, and Dual Processing: The Paradigm Shift in the Psychology of Reasoning." *Mind and Society* 11:27–40.

Elsbach, Kimberly, and Francis Flynn. 2013. "Creative Collaboration and the Self-Concept: A Study of Toy Designers." *Journal of Management Studies* 50:515–544.

Emirbayer, Mustafa, and Victoria Johnson. 2008. "Bourdieu and Organizational Analysis." *Theory and Society* 37:1–44.

Emirbayer, Mustafa, and Ann Mische. 1998. "What Is Agency?" *American Journal of Sociology* 103:962–1023.

Epstein, Seymour. 1973. "The Self-Concept Revisited: Or a Theory of a Theory." *American Psychologist* 28:404–416.

Erickson, Bonnie. 1996. "Culture, Class, and Connections." *American Journal of Sociology* 102:217–251.

———. 2007. "The Crisis in Culture and Inequality." In *Engaging Art: The Next Great Transformation of America's Cultural Life*, edited by Steven J. Tepper and Bill Ivey. New York: Routledge.

Escoffier, Auguste. 1979. *The Complete Guide to the Art of Modern Cookery: The First Translation into English in Its Entirety of "Le Guide Culinaire."* Translated by H. L. Cracknell and R. J. Kaufman. London: Heinemann.

Espeland, Wendy N., and Michael Sauder. 2007. "Rankings and Reactivity: How Public Measures Recreate Social Worlds." *American Journal of Sociology* 113:1–40.

Espeland, Wendy N., and Mitchell L. Stevens. 1998. "Commensuration as a Social Process." *Annual Review of Sociology* 24:313–343.

Evans, James A. 2010. "Industry Collaboration, Scientific Sharing, and the Dissemination of Knowledge." *Social Studies of Science* 40:757–791.

Evans, Jonathan St. B. T. 2010. *Thinking Twice: Two Minds in One Brain*. Oxford, UK: Oxford University Press.

Evans, Jonathan St. B. T. 2012. "Spot the Difference: Distinguishing Between Two Kinds of Processing." *Mind and Society* 11:121–131.

Farrell, Michael P. 2001. *Collaborative Circles: Friendship Dynamics and Creative Work*. Chicago: University of Chicago Press.

Farrer, James, ed. 2010. *Globalization, Food and Social Identities in the Pacific Region*. Tokyo: Sophia University Institute of Comparative Culture.

Fauchart, Emmanuelle, and Eric von Hippel. 2006. "Norms-Based Intellectual Property Systems: The Case of French Chefs." *Organization Science* 19:187–201.

Faulkner, Robert. [1983] 1987. *Music on Demand: Composers and Careers in the Hollywood Film Industry*. New Brunswick, NJ: Transaction Books.

———. 2006. "Shedding Culture." In *Art from Start to Finish*, edited by Howard F. Becker, Robert Faulkner, and Barbara Kirshenblatt-Gimblett. Chicago: University of Chicago Press.

Faulkner, Robert, and Howard Becker. 2009. *"Do You Know . . . ?": The Jazz Repertoire in Action*. Chicago: University of Chicago Press.

Ferguson, Priscilla Parkhurst. 1998. "A Cultural Field in the Making: Gastronomy in 19th Century France." *American Journal of Sociology* 104:597–641.

————. 2004. *Accounting for Taste: The Triumph of French Cuisine*. Chicago: University of Chicago Press.

Ferguson, Priscilla Parkhurst, and Sharon Zukin. 1998. "The Careers of Chefs." In *Eating Culture*, edited by Ron Scapp and Brian Seitz. Albany, NY: SUNY Press.

Ferree, Myra Marx, and David A. Merrill. 2000. "Hot Movements, Cold Cognition: Thinking About Social Movements in Gendered Frames." *Contemporary Sociology* 29:454–462.

Fine, Gary Alan. 1990. "Organizational Time: Temporal Demands and the Experience of Work in Restaurant Kitchens." *Social Forces* 69:95–114.

————. 1992. "Agency, Structure, and Comparative Contexts: Toward a Synthetic Interactionism." *Symbolic Interaction* 15:87–108.

————. 1995. "Wittgenstein's Kitchen: Sharing Meaning in Restaurant Work." *Theory and Society* 24:245–269.

————. 1996. *Kitchens: The Culture of Restaurant Work*. Berkeley: University of California Press.

Fischler, Claude. 1990. *L'Homnivore*. Paris: Odile Jacob.

Fishman, Robert M., and Omar Lizardo. 2013. "How Macro-Historical Change Shapes Cultural Taste: Legacies of Democratization in Spain and Portugal." *American Sociological Review* 78:213–239.

Fligstein, Neil. 1996. "Markets as Politics: A Political-Cultural Approach to Market Institutions." *American Sociological Review* 61:656–673.

Fligstein, Neil, and Doug McAdam. 2011. "Toward a General Theory of Strategic Action Fields." *Sociological Theory* 29:1–26.

————. 2012. *A Theory of Fields*. New York: Oxford University Press.

Fodor, Jerry A., and Zenon W. Pylyshyn. 1988. "Connectionism and Cognitive Architecture: A Critical Analysis." *Cognition* 28:3–71.

————. 1995. "Connectionism and Cognitive Architecture: A Critical Analysis." In *Connectionism: Debates on Psychological Explanation*, edited by Cynthia Macdonald and Graham Macdonald. Oxford, UK: Basil Blackwell.

Frank, Michael J., Michael X. Cohen, and Alan G. Sanfey. 2009. "Multiple Systems in Decision Making: A Neurocomputational Perspective." *Current Directions in Psychological Science* 18:73–77.

Frickel, Scott, and Neil Gross. 2005. "A General Theory of Scientific/Intellectual Movements." *American Sociological Review* 70:204–232.

Friedland, Roger. 2009. "The Endless Fields of Pierre Bourdieu." *Organization* 16:887–917.

Friedland, Roger, and Robert Alford. 1991. "Bringing Society Back In: Symbols, Practices, and Institutional Contradictions." In *The New Institutionalism in Organizational Analysis*, edited by Walter Powell and Paul DiMaggio. Chicago: University of Chicago Press.

Galenson, David. 2007. *Old Masters and Young Geniuses: The Two Life Cycles of Artistic Creativity*. Princeton, NJ: Princeton University Press.

Gardner, Howard. 1993. *Creating Minds: An Anatomy of Creativity Seen Through the*

Lives of Freud, Einstein, Picasso, Stravinsky, Eliot, Graham, and Gandhi. New York: Basic Books.

Geertz, Clifford. 1973. *The Interpretation of Cultures*. New York: Basic Books.

Gieryn, Thomas. 1983. "Boundary-Work and the Demarcation of Science from Non-Science: Strains and Interests in Professional Ideologies of Scientists." *American Sociological Review* 48:781–795.

Giuffre, Katherine. 1999. "Sandpiles of Opportunity: Success in the Art World." *Social Forces* 77:815–832.

Glynn, Mary Ann. 2000. "When Cymbals Become Symbols: Conflict over Organizational Identity Within a Symphony Orchestra." *Organization Science* 11:285–298.

Glynn, Mary Ann, and Rikki Abzug. 2002. "Institutionalizing Identity: Symbolic Isomorphism and Organizational Names." *Academy of Management Journal* 45:267–280.

Goffman, Erving. 1956. "Embarrassment and Social Organization." *American Journal of Sociology* 62:264–271.

———. 1959. *The Presentation of Self in Everyday Life*. New York: Anchor Books, Doubleday.

———. 1961. *Asylums*. Garden City, NY: Doubleday.

———. 1967. *Interaction Ritual: Essays on Face-to-Face Behavior*. New York: Pantheon Books.

Goodman, Nelson. 1955. *Fact, Fiction, and Forecast*. Cambridge, MA: Harvard University Press.

Gould, Roger. 1993. "Collective Action and Network Structure." *American Sociological Review* 58:182–196.

Granovetter, Mark. 1974. *Getting a Job: A Study of Contacts and Careers*. Cambridge, MA: Harvard University Press.

———. 2005. "The Impact of Social Structure on Economic Outcomes." *Journal of Economic Perspectives* 19:33–50.

Green, Adam Isaiah. 2008. "The Social Organization of Desire: The Sexual Fields Approach." *Sociological Theory* 26:25–50.

———. 2011. "Playing the (Sexual) Field: The Interactional Basis of Sexual Stratification." *Social Psychology Quarterly* 74:244–266.

Greenwald, Anthony G., and Mahzarin R. Banaji. 1995. "Implicit Social Cognition: Attitudes, Self-Esteem, and Stereotypes." *Psychological Review* 102:4–27.

Gross, Neil. 2002. "Becoming a Pragmatist Philosopher: Status, Self-Concept, and Intellectual Choice." *American Sociological Review* 67:52–76.

———. 2008. *Richard Rorty: The Making of an American Philosopher*. Chicago: University of Chicago Press.

Hachen, David. 1990. "Three Models of Job Mobility in Labor Markets." *Work and Occupations* 17:320–354.

Hahl, Oliver, and Renée Richardson Gosline. 2011. "When Status Is Not Enough: How High-Status Actors Access the Nonconformity Privilege." Working paper, Sloan School of Management, Massachusetts Institute of Technology.

Haidt, Jonathan. 2001. "The Emotional Dog and Its Rational Tail: A Social Institutionist Approach to Moral Judgment." *Psychological Review* 108:814–834.

———. 2005. *The Happiness Hypothesis: Finding Modern Truth in Ancient Wisdom.* New York: Basic Books.

Hallett, Tim, and Marc J. Ventresca. 2006. "Inhabited Institutions: Social Interactions and Organizational Forms in Gouldner's *Patterns of Industrial Bureaucracy.*" *Theory and Society* 35:213–236.

Hamilton, Dorothy, and Patric Kuh. 2008. *Chef's Story: 27 Chefs Talk About What Got Them into the Kitchen.* New York: Harper Perennial.

Haveman, Heather, and Hayagreeva Rao. 1997. "Structuring a Theory of Moral Sentiments: Institutional and Organizational Coevolution in the Early Thrift Industry." *American Journal of Sociology* 102:1606–1651.

Hechter, Michael, and Satoshi Kanazawa. 1997. "Sociological Rational Choice Theory." *Annual Review of Sociology* 23:191–214.

Hedberg, Bo. 1981. "How Organizations Learn and Unlearn." In *Handbook of Organizational Design,* edited by Paul C. Nystrom and William H. Starbuck. New York: Oxford University Press.

Hegel, Georg Wilhelm Friedrich. [1837] 1997. *Lectures on the Philosophy of History.* Translated by Robert S. Hartman. Englewood Cliffs, NJ: Prentice-Hall.

Hennion, Antoine. 2003. "L'innovation comme écriture de l'entreprise: récits d'innovation au sein d'une enterprise de services." In *Encyclopédie de l'innovation,* edited by Philippe Mustar and Hervé Penan. Paris: Editions Économica.

Higgins, E. Tory. 1987. "Self-Discrepancy: A Theory Relating Self and Affect." *Psychological Review* 94:319–340.

Hirsch, Paul. 1972. "Processing Fads and Fashions: An Organization-Set Analysis of Cultural Industry Systems." *American Journal of Sociology* 77:639–659.

Hollingsworth, J. Rogers. 2000. "The Style and Mode of Research Organizations: Innovation in Science." Keynote Address to the Board of Trustees and Members of the Corporation, Neurosciences Research Foundation, La Jolla, CA.

Hollows, Joanne. 2003. "Oliver's Twist: Leisure, Labour and Domestic Masculinity in *The Naked Chef.*" *International Journal of Cultural Studies* 6:229–248.

Hosking, Richard, ed. 2006. *Authenticity in the Kitchen: Proceedings of the Oxford Symposium on Food and Cookery 2005.* Totnes, UK: Prospect Books.

Hsu, Greta. 2006. "Evaluative Schemas and the Attention of Critics in the US Film Industry." *Industrial and Corporate Change* 15:467–496.

Hsu, Greta, and Michael T. Hannan. 2005. "Identities, Genres, and Organizational Forms." *Organization Science* 16:474–490.

Hsu, Greta, Michael T. Hannan, and László Pólos. 2011. "Typecasting, Legitimation, and Form Emergence: A Formal Theory." *Sociological Theory* 29:97–123.

Husserl, Edmund. 1960. *Cartesian Meditations: An Introduction to Phenomenology.* The Hague: Martinus Nijhoff.

Hutchins, Edwin. 1995. *Cognition in the Wild.* Cambridge, MA: MIT Press.

Joas, Hans. 1996. *The Creativity of Action.* Chicago: University of Chicago Press.

Johnston, Josée, and Shyon Baumann. 2007. "Democracy Versus Distinction: A

Study of Omnivorousness in Gourmet Food Writing." *American Journal of Sociology* 113:165–204.

———. 2010. *Foodies: Democracy and Distinction in the Gourmet Foodscape*. New York: Routledge.

Kadushin, Charles. 1969. "The Professional Self-Concept of Music Students." *American Journal of Sociology* 75:389–404.

Kandel, Eric R., James H. Schwartz, and Thomas M. Jessell, eds. 1995. *Essentials of Neural Science and Behavior*. Norwalk, CT: Appleton & Lange.

Karpik, Lucien. 2010. *Valuing the Unique: The Economics of Singularities*. Princeton, NJ: Princeton University Press.

Katz, Jack. 1999. *How Emotions Work*. Chicago: University of Chicago Press.

Khong, Rachel. 2011. "Nobody Doesn't Love a Cake with a Runny Center." *Lucky Peach*, no. 3: 80–83.

Knorr Cetina, Karin. 1997. "Sociality with Objects: Social Relations in Postsocial Knowledge Societies." *Theory, Culture and Society* 14:1–30.

Kovács, Balázs, Glenn R. Carroll, and David W. Lehman. 2013. "Authenticity and Consumer Value Ratings: Empirical Tests from the Restaurant Domain." *Organization Science* Articles in Advance: 1–21.

Lahire, Bernard. 2003. "From the Habitus to an Individual Heritage of Dispositions. Towards a Sociology at the Level of the Individual." *Poetics* 31:329–355.

Lamont, Michèle. 1992. *Money, Morals, and Manners: The Culture of the French and the American Upper-Middle Class*. Chicago: University of Chicago Press.

———. 2009. *How Professors Think: Inside the Curious World of Academic Judgment*. Cambridge, MA: Harvard University Press.

———. 2012. "Toward a Comparative Sociology of Valuation and Evaluation." *Annual Review of Sociology* 38:201–221.

Lamont, Michèle, and Marcel Fournier, eds. 1992. *Cultivating Differences: Symbolic Boundaries and the Making of Inequality*. Chicago: University of Chicago Press.

Lamont, Michèle, Joshua Guetzkow, and Grégoire Mallard. 2004. "What Is Originality in the Humanities and the Social Sciences?" *American Sociological Review* 69:190–210.

Lamont, Michèle, and Virág Molnár. 2002. "The Study of Boundaries in the Social Sciences." *Annual Review of Sociology* 28:167–195.

Larousse Gastronomique. 2001. New York: Clarkson Potter.

Larson, Magali Sarfati. 1977. *The Rise of Professionalism: A Sociological Analysis*. Berkeley: University of California Press.

———. 2005. "Professions as Disciplinary Cultures." In *The Blackwell Companion to the Sociology of Culture*, edited by Mark Jacobs and Nancy W. Hanrahan. Oxford, UK: Blackwell.

Latour, Bruno. 2005. *Reassembling the Social: An Introduction to Actor-Network Theory*. New York: Oxford University Press.

Laumann, Edward O., Peter V. Marsden, and Joseph Galaskiewicz. 1977. "Community-Elite Influence Structures: Extension of a Network Approach." *American Journal of Sociology* 83:594–631.

Laumann, Edward O., and Franz Urban Pappi. 1973. "New Directions in the Study of Community Elites." *American Sociological Review* 38:212–230.

Lena, Jennifer C. 2012. *Banding Together: How Communities Create Genres in Popular Music.* Princeton, NJ: Princeton University Press.

Leschziner, Vanina. 2006. "Epistemic Foundations of Cuisine: A Socio-cognitive Study of the Configuration of Cuisine in Historical Perspective." *Theory and Society* 35:421–443.

———. 2007. "Kitchen Stories: Patterns of Recognition in Contemporary High Cuisine." *Sociological Forum* 22:77–101.

———. 2010. "Cooking Logics: Cognition and Reflexivity in the Culinary Field." In *Globalization, Food and Social Identities in the Pacific Region*, edited by James Farrer. Tokyo: Sophia University Institute of Comparative Culture.

Leschziner, Vanina, and Andrew Dakin. 2011. "Theorizing Cuisine from Medieval to Modern Times: Cognitive Structures, the Biology of Taste, and Culinary Conventions." *Collapse: Philosophical Research and Development* 7:347–376.

Leschziner, Vanina, and Adam Isaiah Green. 2013. "Thinking About Food and Sex: Deliberate Cognition in the Routine Practices of a Field." *Sociological Theory* 31:116–144.

Lévi-Strauss, Claude. [1962] 1968. *The Savage Mind.* Chicago: University of Chicago Press.

———. 1973. "Structuralism and Ecology." *Social Science Information* 12:7–23.

Lichterman, Paul. 2005. *Elusive Togetherness: Church Groups Trying to Bridge America's Divisions.* Princeton, NJ: Princeton University Press.

Lieberman, Matthew D. 2007. "Social Cognitive Neuroscience: A Review of Core Processes." *Annual Review of Psychology* 58:259–289.

Lizardo, Omar. 2014. "Omnivorousness as the Bridging of Cultural Holes: A Measurement Strategy." *Theory and Society* 43:395–419.

Lizardo, Omar, and Sara Skiles. 2008. "Cultural Consumption in the Fine and Popular Arts Realms." *Sociology Compass* 2:485–502.

———. 2009. "Highbrow Omnivorousness on the Small Screen? Cultural Industry Systems and Patterns of Cultural Choice in Europe." *Poetics* 37:1–23.

———. 2012. "Reconceptualizing and Theorizing 'Omnivorousness': Genetic and Relational Mechanisms." *Sociological Theory* 30:263–282.

Lizardo, Omar, and Michael Strand. 2010. "Skills, Toolkits, Contexts and Institutions: Clarifying the Relationship Between Different Approaches to Cognition in Cultural Sociology." *Poetics* 38:205–228.

Lloyd, Geoffrey E. R. 1966. *Polarity and Analogy: Two Types of Argumentation in Early Greek Thought.* Cambridge, UK: Cambridge University Press.

Long, J. Scott. 1978. "Productivity and Position in the Academic Career." *American Sociological Review* 43:889–908.

Long, J. Scott, Paul D. Allison, and Robert McGinnis. 1979. "Entrance into the Academic Career." *American Sociological Review* 44:816–830.

Lounsbury, Michael. 2002. "Institutional Transformation and Status Mobility: The

Professionalization of the Field of Finance." *Academy of Management Journal* 45:255–266.

Lounsbury, Michael, and Mary Ann Glynn. 2001. "Cultural Entrepreneurship: Stories, Legitimacy, and the Acquisition of Resources." *Strategic Management Journal* 22:545–564.

Macchi, Laura, David Over, and Riccardo Viale. 2012. "Special Issue on: Dual Process Theories of Human Thought: The Debate." *Mind and Society* 11:1–2.

March, James G. 1982. "Theories of Choice and Making Decisions." *Society* 20:29–39.

———. 1991. "Exploration and Exploitation in Organizational Learning." *Organization Science* 2:71–87.

Markus, Hazel R., and Keith P. Sentis. 1982. "The Self in Social Information Processing." In *Social Psychological Perspectives on the Self*, edited by Jerry M. Suls. Hillsdale, NJ: Lawrence Erlbaum Associates

Markus, Hazel R., and Elissa Wurf. 1987. "The Dynamic Self–Concept: A Social Psychological Perspective." *Annual Review of Psychology* 1987:299–337.

Marsden, Peter, and Karen Campbell. 1990. "Recruitment and Selection Processes: The Organizational Side of Job Searches." In *Social Mobility and Social Structure*, edited by Ronald Breiger. Cambridge, UK: Cambridge University Press.

Martin, John Levi. 2003. "What Is Field Theory?" *American Journal of Sociology* 109:1–49.

———. 2009. *Social Structures*. Princeton, NJ: Princeton University Press.

———. 2010. "Life's a Beach but You're an Ant, and Other Unwelcome News for the Sociology of Culture." *Poetics* 38:229–244.

———. 2011. *The Explanation of Social Action*. New York: Oxford University Press.

Marx, Karl. [1859] 1970. *A Contribution to the Critique of Political Economy*. New York: International Publishers.

———. [1867] 1889. *Capital: A Critical Analysis of Capitalist Production*. Translated by Samuel Moore and Edward Aveling. New York: Appleton.

McDonnell, Terence E. 2014. "Drawing Out Culture: Productive Methods to Measure Cognition and Resonance." *Theory and Society* 43:247–274.

McGee, Harold. 2004. *On Food and Cooking: The Science and Lore of the Kitchen*. New York: Scribner.

McLaughlin, Neil. 2001. "Optimal Marginality: Innovation and Orthodoxy in Fromm's Revision of Psychoanalysis." *Sociological Quarterly* 42:271–290.

McLean, Paul D. 2007. *The Art of the Network: Strategic Interaction and Patronage in Renaissance Florence*. Durham, NC: Duke University Press.

Mead, George H. [1934] 1967. *Mind, Self, and Society: From the Standpoint of a Social Behaviorist*. Chicago: University of Chicago Press.

Merleau-Ponty, Maurice. 1962. *Phenomenology of Perception*. New York: Routledge.

Merton, Robert K. 1961. *Social Theory and Social Structure*. Glencoe, IL: Free Press.

Merzenich, Michael, and Koichi Sameshima. 1993. "Cortical Plasticity and Memory." *Current Opinion in Neurobiology* 3:187–196.

Meyer, John W., and Brian Rowan. 1977. "Institutionalized Organizations: Formal Structure as Myth and Ceremony." *American Journal of Sociology* 83:340–363.

Mische, Ann. 2008. *Partisan Publics: Communication and Contention Across Brazilian Youth Activist Networks*. Princeton, NJ: Princeton University Press.

———. 2009. "Projects and Possibilities: Researching Futures in Action." *Sociological Forum* 24:694–704.

Mohr, John. 1994. "Soldiers, Mothers, Tramps and Others: Discourse Roles in the 1907 New York City Charity Directory." *Poetics* 22:327–357.

Mohr, John, and Vincent Duquenne. 1997. "The Duality of Culture and Practice: Poverty Relief in New York City, 1888–1917." *Theory and Society* 26:305–356.

Molotch, Harvey. [2003] 2005. *Where Stuff Comes From: How Toasters, Toilets, Cars, Computers, and Many Other Things Come to Be as They Are*. New York: Routledge.

Monin, Phillippe, and Rodolphe Durand. 2003. "Identity Jumpshipping in French Elite Restaurants: The Influence of Nested and Crosscutting Identities." *Cahiers de Recherche*, École de Management Lyon.

Morrill, Calvin. 2001. "Institutional Change Through Interstitial Emergence: The Growth of Alternative Dispute Resolution in American Law, 1965–1995." Unpublished manuscript, University of Arizona.

Morse, Stan, and Kenneth J. Gergen. 1970. "Social Comparison, Self-Consistency, and the Concept of Self." *Journal of Personality and Social Psychology* 16:148–156.

Moskin, Julia. 2014. "A Change in the Kitchen." *New York Times*, January 22.

Mulkay, Michael J. 1972. *The Social Process of Innovation: A Study in the Sociology of Science*. London: Macmillan.

Mullaney, Jamie. 2005. *Everyone Is NOT Doing It: Abstinence and Personal Identity*. Chicago: University of Chicago Press.

Myhrvold, Nathan, Chris Young, and Maxime Bilet. 2011. *Modernist Cuisine: The Art and Science of Cooking*. Bellevue, WA: Cooking Lab.

National Restaurant Association. 2014. *Restaurant Operations Report*. 2013–2014 ed. Washington, DC: National Restaurant Association and Deloitte.

Needham, Rodney, ed. 1973. *Right and Left: Essays on Dual Symbolic Classification*. Chicago: University of Chicago Press.

———. 1979. *Symbolic Classification*. Santa Monica, CA: Goodyear.

Neisser, Ulric. 1967. *Cognitive Psychology*. Englewood Cliffs, NJ: Prentice-Hall.

Newell, Allen, and Herbert A. Simon. 1972. *Human Problem Solving*. Englewood Cliffs, NJ: Prentice-Hall.

Norman, Donald A. 1986. "Reflections on Cognition and Parallel Distributed Processing." In James L. McClelland, David E. Rumelhart, and the PDP Research Group, *Parallel Distributed Processing: Explorations in the Microstructure of Cognition*. Vol. 2. Cambridge, MA: MIT Press.

Oaksford, Mike, and Nick Chater. 2012. "Dual Processes, Probabilities, and Cognitive Architecture." *Mind and Society* 11:15–26.

Oliver, Pamela, and Hank Johnston. 2000. "What a Good Idea! Ideology and Frames in Social Movement Research." *Mobilization* 5: 37–54.

Ortner, Sherry B. 1984. "Theory in Anthropology Since the Sixties." *Comparative Studies in Society and History* 26:126–166.

Owen-Smith, Jason. 2001. "Managing Laboratory Work Through Skepticism: Processes of Evaluation and Control." *American Sociological Review* 66:427–452.

Owen-Smith, Jason, and Walter Powell. 2004. "Knowledge Networks as Channels and Conduits: The Effects of Spillovers in the Boston Biotechnology Community." *Organization Science* 15:5–21.

Pachuki, Mark A., Sabrina Pendergrass, and Michèle Lamont. 2007. "Boundary Processes: Recent Theoretical Developments and New Contributions." *Poetics* 35:331–351.

Parkin, Frank, ed. 1974. *The Social Analysis of Class Structure*. London: Tavistock.

Parsa, H. G., John T. Self, David Njite, and Tiffany King. 2005. "Why Restaurants Fail." *Cornell Hotel and Restaurant Administration Quarterly* 46:304–322.

Parsons, Talcott. [1937] 1968. *The Structure of Social Action: A Study in Social Theory with Special Reference to a Group of Recent European Writers*. New York: Free Press.

———. 1964. *Social Structure and Personality*. New York: Free Press.

Pearlman, Alison. 2013. *Smart Casual: The Transformation of Gourmet Restaurant Style in America*. Chicago: University of Chicago Press.

People Report. 2013. "Workforce Index Q1." Dallas, TX: TDn2k.

Peterson, Richard. 1997. *Creating Country Music: Fabricating Authenticity*. Chicago: University of Chicago Press.

———. 2005. "Problems in Comparative Research: The Problem of Omnivorousness." *Poetics* 33:257–282.

Peterson, Richard, and N. Anand. 2004. "The Production of Culture Perspective." *Annual Review of Sociology* 30:311–334.

Peterson, Richard, and Roger Kern. 1996. "Changing Highbrow Taste: From Snob to Omnivore." *American Sociological Review* 61:900–907.

Peterson, Richard, and Gabriel Rossman. 2007. "Changing Arts Audiences: Capitalizing on Omnivorousness." In *Engaging Art: The Next Great Transformation of America's Cultural Life*, edited by Steven J. Tepper and Bill Ivey. New York: Routledge.

Phillips, Damon, and David Owens. 2004. "Incumbents, Innovation, and Competence: The Emergence of Recorded Jazz, 1920 to 1929." *Poetics* 32:281–295.

Phillips, Damon, Catherine Turco, and Ezra Zuckerman. 2013. "Betrayal as Market Barrier: Identity-Based Limits to Diversification Among High-Status Corporate Law Firms." *American Journal of Sociology* 118:1023–1054.

Phillips, Damon, and Ezra Zuckerman. 2001. "Middle Status Conformity: Theoretical Restatement and Empirical Demonstration in Two Markets." *American Journal of Sociology* 107:379–429.

Podolny, Joel. 1993. "A Status-Based Model of Market Competition." *American Journal of Sociology* 98:829–872.

———. 2005. *Status Signals: A Sociological Study of Market Competition*. Princeton, NJ: Princeton University Press.

Porac, Joseph F., and Howard Thomas. 1994. "Cognitive Categorization and Subjective Rivalry Among Retailers in a Small City." *Journal of Applied Psychology* 79:54–66.

Porac, Joseph F., Howard Thomas, and Charles Baden-Fuller. 2011. "Competitive

Groups as Cognitive Communities: The Case of Scottish Knitwear Manufacturers Revisited." *Journal of Management Studies* 48:646–664.

Porac, Joseph F., Howard Thomas, Fiona Wilson, Douglas Paton, and Alaina Kanfer. 1995. "Rivalry and the Industry Model of Scottish Knitwear Producers." *Administrative Science Quarterly* 40:203–227.

Powell, Walter. 1985. *Getting into Print: The Decision-Making Process of Scholarly Publishing*. Chicago: University of Chicago Press.

Powell, Walter, Douglas R. White, Kenneth W. Koput, and Jason Owen-Smith. 2005. "Network Dynamics and Field Evolution: The Growth of Interorganizational Collaboration in the Life Sciences." *American Journal of Sociology* 110:1132–1205.

Quinlan, Philip T. 1991. *Connectionism and Psychology*. Chicago: University of Chicago Press.

Rao, Hayagreeva. 1994. "The Social Construction of Reputation: Certification Contests, Legitimation, and the Survival of Organizations in the American Automobile Industry, 1895–1912." *Strategic Management Journal* 15:29–44.

Rao, Hayagreeva, Philippe Monin, and Rodolphe Durand. 2003. "Institutional Change in Toque Ville: Nouvelle Cuisine as an Identity Movement in French Gastronomy." *American Journal of Sociology* 108:795–843.

———. 2005. "Border Crossing: Bricolage and the Erosion of Categorical Boundaries in French Gastronomy." *American Sociological Review* 70:968–991.

Raustiala, Kal, and Christopher Sprigman. 2009. "The Piracy Paradox Revisited." *Stanford Law Review* 61:1201–1225.

Ray, Krishnendu. 2010. "A Taste for Ethnic Difference: American Gustatory Imagination in a Globalizing World." In *Globalization, Food and Social Identities in the Pacific Region*, edited by James Farrer. Tokyo: Sophia University Institute of Comparative Culture.

———. 2011. "Dreams of Pakistani Grill and Vada Pao in Manhattan: Reinscribing the Immigrant Body in Metropolitan Discussions of Taste." *Food, Culture and Society* 14:243–273.

Ray, Krishnendu, and Tulasi Srinivas, eds. 2012. *Curried Cultures: Globalization, Food, and South Asia*. Berkeley: University of California Press.

Rickert, Heinrich. 1913. "Vom System der Werte." *Logos* 4:295–327.

Rosch, Eleanor. 1975. "Cognitive Reference Points." *Cognitive Psychology* 7:532–547.

———. 1978. "Principles of Categorization." In *Cognition and Categorization*, edited by Eleanor Rosch and Barbara L. Lloyd. Hillsdale, NJ: Lawrence Erlbaum Associates.

Rosenfeld, Rachel. 1992. "Job Mobility and Career Processes." *Annual Review of Sociology* 18:39–61.

Roser, Matthew, and Michael S. Gazzaniga. 2004. "Automatic Brains—Interpretive Minds." *Current Directions in Psychological Science* 13:56–59.

Ruhlman, Michael. 2001. *The Soul of a Chef: The Journey Towards Perfection*. New York: Penguin Books.

Rumelhart, David E. 1980. "Schemata: The Building Blocks of Cognition." In *Theoretical Issues in Reading Comprehension: Perspectives from Cognitive Psychology, Lin-*

guistics, Artificial Intelligence, and Education, edited by Rand J. Spiro, Bertram C. Bruce, and William F. Brewer. Hillsdale, NJ: Lawrence Erlbaum Associates.

Sahlins, Marshall. 1976. *Culture and Practical Reason*. Chicago: University of Chicago Press.

———. 1981. *Historical Metaphors and Mythical Realities: Structure in the Early History of the Sandwich Islands Kingdom*. Ann Arbor: University of Michigan Press.

———. 1985. *Islands of History*. Chicago: University of Chicago Press.

———. 2000. *Culture in Practice: Selected Essays*. New York: Zone Books.

Santoro, Marco. 2011. "From Bourdieu to Cultural Sociology." *Cultural Sociology* 5:3–23.

Savage, Mike, and Modesto Gayo. 2011. "Unravelling the Omnivore: A Field Analysis of Contemporary Musical Taste in the United Kingdom." *Poetics* 39:337–357.

Sawyer, R. Keith. 2003. *Group Creativity: Music, Theater, Collaboration*. Mahwah, NJ: Lawrence Erlbaum Associates.

Schütz, Alfred. 1945. "On Multiple Realities." *Philosophy and Phenomenological Research* 5:533–576.

Sewell, William H., Jr. 1992. "A Theory of Structure: Duality, Agency and Transformation." *American Journal of Sociology* 98:1–29.

Shepherd, Gordon M. 2012. *Neurogastronomy: How the Brain Creates Flavor and Why It Matters*. New York: Columbia University Press.

Shingledecker, Clark, David E. Weldon, Kyle Behymer, Benjamin Simpkins, Elizabeth Lerner, Joel Warm, Gerald Matthews, Victore Finomore, Tyler Shaw, and Jennifer S. Murphy. 2010. "Measuring Vigilance Abilities to Enhance Combat Identification Performance." In *Human Factors Issues in Combat Identification*, edited by Dee H. Andrews, Robert P. Herz, and Mark B. Wolf. Farnham, Surrey, UK: Ashgate.

Sifton, Sam. 2010. "A Modern Italian Master." *New York Times*, September 28.

Simmel, Georg. 1904. "Fashion." *The International Quarterly* 10:130–155.

———. 1910. "How Is Society Possible?" *American Journal of Sociology* 16:372–391.

———. 1950. *The Sociology of Georg Simmel*. Translated, edited, and with an introduction by Kurt H. Wolff. New York: Free Press.

———. 1955. *Conflict and the Web of Group-Affiliations*. New York: Free Press.

Smith, D. Randall, and Andrew Abbott. 1983. "A Labor Market Perspective on the Mobility of College Football Coaches." *Social Forces* 61:1147–1167.

Sørensen, Aage B. 1975. "The Structure of Intragenerational Mobility." *American Sociological Review* 40:456–471.

Spilerman, Seymour. 1977. "Careers, Labor Market Structure, and Socioeconomic Achievement." *American Journal of Sociology* 83:551–593.

Spillman, Lyn. 2012. *Solidarity in Strategy: Making Business Meaningful in American Trade Associations*. Chicago: University of Chicago Press.

Stark, David. 2009. *The Sense of Dissonance: Accounts of Worth in Economic Life*. Princeton, NJ: Princeton University Press.

Steinberger, Michael. 2009. *Au Revoir to All That: Food, Wine and the End of France*. Toronto: Doubleday Canada.

Stovel, Katherine, Michael Savage, and Peter Bearman. 1996. "Ascription into

Achievement: Models of Career-Systems at Lloyds Bank, 1890–1970." *American Journal of Sociology* 102:358–399.

Strauss, Claudia, and Naomi Quinn. 1997. *A Cognitive Theory of Cultural Meaning.* Cambridge, UK: Cambridge University Press.

Swann, William B., John J. Griffin, Steven C. Predmore, and Bebe Gaines. 1987. "The Cognitive-Affective Crossfire: When Self-Consistency Confronts Self-Enhancement." *Journal of Personality and Social Psychology* 52:881–889.

Swenson, Rebecca. 2009. "Domestic Divo? Televised Treatments of Masculinity, Femininity and Food." *Critical Studies in Media Communication* 26:36–53.

Swidler, Ann. 1986. "Culture in Action: Symbols and Strategies." *American Sociological Review* 51:273–286.

———. 2003. *Talk of Love: How Culture Matters.* Chicago: University of Chicago Press.

Taylor, Stephanie, and Karen Littleton. 2012. *Contemporary Identities of Creativity and Creative Work.* Surrey, UK: Ashgate.

This, Hervé. 2006. *Molecular Gastronomy: Exploring the Science of Flavor.* New York: Columbia University Press.

Thompson, John B. 2010. *Merchants of Culture: The Publishing Business in the Twenty-First Century.* New York: Plume.

Thompson, Valerie, and Kinga Morsanyi. 2012. "Analytic Thinking: Do You Feel Like it?" *Mind and Society* 11:93–105.

Topolinski, Sascha, and Rolf Reber. 2010. "Gaining Insight into the 'Aha' Experience." *Current Directions in Psychological Science* 19:402–405.

Topolinski, Sascha, and Fritz Strack. 2009. "Scanning the 'Fringe' of Consciousness: What Is Felt and What Is Not Felt in Intuitions about Semantic Coherence." *Consciousness and Cognition* 18:608–618.

Trubek, Amy. 2000. *Haute Cuisine: How the French Invented the Culinary Profession.* Philadelphia: University of Pennsylvania Press.

Tuma, Nancy. 1985. "Effects of Labor Market Structure on Job Shift Patterns." In *Longitudinal Analysis of Labor Market Data*, edited by James J. Heckman and Burton S. Singer. Cambridge, UK: Cambridge University Press.

U.S. Census Bureau. 2014a. "County Business Patterns: 2012." Data released on May 29, 2014. Retrieved from http://www.census.gov/econ/cbp

———. 2014b. "Zip Codes Business Patterns: 2012." Data released on June 12, 2014. Retrieved from http://www.census.gov/econ/cbp

Vaisey, Stephen. 2008a. "Reply to Ann Swidler." *Sociological Forum* 23:619–622.

———. 2008b. "Socrates, Skinner, and Aristotle: Three Ways of Thinking About Culture in Action." *Sociological Forum* 23:603–613.

———. 2009. "Motivation and Justification: A Dual-Process Model of Culture in Action." *American Journal of Sociology* 114:1675–1715.

van Rees, Kees, and Gillis J. Dorleijn. 2001. "The Eighteenth-Century Literary Field in Western Europe: The Interdependence of Material and Symbolic Production and Consumption." *Poetics* 28:331–348.

Velthuis, Olav. 2005. *Talking Prices: Symbolic Meanings of Prices on the Market for Contemporary Art.* Princeton, NJ: Princeton University Press.

Verplanken, Bas, and Rob W. Holland. 2002. "Motivated Decision Making: Effects of Activation and Self-Centrality of Values on Choices and Behavior." *Journal of Personality and Social Psychology* 82:434–447.

Vonnegut, Kurt. 2011. "The People One Knows." In *Palm Sunday: An Autobiographical Collage*. New York: Random House.

Warde, Alan, Lydia Martens, and Wendy Olsen. 1999. "Consumption and the Problem of Variety: Cultural Omnivorousness, Social Distinction and Dining Out." *Sociology* 33:105–127.

Weber, Klaus. 2005. "A Toolkit for Analyzing Corporate Cultural Toolkits." *Poetics* 33:227–252.

Weber, Klaus, Kathryn L. Heinze, and Michaela De Soucey. 2008. "Forage for Thought: Mobilizing Codes in the Movement for Grass-Fed Meat and Dairy Products." *Administrative Science Quarterly* 53:529–567.

Weber, Max. [1920] 1963. *The Sociology of Religion*. Translated by Ephraim Fischoff. Boston: Beacon Press.

———. [1922] 1978. *Economy and Society: An Outline of Interpretive Sociology*. Berkeley: University of California Press.

Webley, Kayla. 2011. "*Top Chef* Dreams: Are Cooking Schools a Rip-Off?" *Time*, July 27.

Wegner, Daniel M., and John A. Bargh. 1998. "Control and Automaticity in Social Life." In *The Handbook of Social Psychology*, edited by Daniel T. Gilbert, Susan T. Fiske and Gardner Lindzey. Boston: McGraw-Hill.

Weick, Karl. 1979. *The Social Psychology of Organizing*. Reading, MA: Addison-Wesley.

———. 1995. *Sensemaking in Organizations*. Thousand Oaks, CA: Sage.

Wells, Pete. 2006. "New Era of the Recipe Burglar." *Food & Wine*, November.

Westby, David. 1960. "The Career Experience of the Symphony Musician." *Social Forces* 38:223–230.

White, Harrison. 1970. *Chains of Opportunity: System Models of Mobility in Organizations*. Cambridge, MA: Harvard University Press.

———. 1981. "Where Do Markets Come From?" *American Journal of Sociology* 87:517–547.

———. 1992. *Identity and Control: A Structural Theory of Social Action*. Princeton, NJ: Princeton University Press.

———. 2008. *Identity and Control: How Social Formations Emerge*. Princeton, NJ: Princeton University Press.

White, Harrison, and Cynthia White. 1965. *Canvases and Careers: Institutional Change in the French Painting World*. New York: John Wiley & Sons.

Whitford, Josh. 2002. "Pragmatism and the Untenable Dualism of Means and Ends: Why Rational Choice Theory Does Not Deserve Paradigmatic Privilege." *Theory and Society* 31:325–363.

Whitley, Richard. [1984] 2000. *The Intellectual and Social Organization of the Sciences*. New York: Oxford University Press.

Whyte, William Foote. 1948. *Human Relations in the Restaurant Industry*. New York: McGraw-Hill.

Wilensky, Harold. 1960. "Work, Careers, and Social Integration." *International Social Science Journal* 12:543–560.

Winship, Christopher. 2006. "Policy Analysis as Puzzle-Solving." In *The Oxford Handbook of Public Policy*, edited by Michael Moran, Martin Rein, and Robert E. Goodin. Oxford, UK: Oxford University Press.

Wittgenstein, Ludwig. [1953] 2003. *Philosophical Investigations*. Translated by Gertrude E. M. Anscombe. Oxford, UK: Blackwell.

Wry, Tyler, Michael Lounsbury, and Mary Ann Glynn. 2011. "Legitimating Nascent Collective Identities: Coordinating Cultural Entrepreneurship." *Organization Science* 22:449–463.

Zajonc, Robert. 1980. *Social Psychology: An Experimental Approach*. Belmont, CA: Brooks/Cole.

Zelizer, Viviana. 1997. *The Sociological Meaning of Money*. Princeton, NJ: Princeton University Press.

———. 2011. *Economic Lives: How Culture Shapes the Economy*. Princeton, NJ: Princeton University Press.

Zerubavel, Eviatar. 1997. *Social Mindscapes: An Invitation to Cognitive Sociology*. Cambridge, MA: Harvard University Press.

———. 2002. "The Elephant in the Room: Notes on the Social Organization of Denial." In *Culture in Mind: Toward a Sociology of Culture and Cognition*, edited by Karen Cerulo. New York: Routledge.

———. 2012. *Ancestors and Relatives: Genealogy, Identity, and Community*. New York: Oxford University Press.

Zucker, Lynne. 1977. "The Role of Institutionalization in Cultural Persistence." *American Sociological Review* 42:726–743.

———. 1987. "Institutional Theories of Organization." *Annual Review of Sociology* 13:443–464.

Zuckerman, Ezra. 1999. "The Categorical Imperative: Securities Analysis and the Illegitimacy Discount." *American Journal of Sociology* 104:1398–1438.

Zuckerman, Ezra, Tai-Young Kim, Kalinda Ukanwa, and James von Rittmann. 2003. "Robust Identities or Nonentities? Typecasting in the Feature-Film Labor Market." *American Journal of Sociology* 108:1018–1074.

Index